The Tone of the Twenties

The Tone of the Twenties
and Other Essays

By Charles Angoff

South Brunswick and New York:
A. S. Barnes and Co.
London: Thomas Yoseloff Ltd

© 1966 by Charles Angoff

Library of Congress Catalogue Card Number: 66-14772

A. S. Barnes and Company, Inc.

South Brunswick, New Jersey

Thomas Yoseloff Ltd

18 Charing Cross Road

London W.C.2 England

6404

Printed in the United States of America

Acknowledgments

Many of the essays included in this volume have been previously published in periodicals, and I am grateful to the editors for permission to reprint:

Literary Review (Autumn 1960) for "The Tone of the Twenties."

South Atlantic Quarterly (Spring 1964) and *The Saturday Review* (August 10, 1965) for portions of "H. L. Mencken: A Postscript."

Atlantic Monthly (December 1962) and the *New Republic* (January 4, 1964) for portions of "George Jean Nathan."

University of Houston *Forum* (Fall 1964) for "Robert Frost."

Antioch Review (Summer 1963) for "Oswald Garrison Villard and the *Nation.*"

Southwest Review (Winter 1963) for "Thomas Wolfe and the Opulent Manner."

Prairie Schooner (Winter 1964) for "William Carlos Williams."

University Review (University of Missouri in Kansas City) (Summer 1965) for "Dorothy Thompson: Kansan in Westchester."

Chicago Jewish Forum (Winter 1963-4) for "George E. Sokolosky."

College English (April 1965) for "Robert P. Tristram Coffin."

New York University *Arts and Sciences* (Winter 1964-5) for "Mike Gold: Leader of Proletarian Culture."

Barcelona *Boletin* (Spring 1965) for "Jim Tully," and (Spring 1966) for "Francis Hackett."

C.A.

Foreword

Much has been written about the traditional strains of the
Author-Publisher relationship. Authors and Publishers are natural
enemies, with the Agent as arbiter, warden, and engineman to keep
the literary train on the tracks. Rather less has been said about the
genuinely warm relationships that often exist between Author and
Publisher, the friendships that depend upon mutual trust and respect.
This is the sort of relationship that I think Charles Angoff and I have
had for nearly a quarter of a century, during which I have published
fourteen of his books. Often these have been published without a contract, but simply on the basis of a continuing understanding between us; sometimes a manuscript is delivered, edited, put
into the processes of printing before I realize that no contract exists.
It is a tribute to our relationship that this state of affairs has never
led to a misunderstanding, argument or bargaining over terms, or
any of the other unpleasantnesses that often exist between Author
and Publisher. It is a tribute also to that relationship that when it
was decided to offer this collection of essays to the public, Charlie
asked me to contribute a brief foreword. It is bracing to a Publisher
to know that his Author thinks him capable of articulate expression.

From time beyond memory, forewords have explained what books
are about. However, it is impossible to explain what this book is

about. It is about a time. It is about a state of mind. It is about the existence of people—giants they sometimes appeared to be—who wrote and thought and behaved in a way peculiar to their own powerful personalities and the pinpoint of history through which they lived. The nineteen-twenties was a pinpoint in history, and although it is within the memory of half the people alive today, it has already receded in its thinking and its manners to a place beside late eighteenth-century England, or the Victorian age. So swiftly has history moved in a brief three decades that virtually no vestige of the thinking of the nineteen-twenties remains with us, and the decade itself seems alien and far far away.

This book is not confined to the decade of the nineteen-twenties. Nor was the decade itself; it died hard, insisting upon intruding into the nineteen-thirties and even the nineteen-forties. Long after the depression and the rise of Hitlerism had rendered obsolete the dominant philosophies of the twenties, they still insisted on remaining alive, appearing incongruous among the more sobering philosophies, like a berouged Victorian old lady dancing the Charleston. Long after the world had passed them by the fallen giants of the twenties still appeared in the public squares looking for a sign of recognition in the faces of passers-by. But the philosophies and manners that nurtured us in the nineteen-twenties had little sustenance in the age of the breadlines and soup kitchens, the gas chambers and atom bombs. There were giants in the land in those days, but the coming of events they could not cope with or even comprehend reduced them to a pitiful life-size.

But the nineteen-twenties was a state of mind and being both beautiful and satisfying. That it was unreal and ephemeral makes no difference—it was wonderful to have been there and to have seen and felt it. Literature was in ferment. A war to end all wars had been fought to a decisive victory for the forces of good and right. Prosperity was rampant: the starving Armenians and the embarrassing Russians had been disposed of. Warren Harding had been swept under the carpet, and the League of Nations was somewhere off in the distance where it could not ruffle the feelings of Senator Cabot Lodge. Sly Calvin Coolidge sat secure in the White House and the sun never set on the British Empire. Socialist stirrings in London and racial stirrings in Munich could have little meaning in a land where the Bible was transmitted daily on ticker tape and *rapport* with a good bootlegger was a status symbol.

It was against this background that the literary ferment of the twenties erupted. In an era in which political justice had triumphed and the world had been made safe for democracy, the muck-rakers could lay about them with mighty swats. Henry L. Mencken could come up from Baltimore to spread terror among the boobocracy, and vanquish weekly the ministers, college professors and chambers of commerce. Sinclair Lewis could follow fashionably and restlessly the paths that had been laboriously carved out by Lincoln Steffens, Ida Tarbell and Upton Sinclair. George Jean Nathan could demolish with a fastidious epigram the tried and true American credos: what the country needed was not a good five-cent cigar but a superb dollar cigar to top off a *gemütlich* evening enjoyed by gentlemen living in the midst of a magnificent state of mind.

And it was a magnificent state of mind. We who grew up in that decade had been born into the best of all possible worlds. The ancient injustices were dead, slain by an enlightened and democratic avenger. There would be no more Hamans, no more Attilas, no more Kaiser Wilhelms. Nations of goodwill were sinking their battleships and demolishing their stores of armaments, and the battles of the future would be fought with the pen, not with the sword. How good it was to grow up in that world, to be nurtured by Mencken, and to believe with him that the true enemies of mankind were the Bible-carrying revivalists and the college professors of English.

It was a world that disappeared all too soon. And as it disappeared it left the giants bewildered. Mencken pretended that the depression didn't exist, that Hitler was a grotesque joke on the fun-loving German people. As the depression deepened and Hitlerism became a world-menacing reality, his bewilderment increased, and he turned bitterly on the liberals who had been his most ardent followers and the mainstay of his strength. He wrote for the scandalous new *Mercury,* calling Roosevelt a despot, referring to him as "King Franklin." He became the darling of the hate-mongers, and in his hallucinations, after his illness, he could not distinguish between Hitler and Roosevelt, Roosevelt and Stalin. Nathan's bewilderment was less virulent, but he too had difficulty in comprehending a world in which the theatre had to take second place to the terrible realities of living drama. In the mid-thirties, when he was its chief editor, the *Spectator* printed the infamous article by Theodore Dreiser "explaining" Hitler's attacks upon the Jews in logical terms of statistics. Nathan could not understand that this was not accepted widely as a reasonable and objective view. Even Sinclair Lewis, who made a valiant attempt to understand the new world of the thirties and forties, could not translate the new ugliness in terms of the America he knew. *It Can't Happen Here* was lumbering and inept, and is now happily almost forgotten. As interpreters of the political and social scene, on a profound level, the literary heroes of the twenties proved themselves almost without exception to be hopelessly incapable. Dorothy Thompson, on the very eve of Hitler's assumption of complete power in Germany, began a new book with the dogmatic assertion that Hitler would "never be Chancellor of Germany." The shame-faced Publisher consigned the book to the remainder counters shortly after its publication.

What then was the charm of the twenties? What was its contribution to America? What makes it worth commemorating in the title of a book? First, of course, there was the insouciance of the time, the hedonism that has been celebrated in songs and plays and books and movies. It was the age of free living and free spending, of the speakeasy and the movie queens, of the climbing ticker tape and the cornucopia that was inexhaustible. Today there is more money available, our average income and gross national product are greater, life abounds in greater luxury than in the twenties—yet nobody can really quite believe in today's prosperity as we believed in that of the twenties. Because then it was permanent, we could build a philosophy upon it. Today's is tempered with uncertainty and unrest, with Berlin and Cuba and China and Korea and Vietnam, with the nuclear bomb and the military draft and the multi-billion dollar army. In an age in which the problems of the world bear down upon us, hedonism is sinful, but in the twenties, when all the world's problems had been solved, hedonism was as natural and right as breathing and singing.

Out of this came a flowering of literature that will stamp the twenties for all time. No period has ever produced anything quite like it. A glance at college level reading lists or the lists of American literature read abroad will quickly confirm that this was indeed the age of the giants. Dreiser, Lewis, O'Neill, Cather, Faulkner, Hemingway, Wolfe, Mencken, Nathan, Anderson, Wilder—these are only a few of the long parade of names that come quickly to mind. Serious fiction, the serious theatre, critical writing—all these reached their zenith, a peak which has never since been surpassed. The procession of banalities we have seen since—from the proletarians to the beatniks, the monstrous, formless excretions that pass for fiction and drama today—serves only to emphasize the richness that we have lost.

Finally, it was an age of personal freedom, when the individual emerged as paramount in the American social scheme. The social reforms of the thirties had not yet reduced every American to a nine-digit number, the income tax was a luxury reserved for the upper income brackets. Politically, Communists rubbed elbows with rugged individualists, prohibitionists, anti-vivisectionists and anti-evolutionists. America had come of age, and the promise of its constitution seemed assured. Not that there were not paradoxes a-plenty—in the immigration quotas, the Oriental exclusion, the "separate but equal rights," the Palmer raids. But self-expression as a political right was as certain then as it is circumscribed today.

This then is what this book is about. It is about the flowering of an age and its withering. It is about people who stamped the impression of their personalities upon that age. It is a tribute, a memorial, a dirge, a paean of joy. It is a souvenir, a trifling recollection of things past. You will search in vain for the plot, the thesis—there is none. It is a string of beads unmatched in size, color or evenness. It does not even have a moral—unless you can find your own. It is about the many people that Charles Angoff met and knew and talked to and worked with in the course of a career that spanned the most fertile period in American literature. Nor are these recollections presented in any formal manner: they were written down all hot as they came from the cauldron of memory.

To each reader who lived through the period these essays will conjure up memories—of a newly "discovered" book or play, of an impression of an individual or a movement. To me as a reader this book has many meanings and brings up many recollections: My discovery of Mencken and Nathan in my mid-teens, when they came upon me like a blinding flash; of my first reading of Saroyan, when I wept over the fate of the vanishing Assyrians; of my discovery through Isaac Goldberg that Mencken was a poet who wrote

.... What to me were all the joys of meadow, brook or down
If I were walking by your side within this joyless town.

It brings back memories of the evenings I spent listening to the fabulous recollections of Madeleine Boyd; of a meeting with George Jean Nathan at the Algonquin, when his hair was already snow-white and he seemed world-weary; of Ernest Boyd, sitting day after day in Pete's Tavern, his messianic white beard slightly beer-stained.

It is especially appropriate that this book should be published at this time. For it is just a decade since the publication of Charles Angoff's book *H. L. Mencken: A Portrait from Memory*, which added to Angoff's already formidable reputation another dimension, that of literary *raconteur*. Angoff's memory of Mencken amounted virtually to total recall. Few people had had the opportunity that he had to see the great debunker over so many years and in such a variety of unguarded moments. He was able to quote him on many of his favorite subjects—on women, religion, college professors, Jews, Negroes, Abraham Lincoln, and even God. It was, by all publishing standards, a successful book, widely read, widely reviewed, widely admired. Mencken himself would have liked it, for, to paraphrase Cromwell, it painted him as he was, warts and all.

But, like all books that draw their heroes life-size, it aroused violent controversy. Many who knew Mencken well have told me privately that the book was an astonishingly accurate portrait of the man. But others professed to see in it a slur on a man who could no longer defend himself. Mencken himself would have roared with laughter at this canard, for he would have been shocked that anyone could have wanted his memory lily-white. Nevertheless, his self-appointed defenders persisted. When the book was reviewed favorably in the *Times Literary Supplement* of London, the review begat a series of letters that regaled the readers of that publication for weeks.

Nor has the controversy fully abated. Even today, a decade later, I sometimes find myself drawn into conversations in defence or in damnation of the book. It is obvious that many of Mencken's defenders are familiar with only a portion of his written work, for they profess themselves shocked at quotations that may be found almost verbatim in his own publications.

None has joined the controversy more fiercely than Mencken's own publisher, who has denounced the book as a vicious and unrecognizable caricature of the man. His vendetta against both the Author and the Publisher has become a part of the literary legend of our time. When I myself held out the olive branch to him several years ago, he scorned it, replying that he did not want the friendship of the publisher of that book. His vendetta has received tacit recognition throughout the publishing fraternity; so much so, that on a recent occasion, when a friend invited me to a party, he thought fit as a matter of course to warn me that Mr. Knopf would be present, affording me an opportunity to decline gracefully, thus averting an historic confrontation.

THOMAS YOSELOFF

London
February 1966

Contents

Foreword *by Thomas Yoseloff*   7

The Tone of the Twenties   17

H. L. Mencken: A Postscript   29

Prejudices and Prophecies   43

George Jean Nathan   47

Robert Frost   62

Sinclair Lewis   69

Oswald Garrison Villard and the *Nation*   74

Thomas Wolfe and the Opulent Manner   84

William Carlos Williams   93

Ernest Boyd   99

Dorothy Thompson: Kansan in Westchester   114

George E. Sokolsky   122

Oliver St. John Gogarty   137

Robert P. Tristram Coffin   145

James Michael Curley: Boston's Falstaff   150

Joshua Liebman and Peace of Mind   156

Louis Weitzenkorn   162

Thomas Beer   169

Vincent Lawrence   176

Mike Gold. Leader of Proletarian Culture   182

Jim Tully   189

Isaac Goldberg   197

William Saroyan: Some Footnotes   203

Francis Hackett   209

Prohibition Days   217

The Proletarian Bohemia   228

The Tone of the Twenties

I HAVE HAD OCCASION RECENTLY TO SPEND SOME TIME IN THE neighborhood of the Algonquin Hotel and the Royalton Hotel on West Forty-Fourth Street in New York City, and my heart was heavy as the memories tumbled one over another. I walked into the Algonquin lobby, looked into the room, well within hailing distance of the bar, where Alexander Woollcott and F.P.A. and George Kaufman and Wolcott Gibbs and Heywood Broun and so many others used to meet and play cards and talk and drink for hours unending . . . and the talk was, as Johannes Brahms would have said, unbuttoned . . . it was about books and ideas and women and about love and "the soft sorrow" (a phrase I heard F.P.A. use) that announces love's arrival, hovers over its mysteries, and follows it as it glides into the arms of the past.

And I came back to the central lobby where, a few weeks before his death, George Jean Nathan, at a little table, gave what was probably his farewell to life and, at the same time, a benediction to a whole era in American history. . . . Earlier we had gone to one of his favorite restaurants on West Forty-Fourth, the Blue Ribbon, then to sit on a bench in Bryant Park, behind the Central Library. He said, "I love this city. Don't let anybody tell you that America is more than New York City. It isn't. Whatever sense and decency the hinterland has—and all America west of the Hudson is hinterland—it gets from New York City. New York City is the capital of the Twentieth Century. Mencken called New York Babylon and a mess of chicken coops unfit for civilized living. That was the small town man in him talking. That's what kept him from being what he might have been. Anyway, Angoff, remember this. The only things that grow in the deserts and backwoods are religions. Civilization grows in the cities." He stopped, smiled, then added, "I was going to let you think this is my idea. I read it somewhere. It's a little hard to lie to you at my time of life."

He suggested we go to the Algonquin for a nightcap. People walked in and out, looked at both of us, and continued on their way. I sensed that they made him feel lonely. He said: "These people who live here now, who drink here now, are merchants, scavengers, they live from aspirin to aspirin, they have to get drunk to make love. Think of it! The era that blossomed here was alive with silver bells, little ones and somewhat bigger ones, and there were magic lanterns and there were girls and there was the night. The wondrous lovely madness of the night went out of American life with the Twenties. You're a lucky man you got a taste of it. I was luckier. I got more . . ."

I walked into the lobby of the Royalton where Nathan died not long after, and sat down and waited for Nathan to come down from his apartment to meet me, as he had so often done, but he did not come down and I couldn't believe that he never would . . . And I noticed that the old charm of the Royalton—it had been quiet and gentle and soft when I had first entered it more than three decades before—had also gone, long before Nathan himself went, as a matter of fact . . . and my mind glided back in memory and my heart grew heavier and heavier . . . It was here that I had seen Robert Benchley and Jim Tully and F. Scott Fitzgerald (in his last sorrowful days, when he looked like an elderly college boy back from a night of heavy-drinking and other forms of merry-making) . . . and it was here that I had often seen and spoken to Ernest Boyd, now virtually forgotten, but a man of fantastic erudition in literary history . . . and James Thurber and Harold Ross and

Dorothy Parker and James M. Cain and Carl Sandburg and Theodore Dreiser and Sherwood Anderson . . .

The Royalton and the Algonquin formed the axis of most that was wonderful in the Twenties. They were the twin capitals of that era, more important by far than Washington or Wall Street or Chicago or San Francisco. It was from them that the pronouncements of the decade issued, and not by way of ukases or bulls, but in whispers and chuckles and smiles and silences . . .

Was it all a happy and gay time? It was not. Times of vital leaping imagination are not times of unalloyed happiness. No happiness is ever unalloyed. The sense of fleeting time and the apparent purposelessness of the entire scheme of things surround all calm and all joy with an inaudible sigh. This seems to be the divine plan.

But it was a time of dominant concern for yearnings, for dreams, for things not seen, for things hoped for, and this is what stamped it. It was a time that lived by the call of the heart, it was a time that was suspicious of the arrogant claims of the mind.

Certain people and certain events stand out in the memory. In the lower forties there used to be a basement bar-restaurant called various names in order to elude new policemen on the beat and Prohibition agents who were overly inquisitive. It was dark, lush, plush, and the food and drink were wonderful. Bankers, Broadway producers and business men often took their new girls there for the first time to make an impression. Its names were on the order of The Seven Sins, Royal Flush, Left Bank, Right Bank, Virtue Triumphant, Inc. I was there once in the small hours of the morning. Nathan had taken me along. We went to a huge table where there were a dozen men and women assembled. As the night wore on about a dozen more people joined us.

For some three hours Robert Benchley held forth. He looked so young, so boyish, so happy, so full of words, so eager to talk . . . and as he talked one or another of the girls would come over and kiss him, and after each such kiss he would say, "The accolade of the angels, my love!"

What did he talk about? After more than thirty years I do not remember the details, but its aroma, its direction, its timbre, its contour linger with me. Toward the end (it must have been almost five in the morning) he and Nathan debated on the relative merits of the night and evening, Nathan championing the supremacy of the night, Benchley pushing the claims of the evening.

"I will say this for George Jean Nathan of the great State of Indiana and of Cornell University, a well-known fencing academy," said Benchley, "I will say this, he uses the right similes and antonyms and the subjunctive. It is impossible to talk about eternal things without bringing in women. Now George says the essence of woman is night, and hence night wins. I am not one to gainsay the many virtues of night. Where, indeed, would we all be without the night? But, and I wish you would all listen to me, it's the memory of a woman at eventide that you kiss at night. Twilight, my friends, that's what makes all the difference between the ordinary world and God's world, between barbarism and civilization, between man and woman."

A woman who was sitting next to me, said, "He should have been a poet or a musician. He's too good to be a humorist or a dramatic critic."

There was another time, when a publisher's editor took me to a party given, I believe, by Lewis Gannett, former book reviewer for the *New York Herald Tribune*. In one corner a group was arguing about Marcel Proust: whether he was a novelist or a prose poet, or a writer at all, and how he compared with Anatole France. In another corner a woman was reciting Emily Dickinson's poems by the dozen. Then there was a group in the middle of which a huge man was holding forth with great animation, and right in front of him, looking up at him, in a kindly, bewildered aura of admiration, was a shorter man. I approached this group, fascinated by the bulk of the man in the center; in fact, I was so fascinated that I didn't hear what he was saying. He had a head like a squash and his eyes bulged, yet there was something tender in his face and in his talk. I asked who the man was, and was told that he was Diego Rivera. I was not an admirer of his work, though I appreciated its power. In painting and sculpture, as in poetry, I am more attracted by the lyrical than the dramatic.

Then somebody told me the shorter man facing Diego Rivera was Sherwood Anderson. My heart leaped at the name, for I thought then (and still do) that he was one of the supreme literary artists of the English language in the past one hundred years, a man who in range, intensity, and genuine creativity is on a plane with Chekhov, De Maupassant, and Thomas Hardy. I followed Anderson around the room as unobtrusively as possible. I was pleased with him. He looked just as I wanted him to look, serene, bedazzled by all the talk and commotion, present yet far away, the very personification of total unconcern with what the world calls practical things. He spoke very little. All I remember his saying that night is, "I would like to be on a boat now."

That one line, in some mystical way, defines Anderson and also stamps the era. All America wanted to be on a boat . . . all America sensed there was more solidity on the ocean than on the bedrock of its cities. America wanted to flee from the products of its sciences, even as Anderson did flee from his office as he entered into middle age. This yearning for the joyous madness of the unfettered heart reaching for warm oblivion or infinity was the key of being in those years. The key was sounded in New York and its echoes reached every soul across the land, adding a glow to every woman's face and inches to every man's stature.

It was a time of plentitude in the arts, because the heart of America was plenteous. There were three times as many theatres as now, and the whole theatrical world was off-Broadway . . . experimentation everywhere side by side with old gold. There were theatres in the bowels of the Bowery. There were theatres east and west of Broadway extending into the sixties, and there were theatres in Washington Heights—and Forty-Second Street, between Times Square and Eighth Avenue and even extending half a block to Ninth Avenue, was an avenue of enchantment. Presiding over all the theatres was the Amsterdam, long the home of the "Follies" and for long the temple where young men, whole generations of them, lost their hearts to Adèle Astair and Marilyn Miller.

A word about the "Follies" and the "Scandals" and the "New Faces" and the "Gaieties." Weren't they sheer fluff? Of course they were. And that was their glory. At their best they were a reflection of what was happening in the heart of America. America had found herself on a national scale as Walt Whitman had found himself three quarters of a century before. Whitman had been a prophet:

> "One's self I sing, a simple separate, person,
> Yet utter the word Democratic, the word En Masse.
> Of physiology from top to toe I sing, . . ."

How Whitman would have loved and sung and loved again and sung again the Twenties!

> "I hear America singing, the varied carols I hear,
> Those of mechanics, each one singing as it
> should be blithe and strong. . . ."

But was it only New York that was singing? It was not. New York was only leading the chorus. The melodies of the "Gaieties" and "Vanities" and "Follies" were soon heard around the land, and in every home, in every hall, in every bar, in the parks and on the hills and in the valleys: "Clap Yo' Hands," "Strike Up The Band," " 'S Wonderful," "Oh, Lady, Be Good!" "That Certain Feeling" . . .

The musicals and the popular tunes were of a quality that echoed the tenderness in the people and the wondrous common humanity in those more blessed with knowledge and conscious perception. But these latter more blessed men and women had special reasons for rejoicing—and the special reasons were good for the whole nation, for taste and manners and attitudes and inner delights do spread and do seep into the farthermost nooks and into the apparently most unlikely folk. What comes out of silver bells is heard round the world.

And what mighty and heroic and heart-invested days those were for those who look to the drama and music for guidance as well as comfort. Eugene O'Neill came into his own in that decade. Broadway, and hence America, at long last accepted him, seeing him for the monumental creator he was. When *Desire Under the Elms* and *Beyond the Horizon* finally reached Times Square, America came of age in the art of dramatic writing. And when *Strange Interlude* and *Mourning Becomes Electra* followed it, the American theatre joined the stream of world dramatic history. And it was the same decade in which other playwrights, notably Maxwell Anderson, did their finest work. Let us not forget that the early Anderson was a poet, a minor O'Neill, but a minor O'Neill is also wonderful, as *What Price Glory?* and *Saturday's Children* are also fine and enduring dramatic poems to two great events in American history: World War I and the moral, spiritual upheaval that followed it.

Music? Had America ever before been so rich in musical organizations, in opportunities for all people to enjoy great music as in the Twenties? For some mysterious reason our composers have not yet come forth with compositions of the stature of those of Melville and Whitman and Hawthorne and Emily Dickinson and Willa Cather in literature. But there is now a receptive public for great music, and when there is such an audience great works cannot be far behind. The history of culture attests to that.

I can personally attest to the maturation of the audience, for my own maturity largely came about in the Twenties. For years the Boston Symphony Orchestra, under the proud, austere, and almost Prussian direction of Karl Muck, was pretty much the private pleasure of the Back Bay élite. But after the First World War something happened in the Boston musical world, as it happened in every other area of Boston culture—all American culture. If America and its Allies had not been overly successful in making the world safe for democracy, America did manage, through the inscrutable workings of historical forces, to democratize its major institutions of culture. It is one of the curiosities of American history that it achieved political democracy long before it achieved true, widespread cultural democracy. Andrew Jackson came a century before Stephen Crane, and Harvard had been in existence for almost two centuries before the state universities became full-fledged bodies of higher learning.

But back to music. My mother once took me to hear Karl Muck play Brahms' *First Symphony,* and the feat was the talk of the Boston Ghetto. Suddenly, almost as if overnight, as the Twenties came into being, many of my friends had season tickets (or pooled their resources for one or two season tickets to be shared by several) for the Boston Symphony Orchestra. And soon there were several smaller symphonies that came and went.

New York now has one major orchestra, the Philharmonic, but in the Twenties it had several more, among them the New York Symphony, whose chief conductor was the late Walter Damrosch, and the Beethoven Symphony. It was Walter Damrosch who introduced Gershwin's *Concerto in F.* and it was Fritz Busch who was on the podium when the eight (or was it ten?)-year-old Yehudi Menuhin made his New York début as soloist in Beethoven's *Violin Concerto.*

The Metropolitan Opera House had an institution in the Twenties, the Sunday Night Gala Concert, which I attended regularly. I used to sit in one of the last rows in the topmost balcony, and I paid fifty cents for my seat. I met there pretty much the same people Sunday after Sunday. They were of all ages, of various races and religions. They came from Manhattan and Brooklyn and the Bronx, others came from Newark and Philadelphia, and there were individuals and couples from all over the United States who had come to New York for a visit. We all had in common two things: we were deficient in financial resources and we loved music. The administrators of the august Metropolitan Opera Company had learned about us and apparently had decided that there wasn't too much loss in our "trade." But I think there was another reason why the Metropolitan was good to us. It heard America singing, and it wanted to join the chorus, so to speak. It became just as smart, as the phrase goes, to lose money on the common people as to lose it on the carriage trade.

And what did we hear at the Sunday Gala Concerts? What glorious vocal music and what glorious instrumental music. We heard Giovanni Martinelli and Tito Schipa and Antonio Scotti and

Edward Johnson and Lawrence Tibbett, and we heard Elizabeth Rethberg and Sigrid Onegin and Lucrezia Bori and Lily Pons and Frances Alda . . . we heard arias from *Aïda* and *The Magic Flute* and *La Bohème* and *Carmen* and *La Traviata* and *Boris Godunov* and *Il Trovatore* and *Louise* and *Parsifal* and *Der Rosenkavalier* and many of the other golden treasures . . . and we heard *lieder* . . . and the memory of Sigrid Onegin singing Schubert's "Der Erlkönig" and *Die Winter Reise* will always be with me . . . She sang them like an angel sorrowing for the evanescence of the loveliness of this world . . . and I saw a young couple holding hands and moved to tears by the otherworldly wonderment of what they were hearing, and this, too, will always be with me . . . and as we all walked slowly down the hundreds of stairs to Broadway, we were silent, for we all felt a little closer to the divinity that shaped us.

There was so much else. But one more aspect must be mentioned: the vitality in the newspaper, magazine and book worlds. New York City had three times as many newspapers as it has now, and what papers some of them were. *The Morning World* of blessed memory was like no other paper in all American journalistic history. It generally printed the news in succinct form, but in the case of subjects that interested it, it went to enormous lengths. Its investigation of the Ku Klux Klan remains one of the masterpieces of American journalism. Then there was its editorial page. It was not written in the "however, nevertheless" spirit. One could never find in it a paragraph congratulating some dull politician or preacher for having reached the age of eighty and thus beaten the calendar. The page was alive with imagination, with courage, and with good writing—often brilliant writing. And the cartoons by Rollin Kirby were *sui generis*. Kirby, as a cartoonist, was probably our nearest approach to Daumier. His portrayal of Mr. Prohibition—a tall, lanky, sleazy, lascivious-lipped man with his umbrella—is already a part of our body of national symbols.

But it was the Page Opposite the Editorial that stamped the *World*, that reflected the Twenties, that set a standard for American creative daily journalism, that gave the newspaper men the country over something to dream about with respect to their own papers.

There was The Conning Tower, a column conducted by the recently departed F. P. A. (Franklin P. Adams)—a column of lovely and stinging light verse, of pleasant or sharp comment upon the passing scene, of crusades for minor civic improvements (such as the more prominent display of street numbers on homes), of factual corrections of speeches by pompous statesmen. Everything was put down *con amore*, with good humor. There was no indignation, no malice. The spirit of the boulevard, of the drawing room, of the literary coffee shop hovered over it.

And the same civilized note was in the music criticism, first by Deems Taylor and then by Samuel Chotzinoff, and in the book reviews by Laurence Stallings, and of course in "It Seems To Me," a daily column of brief essays and remarks about everything at all, conducted by Heywood Broun before he became an amateur radical.

This was the *Morning World*, and this was the *Evening World* . . . and equally wonderful in their own ways were the *New York Evening Post*, which must never be confused with the embarrassing thing it is now, and the *New York Sun*. Along with the monumental *Times*, they set the pace for the newspapers west, north, and south of the Hudson.

A final word about magazine and book publishers. With many of our current mass circulation magazines (as with *Life*, for example) it is not always easy to differentiate between the advertisements and the editorial matter. And there are only two monthlies that pretend to offer any interpretation of the news—and they are more monthly newspapers than magazines. What could one read in the Twenties, where could a beginning writer or a veteran writer send his stories and essays and poems? Was he often bewildered as he is now? He had a choice, and what a choice: *Scribner's, The Forum*, the *Century*, the *Dial, World's Work, Review of Reviews*, the old *American Mercury, McNaught's Monthly, Plain Talk*, the *North American Review*, the old *Atlantic*, the old *Harper's*, and outside of New York there were the "little" magazines which were then in their glory: the old *Prairie Schooner*, the *Midland*, the *Double Dealer*—but why go on? You can get the names in any history of American magazines.

As for book publishing, the tendency now is for publishers to combine, as newspapers are combining, with the resulting organization often being a plant without a soul, a post-office, a paper factory, where, alas, manuscripts are frequently accepted by the vote of salesmen, not by the enthusiastic choice of an editor to whom publishing is an adventure in ideas and in literary imagination, who spends his evenings at home looking for pearls of great price in the accumulated manuscripts, who would be offended if he were invited to become a panel member of an "intellectual" TV or radio show helping to sell some deodorant or laxative. The Twenties were the days of those wonderful pioneers of culture, small publishers. Alfred A. Knopf was one such publisher then, Covici-Friede was another, Horace Liveright a third and there were a dozen others who would rather print the first book of Edna St. Vincent Millay and Sinclair Lewis than all the volumes by Robert Chambers and Kathleen Norris. It is these little publishers who helped carry the flag of American literary culture further North.

Books and music and the theatre were not merely parts of one's life: they transfused the whole of one's life. It became fashionable to talk about philosophy and Humanism in Literature and about Toscanini's interpretation of Beethoven's *Seventh* as contrasted with Mengelberg's, and about the "real" meaning of Joyce's *Ulysses*. While it is true that not all were privy to the complexities involved, it is also true that the interest of so many people in such matters indicated something that was wonderful. America had become one huge Bohemia—singing and dancing and yearning and feeling totally unfettered and eager to give expression to this glorious carefreeness that one could sense in the faces, in the very gait, of people.

And there was another meaning to this wonderful, soft commotion: America had at long last become fully conscious of its grandeur: of the magnitude of its history, of the special stature of its great men and women . . . America discovered that Washington and Lincoln and Jackson and Jefferson were not wax figures set up as models for school children, but that these men could walk beside Burke and Peel and Locke and Montesquieu . . . and it discovered that Whitman and Dickinson and Melville and Crane were not just the authors of pieces to be declaimed at school graduations, but men and women of great song and profound insight.

These were the Twenties. These were its legacies. What happened toward the end of October 1929 only meant that some of the economic underpinnings of our way of life had become a bit shaky. The basic treasures of what for a decade had been our new and glorious Bohemia, our full awakening to our national magnificence, remained intact, and set in motion a cultural development that, as the English already know insofar as our literature is concerned, will flower into something tremendous in history. Remember this: on the very same day in 1929 that Wall Street was probably in its most confused state there was published a first novel called *Look Homeward Angel*.

H. L. Mencken: A Postscript

MENCKEN HAS BEEN DEAD NOW ABOUT A DECADE, BUT SO FAST has the world moved, and literary fashions with it, that he already seems to be a figure from out of the distant past. He is being praised by textbook writers, a circumstance which would have pained him, and he is being ignored by writers for the "little magazines," a fact which would have pained him just as much. His heroes are nearly all forgotten or sneered at. Dreiser is now being discussed in college classrooms, but, were Mencken alive, he would hardly be pleased by the quality of the discussion. A man was recently given a Ph.D. in a Middle Western university for a thesis on Dreiser, in which he argued that Dreiser was a religious man, and deeply moral, too— whereas Dreiser devoted his life to ridiculing religion as an organized establishment and questioning the major bases of the accepted moral code. Two big books have been written about Sherwood Anderson, and neither author understands Anderson the way Mencken understood him. To both authors, Anderson was something of a good-natured *shnook*. To Mencken, Anderson, at his best was a great artist and a profound commentator on the American scene. There are few hardy enough in the contemporary critical world to say a good word for Joseph Hergesheimer or James Branch Cabell or Elizabeth Woodworth Reese or John McClure or Ruth Suckow—

and Mencken had predicted immortality of one sort or another for each of them. Worst of all, Sinclair Lewis, who, in his opinion, was the greatest novelist of his generation, is seldom discussed by the critics who temporarily wield influence, and when they do discuss him, they call him a journalist at his best and a vaudevillian at his worst.

As for Mencken himself, who has had at least two biographers, did anybody really know him? Very few people did. He knew many people across the years and visited with them often, but hardly any one of them had any notion of what went on within him. Gerald W. Johnson, the "liberal" journalist, who writes so often about him, is a humorless man, whom Mencken used to call "an emancipated Baptist, but not a bad sort." Mencken was close to the Owenses of Baltimore—several of them were associated with the Baltimore *Sunpapers*—but they knew not of Mencken's bounce, of his deepest prejudices.

Mencken's publisher, Alfred A. Knopf, was very good to Mencken most of the time—though he made his life miserable, insulting him before Mencken's own office help, in the dark days of the old *Mercury*—and he did continue to publish his books long after Mencken had lost his vogue. But the two men were the proverbial poles apart. Mencken looked upon Knopf as a dullard, though a good, if somewhat lucky, publisher. Knopf appeared to be for the old *Mercury* as long as it made money and was talked about; when it began to lose money and was not so popular, Knopf criticized it. Mencken resented the criticism, for he maintained, and rightly so, that the magazine remained essentially the same. The world, the country had changed, a fact that Knopf didn't seem to appreciate. Mencken's philosophy, such as it was, was as dubious in the Coolidge-Hoover days as it was in the Depression. Few readers of the old *Mercury* respected Mencken's ideas, even when the *Mercury* had its largest circulation; they only respected Mencken's humor—and the Twenties were a time of carefree humor and not too great an emphasis on ideas. This, too, Knopf didn't realize. But Knopf simply didn't know what sort of man Mencken was. He didn't realize that Mencken was essentially not a literary critic or a political commentator, but rather a philosophical anarchist, a literary stylist, a vaudevillian, a life-long irresponsible boy whose chief delight in life was, to use his own words, "to stir up the animals." The Knopf-Mencken relationship was an unwise marriage that yet made sense to both parties. Mencken could barely tolerate Knopf's dullness, but he respected him as a publisher and, as he often told me, "Well, he's nobody to take along on a drinking party, but he shows good taste in continuing to publish me, and that, my boy, is a very great virtue in my eyes."

Only two people truly understood Mencken, and with both he had battles so bitter that they virtually abandoned him—and Mencken's last fifteen years were very lonely ones. One of these men was Philip Goodman, the other was George Jean Nathan. Mencken's name has been so often coupled with Nathan's that many think they were inseparable all their days. The truth is that from 1925 on they were never more than friendly enemies and for the greater part of that time they did not talk to each other and even passed each other by on the street.

Mencken and Nathan were close while they co-edited the *Smart Set*. This magazine was a perfect reflection of each of their personalities. It was a raffish magazine, with every page a barrel of spitballs at the sacred assumptions of every-day life. It sneered at the sexual code, it sneered at ministers, it sneered at politicians, it sneered at colleges and universities, it sneered at psychology and the science of education, it sneered at motherhood, it sneered at the Bible. In addition, it printed the fresh stories and poems of young writers who, in their writings, also sneered at these same institutions. It printed Ben Hecht and it printed D. H. Lawrence and it printed James Branch Cabell and it printed James Joyce. And all these sneers were packaged, as the modern phrase would have it, in rather dubious advertisements: advertisements of love powders and bust developers and "scientific" trusses and magic lanterns and mail-order spectacles and "male pills" and "female tonics" and hair permanents. This sort of juxtaposition was just what Mencken and Nathan liked: a story by James Joyce right next to an advertisement for a bust developer.

But Lord Acton's dictum about power applies not only to statesmen; it also applies, apparently, to the purely intellectual. Mencken
and Nathan achieved an enviable reputation with the *Smart Set,* a
magazine which wielded a considerable influence. But this very
success turned the heads of the two *enfants terribles.* They wanted
to become respectable. They wanted their magazine to print
advertisements of high-priced automobiles and perfumes, not of
love powders and trusses. They interested Knopf, who liked fancy
types and book jackets. Knopf agreed to put out the *Mercury,* a
title suggested by Nathan, and he put out a magazine which
physically left nothing to be desired by the prestige-seeking Mencken
and Nathan. And that's where the trouble began. Nathan had
changed only a little. He yearned for literary society, but at heart he
remained a literateur of the rather raffish sort. He still had little
interest in politicians and politics, except to sneer at them. Mencken
changed far more. His former raffishness became more respectable,
his interest in belles lettres declined, and his interest in politics and
politicians increased; he now studied them as well as sneered at
them, he now followed their antics in the city councils and the state
legislatures and the Federal Congress. This appalled Nathan; soon
they were having battles, and soon Nathan was out of the *Mercury.*

Nathan insisted almost to his dying day that Mencken had been
untrue to himself; that he, Mencken, really was not interested in
politics; that, at bottom, he always was a raffish man, a literary
man, just like Nathan. Nathan could have written perceptively
about Mencken, and he did in his various books, but only on the
run, so to speak. Only Nathan could have written a true portrait
of Mencken, that is, a full-length portrait, but he never got around
to it, and at the end he wisely refrained, for by then he was angry
with Mencken, and whatever portrait he might have written would
have been marred by some unconscious animosity. By that time
there was something else involved which kept Nathan from writing
about Mencken. Mencken's marriage to Sara Haardt in 1930 had
rather astonished Nathan, who himself didn't get married till he
was past seventy and already quite ill. But what had annoyed
Nathan was that Mencken had been married in the Episcopal

Church, after years of denouncing all organized bodies of religion. Mencken insisted that he didn't want to, but that in Maryland only religious marriages were recognized by the state. This wasn't quite true, as Mencken and Nathan knew. Nathan simply asked why, in that case, Mencken didn't go to a state where a religious ceremony was not required. After all, he said, a principle was involved. Mencken became angry, and they didn't discuss the matter any further. But it rankled in both their breasts. Nathan thought that by his act Mencken had betrayed his principles with respect to the authority of the church. In view of Nathan's own virtually last-minute conversion to Catholicism all this is certainly ironical.

Philip Goodman, in some ways, was even closer to Mencken and in some respects understood him better than did Nathan. Goodman, who merits a full-length novel, was in a class all by himself. He was more than raffish. He was superatheistical, supercynical, utterly amoral, extremely sensual, sybaritic, a loafer by choice and conviction, a man of vast superficial learning and the most profound intuitions. Villon and Verlaine and Modigliani and Socrates and Edgar Allan Poe and Lorenzo da Ponte and Mozart and Beethoven and Casanova and Cagliostro and the Medici popes would have loved him. Goodman thought that all civilization was one hoax, that all morals were worthless and dishonest, that all women were basically both saints and whores, that all men were basically saints and swindlers and lechers and thieves and reservoirs of malice and vaults of the utmost kindness. If pressed, Goodman would have said that the "evil" generally predominated, and he would have added, as he often told me, "That, my boy, is what makes it all so wonderful. The devil sings the best tunes, yes sir, the very best tunes. Every woman knows it as she looks at a shapely man, no matter how long she is married, and every man knows it when he sees a girl with firm breasts and firm hips, no matter how long he has been married, and even if he's a priest. Never forget that, and life won't fool you."

Goodman was not a man without illusions. He cultivated illusions, for he claimed that without illusions life would be impossible. "No man," he said, "ever thinks of the girl or woman he's with in bed as anything but a virgin. Every man has to believe in the Ten

Commandments, especially the Seventh, but no man can live by the Seventh Commandment and remain sane. Monogamy is a dull institution, a silly institution, impossible and cruel, especially to the man. Women haven't a man's imagination, but the Seventh Commandment is necessary, for illusion's sake."

Nobody knew exactly how Goodman made his living, nobody knew exactly how he spent his day. He would sleep till about noon, take two hours for breakfast, and then disappear till seven or eight. This schedule he followed not merely now and then, but a good deal of the time. His wife and daughter Ruth knew almost as little about him as did his friends. He adored his daughter, but he remained largely mysterious to her. He built up all sorts of legends about himself: that he was a direct descendant of Spinoza (though Spinoza had never married), that one of his ancestors had become a Morrano in Spain and that this Morrano had had seven sons, one of whom became a Cardinal in Spain ("I think this same Cardinal later became a Pope, Sixtus the Ninth or something, but I'm not sure, and what I'm not sure of I never state as a fact. Knowledge should be holy"). He also claimed that a distant cousin of his had married into the English royal family ("through the backdoor, he was in the delivery profession"). He told fantastic stories about his father: that he had inherited millions, that he was a self-made man ("He made a wealthy jackass out of himself, but he had good taste in women"); that he was very religious ("He supports all the *shuls* in Philadelphia"); that he was totally and utterly irreligious.

Goodman also had strange theories about health. He claimed that eating never hurt anybody (he himself weighed well over 200 and died of diabetes), that drinking never hurt anybody ("If you nip at a quart all day long, you'll live a long time"), and he was in favor of constant love-making ("Of course, there should be intervals for summing up"). He would spend much time during the day, as he freely confessed, watching buildings going up and bridges being built. He was one of New York City's most assiduous sidewalk superintendents.

He and Mencken took to each other like the proverbial Gold Dust Twins. Apparently Goodman reflected whatever was deepest in Mencken, and Mencken freely confessed to having "borrowed" some of Goodman's phrases and ideas. Goodman didn't mind: "I don't mind seeing the wrong man get the credit," he would say to Mencken. "That's only history. All history is objective misinformation." He and Mencken traveled in Europe together, and they spent whole evenings together in New York when Mencken would come up from Baltimore. He regretted the evenings that he didn't spend with Goodman. What did Mencken and Goodman do on their evenings together? During Prohibition they would go to Union City in New Jersey to some speakeasy and drink stein after stein of beer and gorge themselves with boiled beef and knockwurst and sauerkraut and mashed potatoes and cheese cake and drink cup after cup of coffee, and then they would come back to Manhattan and tell each other, immediately upon putting foot on the other side of the Hudson, that they were hungry and they would drop into the Blue Ribbon Restaurant on West Forty-fourth Street or into Seven Stars on West Forty-seventh Street and consume more cheese cake and possibly some strudel, too, and more coffee and more beer. Just before leaving they would, often, each have a double martini. I have been out with them on such expeditions, and one actually had to see them eat to believe how much they ate. Goodman had a theory about the martinis: "The gin oxidizes the food." "What does that mean?" I once asked innocently. "Why," said Goodman, "I'm surprised you don't understand. It's the molecules and the atoms, those things."

This wonderful relationship was, I honestly believe, the deepest one that Mencken ever had; it lasted for fifteen years. Nathan was, I believe, jealous. He tried to break up the friendship. He ridiculed Goodman. He called him a vulgarian, a liar, a worthless fellow, a dishonest man, and on more than one occasion he called him "a damn Jew," though Nathan himself was at least 50 per cent Jewish. But Mencken only looked at Nathan and said, "Come, come, George, stop that." Eventually Nathan did stop. He surrendered to Goodman. Slowly it became apparent to me that the Goodman-Mencken relationship was, in some respects, one-sided. Mencken adored Goodman and felt enormously comfortable in his company.

But Goodman wasn't too sure about his feelings toward Mencken, at least toward the end of the Twenties. One factor may have been Goodman's deteriorating financial position, which added a strain of seriousness to his outlook on life. But there was something more profound. For all his carefreeness Goodman was a man of pity and compassion. The sight of the soup lines in Times Square, the reports of the homeless and the hungry and the dispossessed all over the country filled him with sorrow and anger—anger that a country as rich as the United States should come to this state.

Goodman spoke about this to Mencken, but Mencken pooh-poohed such talk. "It will all blow over," he said. "A temporary thing. A period of adjustment." Goodman saw something more serious. He saw a basic flaw in the whole system. He was not a socialist, he certainly was not a Communist. He was a liberal. He took pride in calling himself "a confused and fuzzy liberal. I like that. Freedom is a fuzzy thing, not clear. All good things are not entirely clear." Mencken persisted in making light of the whole situation. Goodman got angrier. Soon Mencken got angrier. Soon they didn't talk about the economic state of the country any more. The silence did not rest easily with either of them. In the *Mercury* office Mencken would say now and then, more to himself than to anybody, "Goodman has gone crazy. He believes all this newspaper talk about a deep depression. There's no such thing." At other times Mencken would call Goodman a Communist—not to his face, but in the office. Then it was obvious that when he called Goodman to arrange a place and time of meeting, the old bounce in his voice was missing, and the laughter was mechanical. Goodman, on his part, was saying unfriendly things about Mencken. He began to tell me that "Mencken is a fat-head." After a while he said, "Well maybe I shouldn't have expected more from a stupid German. Germans are a cruel race. Fat and cruel."

Then the two began squabbling about the *Mercury,* which was losing circulation at a rapid pace. Mencken made light of that, too. "Oh, come on, Phil, you know as well as I do that a great many of our readers have no business reading the *Mercury*. They buy it for show. I always told Knopf that our circulation was too big. As the circulation mounted, he was glad, but I was troubled. The wrong people were reading us. And they complain about what's in the magazine. They want a sort of monthly *Nation*. That we'll never be. I think our optimum circulation is 10,000, maybe less, but surely not more. When we reached 75,000 Knopf, who's always looking out for the shekels, and rightly so, by his lights, was in heaven." "You were mighty pleased yourself, Henry," said Goodman. "Oh, well, I wanted to please Knopf. Anyway, I'm glad the circulation is going down. I want only readers whom I respect."

The argument over the *Mercury,* in time, became more bitter. Goodman claimed that the *Mercury* was losing in circulation because readers thought Mencken was out of step with the times. "You give them that stuff about Baptists and Methodists, when they want to read about the horrible state of affairs." "The state of affairs isn't horrible," said Mencken. So the two slowly ceased talking about the depression. They also ceased talking about the *Mercury* and about world affairs in general, for Goodman was veering more and more to the view that the government should take a firmer hand in the way business was conducted, whereas Mencken saw no need for any change in the way business was conducting itself. The time soon came when Mencken and Goodman had little to talk about, and they soon saw less and less of each other. Then came a time when neither discussed the other. And when Goodman died, there went with him the second man who could have written fully and truly about Mencken.

Mencken was essentially a newspaper man, eager to get on paper "the passing show," a favorite phrase of his. Deeper meanings of "the passing show" did not interest him very much, and they were probably beyond him. This is why the novelists who portrayed "the passing show" in garish colors, especially those who commented adversely upon life in the United States, appealed so much to Mencken. In the deepest sense of the word he was not at all a literary critic, for aesthetic values largely eluded him. He didn't write about Emily Dickinson and Tolstoy and Flaubert and Dostoevsky and Thomas Hardy, because these writers annoyed him with their symbolism and their probing. He was all for Dreiser and Sherwood Anderson and particularly Sinclair Lewis. Lewis, to him, was probably the greatest novelist America had produced. Lewis was at heart little more than a newspaper reporter, and Mencken was at heart little more than a newspaper editor. The two saw eye to eye. Melville and Hawthorne were, to Mencken, "Puritan dullards."

Lewis, of course, had the additional advantage of making fun of the United States—of its Babbitts and Elmer Gantrys and Carol Kennicotts. Why was Mencken so interested in sneering at his own country? There are many reasons. Actually, he loved America. He felt more at home here than anywhere else. But he was of German origin, and he couldn't get rid of the *Deutschland über Alles* feeling. He claimed that Germany was the most cultured land in the world, and that there wasn't even a close second. He became even more strongly attached to Germany after the Allies defeated her in World War I. Mencken was outraged that such "inferior" nations as England and France and the United States should have laid his beloved Germany so low. So that anybody who made fun of so "inferior" a country as the United States was that much of a good writer to Mencken.

Then there was the much simpler matter of attracting attention. Mencken had learned, when a young man, that the first thing a writer had to do was to get an audience, and that one way of getting an audience was to poke fun at its most sacred personages and ideas. That is pretty much what Lewis did, and that was fine with Mencken. Lewis exaggerated, and Mencken knew it. Lewis was hardly a stylist, he wrote flamboyantly and Mencken knew it. Lewis was surfacy, and Mencken knew it. But he also knew that Lewis drew attention, the people who read newspapers read Lewis, and that was pretty much all that Mencken wanted to know.

Mencken claimed he was for civil liberties, but there was a catch to his claim; he was for civil liberties largely for those who agreed with him. He saw nothing wrong in denying civil liberties to German Jews, and he saw nothing wrong in the Nazi book burnings; he didn't like it, but he was not so opposed to it that he felt impelled to print articles denouncing Germans for doing this or allowing the Nazis in their midst to do it. Mencken was not a vulgar Nazi; he did not throw stones at synagogues, he was offended by the report of Nazis pulling the beards of orthodox Jews. Yet he was strongly sympathetic with the whole Nazi philosophy, as Herbert Bayard Swope said on a national radio hook-up shortly after Mencken's death. As a matter of fact, Mencken entertained several of the same ideas entertained by the Southern segregationists. Swope, former editor of the *New York World,* reported that Mencken made fun of his anti-Ku Klux Klan crusade.

But despite all this, there was a strangely tender streak in him. A good deal of the time he was lonely; a good deal of the time he considered himself a complete failure. In his early days he had many friends, among them Nathan and Goodman and several members of the faculty of the Johns Hopkins University, but these friends died off or they abandoned him because they couldn't stand his harsh feeling toward those who were caught by the depression, or they couldn't stand his strangely calm views respecting Hitler. This doubtless is one of the reasons why he married Sara Haardt. He had long been fond of her, but it is doubtful that he would have married her if so many of his men friends hadn't left him; and as he went into his fifties he began to fear death more and more and he began to feel the need, more and more, of what he called "woman's softness, every man has to have it in this world of sin and corruption." In Sara he had a loyal and comforting companion who listened to his tirades against "Roosevelt the Communist" and against "the rabid anti-German press." Sara Haardt did not agree with much of what he said—she was far more liberal politically—but she loved him and she listened and she listened, and he felt more at ease. She had difficulty in agreeing with him about his feelings toward all the friends who were leaving him. She liked Goodman very much personally, though she was not inclined to be as liberal politically as he was; hence, when Mencken railed against Goodman as a Communist or a "fool who's fallen for the *New Masses* hogwash" she found it difficult to keep silent. Besides, she knew that Mencken didn't quite mean everything he said: his violence against Goodman only reflected his continuing need for the company of that fantastic man. It was easier for Sara to agree with her husband about Nathan, for she disliked Nathan intensely: she thought he was a snob and "a clothes horse."

Sara Haardt did not live a long time. She died five years after she and Mencken were married. He mourned her sincerely, but I have always thought that toward the end of their life together he was disappointed, not in her personally but in the institution of marriage that he had shunned for so long. He often talked to me about the institution, before Sara died and afterward.

We were at Lüchow's once, and he was in a moody frame of mind. He made a comment about a girl who passed our table. "She looks like a cutie that George Nathan used to diddle when we were on the *Smart Set*," he said. "The same silly, quick, hurried walk, the same small, tight fanny. George liked them that way. He used to call them sweet pickles. Not bad. Lillian Gish used to look like that, except that she didn't smile or giggle, she'd just sit. I always had the funny feeling that any minute she might turn into a nun. I don't know. Maybe she was a nun all the time." He looked off into the distance, and I said nothing, for I had the feeling that he didn't want to be interrupted, that a talking spell had come upon him. Besides, there wasn't much I had to say. I did not know any of Nathan's girls at the time he was on the *Smart Set*, and while I had met Lillian Gish a few times, she made little impression on me.

He turned to me and continued, "Well, it's all very strange. The ways of God make no sense to me. As one gets older, he finds less and less comfort in bed with a woman. When a man's younger, it's the woman who gives him comfort. When he gets older and his woman gets older, it's she who looks for comfort in him—and all the time he still is looking for comfort in a woman. A man and woman looking for comfort in each other end up by giving each other only disappointment. Why that should be so, I don't know. Do you?"

After a while, he looked off into the distance again. Then he said, "Well, marriage is supposed to help out a man in misery, give him a warmth, a haven, make it easier for him. But I don't know." "I've never been married." "But you hear people talk, you see, you smell"

"Yes, I hear and smell and see. But—well, I'm afraid to talk."
"Come, come." "It sounds funny. Whenever I'm in a married man's
home, I mean most of the time, most such homes, or many of them,
I get the funny feeling that the wife has her eyes on me."

"I know perfectly well what you mean, and I regret to say you're
right, not because you're such a handsome buck, but because you're
a man. A woman is by nature an adulteress, and a man is by nature
an adulterer. And the sooner society gives adultery, on all levels,
a chance to express itself, the better will it be. It will mean, first and
foremost, that sex will play less of a part in a man's life, and he'll
have energy left over to think about more important things. Once
an intelligent man has had his fill of a woman, he's a free man for a
week or even two weeks, and in that time he can attend to his
business, without having a woman's nipples dangling before his eyes
all the time."

He stopped again, looked off into the distance, "Well, this is
all distant talk anyway. The world is getting colder." Suddenly he
stopped. Then he added, "That's where Goodman and Nathan
differ from me." He looked at me, and I tried to appear calm.
Actually, I was considerably surprised. He hadn't mentioned those
names in this precise connection, for many months. He had "broken"
with them a considerable time before. Then he went on, "Goodman
and Nathan still find comfort in a woman's arms. That puzzles me."
The chamber orchestra of Lüchow's was playing the Blue Danube
waltz; Mencken and I noticed it for the first time. Before, the
orchestra had played something that didn't seem familiar. A smile
went over Mencken's face. He turned to me, "It's still good, very
good, eh?" "Yes. It is." "I wish I had lived then. This world is not
for me. Too much democracy, and the democrats show their influence everywhere. There's no delicacy, no tenderness. It's all boiled
beef and cabbage. No wine. No Liebfraumilch. You know, bad as
Franz Josef was, and he was pretty bad, the life around him was
elegant, and that's what we miss now, I miss now, elegance. I don't
think an aristocratic government is bad at all. Even at its worst it's
better than a good democracy."

He turned to face me squarely. He knew I disagreed with him.

He knew I was a New Dealer, and he didn't like the New Deal at all. He also knew that I didn't like the proletarian literature of the time. But he enjoyed annoying me by implying that I did like the proletarian writers. "Well," he said, "You can have your Michael Gold. I'll take James Branch Cabell." I reminded him that I had objected to printing excerpts from Gold's *Jews Without Money* in the *Mercury,* that it was he, Mencken, who was for it. "Well," he said, "that's so, and it isn't so. You didn't object hard enough."

Then he said, "Sara didn't like this place very much. I never understood why." He said this not out of dismay, or even out of affection, or even as an indirect tribute to her memory. It was only a statement of fact. He smiled, then he said, "That slop she used to drink. Coca-Cola. Imagine that. Sometimes she used to mix it with a little rum. I think she called the concoction Cuba Libre, and she liked that. Nothing any good ever came out of Cuba, and I never drank it. I let the cook drink it, and I warned the cook not to slip it into the soup. You can't tell with these Baltimore cooks."

After a bit more talk: "Let's have another round of beer and call it quits. I feel tired." He kept silent for most of the next five or even ten minutes. I looked at him through the corner of my eye. I had never before seen him look so lonely.

Prejudices and Prophecies

MENCKEN'S ACHIEVEMENT AS AN EDITOR IS SECURE, AS EVEN his more severe critics must admit. His editorial greatness lasted over a very short period, actually for the years 1924–28, about five years. With the stock market collapse of 1929 he seemed to have lost his grip and thereafter till his retirement at the end of 1934, he did little more than fumble. His stock of ideas was unequal to what was happening in the world. But those five years were, in many ways, golden ones in the journalistic history of the United States, and largely because of Mencken's efforts.

But only great editors can make great mistakes in editorial judgment, especially when holding forth about other magazines. Mencken knew he made these mistakes, and he often laughed about them—at least some of them.

There was, first of all, *Reader's Digest*. I remember the very first issues that reached the office of the *American Mercury*. I remember seeing Mencken looking at one issue, riffling the pages, and then shouting across the room to me, "Here's something else that won't last a year; well, as long as some fat rich lady's money holds out." Mencken had no idea who was supporting the *Digest*. He was merely expressing his contempt in one of his own ways. He had a theory that all little magazines were supported by fat rich ladies. It was pure fantasy on his part. If anybody asked him to prove his theory, he would say, "Well, I have my own statistics and file of information."

"You know, Angoff," he continued, "this sheet really depresses me. The little, smelly poetry magazines are earnest and dull and worthless, but at least there's an attempt at a semblance of literature in them. This *Digest* is just a service magazine, and it performs its service by taking the life out of articles. And what articles! How to cure colds with faith and how to be happy though miserable, and rubbish like that. Mark my words, it won't last."

I agreed with him. Some months later DeWitt Wallace came to the office to arrange one of his celebrated deals. I don't remember all the details, but he did suggest this arrangement: he would pay us a yearly amount—about $1,000, I think it was—and for this he would have exclusive right, for a period of about three months after an issue of the *Mercury* was put on the news-stands, to digest whatever articles he wished. Once an article was digested he would pay the author a certain amount of money and he would also pay us an additional sum of money. Mr. Wallace looked like an honest and earnest man. I rather liked him, which is why I spoke to him as I did. I said to him in effect (for I was sure he would fail in a short time and I didn't want to hold him to his contract and get him into financial difficulties), "Mr. Wallace, your proposal is a fair one in every way, but frankly I'm worried about it for your sake. Before I say what I want to say, I want to add that your offer is far better than what other, similar digest magazines have offered." (At the time there were several digest magazines; most of them have disappeared.) I went on, "You're new and young at this business. Suppose we leave it this way: let's not sign any contract. You give us no lump sum of money. But I give you my word that if you want to digest anything in the *Mercury,* within a month after an issue is on the stands, I'll accept your offer first, ahead of any offer made by anybody else. And the reason for that is simply this: that your offer is best for the authors of the articles. As for paying the *Mercury,* you pay us whatever you pay the author."

Mr. Wallace pressed me to agree to his proposal. I refused because

I was sorry for him. I was sure, as Mencken was sure, that he couldn't possibly last more than a year or so, and I didn't want to tie him up financially. I told Mencken about my talk with Wallace when he next came up from Baltimore. Mencken looked at me and said, "Well, don't tell Knopf. We could use that $1,000. But it would be blood money. You were far more decent than I would have been. Sometimes I think you're a do-gooder at heart. Well, the poor bastard will lose his shirt. On the other hand, there's no telling. His magazine is so bad it may go over. There's no underestimating the intelligence of the American public."

Mencken also discussed with me the future of *Time* magazine. He told me that two young men, apparently Britten Haddon and Henry Luce, had seen him in Baltimore and asked for his opinion of a magazine like *Time*. He was not enthusiastic. As he told me, "They looked like nice Yale boys, more interested in making money than in putting across a really valuable idea. I didn't want to discourage them, so I didn't tell them outright their idea was worthless, but I certainly wasn't enthusiastic." Later he said to me, "The *New York Times* may be dull and repetitious, but it does give the news. What these two young geniuses are doing is condensing the *Times* and adding some mistakes of their own. But there's no telling. If the American people can elect Warren Gamaliel Harding as President, then they may very well fall for *Time*. But I don't think it will go over. It's hard to imagine."

Mencken's opinion of the future of the *New Yorker* was not a very sanguine one. "Just a wise-guy magazine," he called it. He had almost no use for the fiction or the poetry, though he did like the cartoons. He also liked some of the early book reviews of Clifton Fadiman. Mencken would sometimes talk about the Robert Benchley theatrical critiques, always favorably, and he would sometimes talk about Dorothy Parker's stories and reviews, usually unfavorably.

The one time Mencken was angry with the editor of a new magazine was when *Plain Talk* was founded by Geoffrey D. Eaton. Mencken claimed, and rightly, that *Plain Talk* was an outright imitation of the *Mercury*. "Plain stealing, plain ordinary stealing," he said to me. When Eaton asked him for a contribution to *Plain Talk,* Mencken wrote to him that he didn't have the time at the moment. To me he said, "That's gall." When Eaton died, Mencken said, "Eaton was a fool. He was a fair short story writer, and he might have become a good novelist. Why he wasted his talents on a shabby magazine, and also made enemies with it, stumps me. But, then, people are their own worst enemies, I suppose." *Plain Talk* eventually vanished.

The only magazine published in New York that Mencken read carefully and liked very much was the *Nation,* edited and published at the time by Oswald Garrison Villard. A conservative in politics and economics, Mencken sneered at Villard's "Messianic liberalism and offensive do-goodism," but he would add, "Still, all in all, he puts out a fine magazine. He gets news the newspapers don't get, he prints good articles and good reviews and good editorials. I hardly agree with a thing he says, but he stimulates me. His Prohibitionism, of course, is uncivilized, but I read his magazine." Mencken often wrote for the *Nation.* I used to see him slave over reviews for the magazine, reviews for which he would get about $7.85. I once asked him why he worked so hard on these reviews. He said, "Well, I work hard on everything I do for that magazine, not just reviews. I don't want to let them down. If I lay down on the job, they send the stuff back to me and ask me to rewrite, and I like that. It keeps me on my toes."

George Jean Nathan

HISTORY, UNFORTUNATELY, IS OFTEN WRITTEN BY MEN AND women who have access to secondary sources alone, who have never known their subjects personally; and thus they commit gross errors of fact and of judgment—as is evident in the spate of biographies that have appeared about Mencken and Fitzgerald. Most of them have little value. Nathan will probably suffer from the same kind of bogus scholarship. I knew him, at times intimately, over a period of nearly thirty-five years. I have no intention of writing a biography of him, but I would like to put down some facts and impressions that may keep future biographers from making fools of themselves.

Nathan tried to give the impression that he never voted, never served on juries, and found special pleasure in being a bad citizen. This was only one of his poses. Near the end of his life he confessed to me that he voted often and served on juries often, and I had the feeling that he took his voting and jury service seriously. What were his politics? In the main he was a Republican. He voted for Eisenhower twice, and I believe he was disappointed in him twice. He didn't take to Adlai Stevenson. I never knew why. All Nathan ever said was, "Well, Eisenhower is better for the country, for business, and I trust him more."

When Nathan was seventy-one I asked him why he didn't marry Julie Haydon, since he had told me he had been in love with her for years. "Now, now, Angoff," he said. "Hold your horses. What's your rush?"

One of Nathan's most unpleasant duties was to comment upon the plays of friends such as Dreiser and Anderson. "They think," he once said to me, "that a novelist can write a few plays between his novels. They just don't know how hard it is to write a play. The real trouble is that, deep down, they don't take playwriting seriously. Well, Henry James made the same mistake, and so has Hemingway, who is one of the worst playwrights who ever lived. He made the special mistake of thinking that all a play needs is dialogue. It also needs a dramatic mind, and that Hemingway hasn't got."

The critical and psychological mystery about Nathan is a simple one: how did this fop, who knew nothing about slum life, who prided himself upon being above the vast and silent majority of misery—how did he come to be the champion of O'Neill and O'Casey, both of whom wrote so dramatically and so sincerely and so lovingly about the people of the slums? And how was it that this same fop and boulevardier and snob saw through Noel Coward so readily—Noel Coward, who wrote almost entirely about snobs and fops? There is still another mystery about Nathan: how was it that this same man who saw through Noel Coward and who so admired O'Neill and O'Casey could see through the pretentiousness and hollowness and falseness of Clifford Odets? Time and again Nathan told me, as he wrote in his articles, that Odets was a third-rate writer who didn't know the people of the Bronx but wrote about them as they were reflected through Odets' Hollywood mind.

Nathan had the highest opinion of his own critiques. He thought that they were far superior to those of any other critic of his time, or of any other time in American dramatic history. Yet, he nearly always asked the elevator operator at the Royalton Hotel what he thought about his last review. And if the elevator operator was not entirely enthusiastic—often he hesitated in expressing his opinion simply because he hadn't read Nathan's last review and didn't dare to say so—Nathan's whole day would be spoiled. I doubt that he ever learned to take criticism, real or fancied, from anyone.

I went with Nathan to the opening night of *Grand Hotel*. The applause had been tremendous. Sam Jaffe and Hortense Alden, the principals, took curtain call after curtain call.

As we walked back to the Royalton for a nightcap, Nathan said, "So what do you think, my dear Herrn Professor Doctor?"

I was afraid to express my opinion. He insisted that I talk. I said, "Well, I thought it was a piece of cheap pulp."

"For once you are right," he said. "Now listen to an even greater professor. My dear friend X on the New York —— will say of it, 'A deep and penetrating slice of life, wonderfully acted.' And my dear friend Y of the New York —— will say of it, 'A deep and heartwarming insight into life magically acted.' "

Nathan was absolutely right, to the last comma and period.

Later that same evening Nathan said, "Remember this. Whenever a critic says something is 'heartwarming,' he means he is bewildered by what he saw or read or is ashamed for having liked something that his better sense tells him he should not have liked. In other words, he is confessing mediocrity."

Why did Nathan join the Catholic Church toward the end of his life? I don't know. He had sneered at the "superstitions" of the Church for many years, as anybody who reads his various books, and especially the Clinical Notes department in the old *American Mercury,* can see. It is true that he never denounced the Catholics as much as he denounced or made fun of the Methodists and the Presbyterians and the Episcopalians, but he had never revealed to me that he planned to join the Catholic Church. The feeling I had was that he would never formally join any church. Further, I had the impression that he was totally "non-church." This was confirmed for me by his attitude toward Mencken's marriage in an Episcopalian church. Nathan said to me several times, "Mencken's marriage in church I don't understand at all."

Some things may throw light upon Nathan's very late conversion to Catholicism. On several occasions he had told me that his mother was friendly with the late Cardinal Dougherty of Philadelphia. He also told me that his mother was friendly with a parish priest in Philadelphia.

Nathan frequently spoke in a very sympathetic manner of Catholic customs and rituals. When a friend of his, Curley by name—I do not remember his full name; I believe he was associated with the Hearst publications—died, Nathan went to his funeral, and Nathan spoke movingly of the Catholic funeral service. "It was rather impressive," he said to me.

Nathan was too much of the civilized, metropolitan man to denounce the violent anti-Catholicism of Sean O'Casey. for whom he had not only vast respect but deep affection. But he did say to me, "You know, Sean is a little unfair to the Catholics. They're much better than he makes them out to be."

In all the time that I was close to Nathan, and we saw a good deal of each other over a period of many years, never, not even toward the very end, did he give me any inkling that he was taking lessons leading toward conversion to Catholicism. He told me several other intimate matters. But this he did not tell me.

Was Nathan of Jewish origin? He was, but exactly how deep his Jewish origin was I don't know. Early in my relationship with him, he told me that his father was Jewish. Several years later he told me that his mother was "partly Jewish." He never elaborated on this statement. When the Hitler madness came upon the scene, Nathan was perturbed—I fear I cannot use a more powerful word. On one occasion he said, "You know, Angoff, as I walk down Fifth Avenue, I can see the Mischa Elman in every Jew's eyes." But as the Hitler madness intensified and the persecution of the Jews increased, Nathan talked less and less about "the Mischa Elman in every Jew's eyes." In 1934 he ceased talking about the Jews altogether.

Early in my association with Mencken he told me that in the very first editorial of the *American Mercury* he had referred to Nathan as "my unbaptized co-editor."

"This may and it may not surprise you, Angoff," Mencken said to me. "But George objected to this phrase. Apparently he didn't want people to know he had any Jewish blood. So I took the phrase out."

A few months before he died, I had tea with Nathan at the Algonquin; he was (as far as I knew him) more a tea drinker than a coffee drinker, though toward the end of his life he took to frequent coffee drinking on the ground that his doctor had told him that coffee was better for the circulation than was tea. My book on Mencken, *H. L. Mencken: A Portrait From Memory,* had just gone to my publisher, and I wanted to get Nathan's view on a very touchy matter concerning Mencken.

I decided to come right out with my question: "Was Mencken anti-Semitic? I think that in a very real sense he was, and I say so in my book—anyway, I strongly hint at it."

Nathan was silent for a few seconds, then said, "If you say what you have just told me, you won't be wrong. Perhaps I can put it this way. Menck was a Prussian." Nathan hesitated again. Then he added, "I guess it would be right to say that he never wholly liked Jews. He respected them, he was amused by them, he was even afraid of them, but he didn't like them. Maybe he even disliked them. I suppose that's anti-Semitism."

In his theatrical criticism Nathan was a genuine scholar. It would probably be correct to say that he was one of the best-read dramatic critics in our history thus far. But in his other writings his learning and integrity were of a lesser order. For a while he conducted the department of Clinical Notes in the old *American Mercury* all by himself. Hitherto it had been conducted by both Mencken and Nathan. Mencken told me to watch Nathan closely, to read his copy carefully, because "George just knows nothing about anything except the theater, and he insists upon writing about the things he knows nothing about. So watch him." Mencken was right. Nathan perpetrated several bloomers in his copy. Once he wrote about Samuel Gompers of the American Federation of Labor as if he were still alive. I pointed out his error to him.

"When did he die?" Nathan asked.

"Two years ago," I said. "No, three years ago."

Another time Nathan wrote a paragraph about military men in the White House and wrote of George Washington that he had been born in England. I changed this, and said so to Nathan. "Now, I always thought he was born somewhere outside London."

Nathan read little fiction. My belief is that he only ran through the novels of Lewis and Dreiser and Anderson and Fitzgerald. But there were two novelists who, I incline to think, interested him above all others—namely, Joseph Hergesheimer and James Branch Cabell. He didn't express his admiration in public very often because (and this is only a hunch) he wasn't too sure of his critical standards with respect to fiction, and he simply didn't want to stick his neck out.

Why did Nathan found the *American Spectator,* the monthly magazine in newspaper format, whose editorial board included Dreiser, Anderson, Boyd, O'Neill, and Cabell? I fear the answer is very simple: to annoy Mencken, who had pushed him out of the *American Mercury* and who was having trouble on the magazine. Mencken knew it, Knopf knew it, but Nathan didn't know that Mencken and Knopf knew it.

Why did Mencken and Nathan finally break up on the *American Mercury?* One reason was that their interests changed; Mencken was abandoning literary criticism and going in for political commentary, while Nathan remained interested chiefly in literary matters. But there was still another reason—Nathan's laziness and selfishness. Nathan spent an average of about an hour a day in the office of the *Mercury.* He answered a few letters, glanced at a few short stories and poems, and sent most of the manuscripts and a good deal of other correspondence to Mencken. Mencken pleaded with him to do more work. Nathan refused. Then came the two political conventions in 1924, and Nathan continued to send Mencken the manuscripts and correspondence while Mencken was covering the conventions for the Baltimore *Sun.* When Mencken came back from the conventions, he decided to get rid of Nathan. Nathan fought back, but Mencken won out, with the aid of Knopf, who eventually sided with Mencken.

Nathan occupied a desk in the Knopf offices adjacent to the *Mercury* offices for some time after he was pushed out of the editorial conduct of the magazine. Several of the secretaries would do his dictation or otherwise help him out. Not once, as far as I knew, did he give a single girl a Christmas gift. Mencken was the opposite. He loved to hand out gifts.

Nathan, who generally had good intuition about people, especially women, was completely wrong about Sara Haardt, Mencken's wife. Nathan thought she was a great admirer of his. Actually she sneered at him, often calling him "a fop and a clotheshorse."

Nathan's reputation, at least in his earlier years, of being something of a Charlie Chaplin in his attraction to very young girls was based on fact. He apparently felt relaxed in the company of seventeen- and eighteen-year-olds. A girl in her twenties was very old to him. Mencken, on the other hand, was attracted to older women. Mencken said once, "George likes them while they're still giggly and itchy. I like them over thirty, when they're beginning to get a little ripe and moldy. I look for a touch of gray in a woman."

Perhaps this is the place to say something about the difference between Mencken's and Nathan's views of virginity. It was my impression that Mencken was inclined to take what may be called the traditional view. Deep down in his heart, he probably had grave doubts about marrying any woman who had had sexual experiences in or outside of marriage. In his liquored moments he did call such women sluts. As a matter of fact, this very tendency of his was the cause of a serious squabble between him and Nathan. Eugene O'Neill had just married one of his later wives. Nathan, who was always anxious about O'Neill's happiness, said he was delighted, on the ground that O'Neill's new wife might bring him some of the personal happiness that he was so deeply in need of but had never before wholly achieved. Mencken laughed and said, "That's something, George! The new wife is like his former wives, or his former girls, just a cutie, just a slut." Nathan burst out, "That's barbaric!", and stalked out of the room.

One of the several mysteries about Nathan's criticism was his violent dislike of Thornton Wilder. I seldom argued with him, because I was more eager to listen; besides, my knowledge of the theater, compared to his, was paltry. But I was (and still am) so sure that *Our Town* was a great play—in itself, perhaps, greater than any single play that O'Neill had done—that I felt impelled on occasion to object mildly. To most of my objections Nathan would say, smiling, "Now, now, you are falling for all that Brooks Atkinson hogwash. *Our Town* is a steal from Joyce." I asked what he meant by "a steal from Joyce." He answered, "Now, now, don't talk like a professor." Apparently he referred to some article that pointed out Wilder's indebtedness to Joyce's general method. I said that such indebtedness was obvious and nothing to be ashamed of, that such indebtedness, in literary history, was as common as the sunrise. When I said this, Nathan would say, "Let's call a halt to this nonsense. You'll learn when you get older."

Was Nathan always above personal attachments in his criticism? Of course not. Somewhere, in one of his books, he says something to this effect: "Critical objectivity is a wonderful thing, and all decent critics try to abide by it. But let a man's childhood nannie write a play, and out of the window flies all critical objectivity."

I saw Nathan in the company of enormously wealthy people, including one man who is reputed to have made millions in the stock market. I saw Nathan in the company of individuals, both men and women, high in society; and there was a wide streak of social climbing in Nathan. I saw Nathan in the company of nobility— members of the former Russian royal family, members of the former Spanish royal family, members of the family of French pretenders to the French throne, members of the former Yugoslav royal family and of the former Bulgarian royal family and of the former Rumanian royal family. But I never saw him so happy and so relaxed and so utterly at home as he was on the three occasions when he, Sean O'Casey, and I were spending a couple of hours or more at the Blue Ribbon Restaurant on West Forty-fourth Street in New York City, one of Nathan's favorite cafes. O'Casey was encased in a turtleneck sweater, his fingers occasionally went into his coffee (O'Casey's eyesight was very poor); and Nathan obviously loved it all. Nathan did a great deal for O'Casey, and that is one of his eternal glories. But O'Casey also did a great deal for Nathan. He brought out all that was lovely and all that was true and all that was beautiful in him, deeply buried as it was under heaps of all sorts of rubbish.

Nathan was a hedonist, a flaneur, a boulevardier; a superlative dandy, with his French cuffs extending beyond his jacket sleeves, and large cuff links emphasizing their dandiness. He was one of the last to sport a cane on Fifth Avenue. And yet—so contradictory was he—he lived for 50 years in the Royalton Hotel in a small two-room apartment which looked like a second-hand book-store. There were books underneath his sofa—books piled high on rickety chairs. Busts of himself and others were strewn all over.

His outlook on life was that of the Fifth Avenue of the Golden Twenties, when there were double-decker busses, traffic towers and wonderful old mansions at the corner of Fifty-First Street and the corner of Fifty-Seventh Street and Forty-Eighth Street.

We met for the last time when we dined at the Blue Ribbon, on West-Forty-Fourth Street, not far from the Royalton. I had picked him up in the lobby of the Royalton and we walked slowly further west, he almost dragging his feet. He hadn't been out of his apartment for several days; the doctor had told him to move around more, to take short walks on his block and even a bit beyond. But he hesitated. He was afraid of getting dizzy.

"The traffic is getting pretty heavy," he said, as we waited to cross Sixth Avenue.

"Yes," I said, recalling how we used to disobey the traffic lights on this same corner 20 years earlier.

"The lights are pretty dim, aren't they, Angoff?"

"Yes, they are."

He had a favorite spot on the second floor of the Blue Ribbon, a corner table.

He ordered soup immediately. As usual I balked. I didn't like soup. I still don't like it. "You've been poorly brought up, my boy," he said. "Soup is what keeps you alive. You know something?"

"What?"

"I don't believe there's been a day in the last 50, no, it's probably 60 years that I haven't had soup at least once a day. Dr. Christiansen approves of it." Dr. Christiansen was his physician.

I had soup.

"Isn't it a little dark here?" he said.

"A little."

He had told me some months before that hardening of the arteries might affect his vision.

He ordered Yankee pot roast, and so did I. He ordered ice cream, so did I. Then he ordered demitasse, and I ordered a large coffee.

"Well, what do you think Heinie's doing now?" Heinie was Mencken, who had been dead about two years.

"Reading a Baptist weekly, I suppose."

He smiled. "Could be."

Suddenly Nathan began to talk about Cornell, his Alma Mater. He began to repeat an old line he had used with me, that Cornell was a better university than Harvard, that its campus was more beautiful, and so on. He had once asked me, indirectly, to be sure, but plainly just the same, to try to get him an honorary doctorate from Harvard. I pleaded that my word with the hierarchy at Harvard was worthless, but he implied that a word properly placed wouldn't do any harm. I did place such words in various places, in vain. Nathan did get an honorary degree (an Litt.D., I believe) from the University of Indiana.

He put two pills in his mouth, and washed them down with coffee. "My doctor says they will help my blood pressure and my neuralgia, and all sorts of other things that are wrong with me. I don't believe him but I'm afraid not to. I begin to think, along with Heinie, that medicine is about 99 percent superstition. The only medicine I believe in is veterinary medicine. Our dog has been ailing, too. But you should see how the hound jumps around, all because of the pills the vet prescribes. I may try some of the same pills. Don't tell Julie." (Julie Hayden, his wife).

"Are you off liquor altogether?"

"Well, yes and no. I don't think the doctor wants me to take any, or just a little. When nobody's looking I take a nip now and then. But I feel like the character in O'Neill's *The Iceman Cometh*, the alcohol seems to have gone out of the liquor these days." He smiled.

"Do you think it's Eisenhower's fault? You're an anti-Eisenhower man."

"It could be his fault. Truman would never take alcohol out of any liquor."

"You're right there, my boy. Truman never would."

A waiter came along. "Was everything fine, Mr. Nathan, I mean good?"

"Yes, yes," said Nathan. "Only I wish you would teach my friend here, Mr. Angoff, to learn to like your marvelous soup."

Now began the usual battle as to who would pay, whether we should go dutch, or toss up a coin.

"Angoff, I'm so close to being an angel, that you should really let me pay. Please."

I let him pay.

We walked toward the Royalton. He looked at his watch and said, "Have you time for a nightcap at the Algonquin?"

"Sure. But you mustn't drink."

"Who told you that?"

"You did."

He smiled. "The doctor didn't say *absolutely*, did he?"

"Well. . . ."

He seemed tired as we entered the Algonquin. It was about ten-thirty and the lobby was virtually empty.

"What will you have?" I asked.

"Oh, stop that nonsense, Angoff. This is on me."

"No. This time, this one time. I want to."

"Well, you're stubborn. Just for that I'll shock you. I'll just have a coffee."

"Oh, no, you can't do that."

"No, that's right. Make mine beer, High Life, but only on the condition that you order one, too, none of your pansy drinks like sherry or port."

I ordered two High Lifes.

"Fine beer," he said. "How a man called Miller came to make it, is beyond me. Do you know?"

"No."

"God is a comedian. A good beer should be made by a man called Kuggelwasser or Adolf Hetmeyer or Otto Kleinman or Otto Grossman. But God's humor has always puzzled me."

Some people began to come in and out of the hotel. Nathan watched them. He took another drink of his beer. "There isn't a flutter or bounce in any of them," he said. "Travelling salesmen, professors, small town bankers, and the terrible women these men generally have. They're all silently hysterical, not an ounce of real happiness. Can you imagine the mutual disappointment that goes on in bed? They make love with the aid of aspirin and alcohol. Alcohol is for the memory, it isn't an aphrodisiac.

"You know something, Angoff? That's where Heinie and I differ sharply. No matter what he says, he likes these people, he says they're solid, pay their bills, and all that. Did you know that deep down he's a Babbitt, that he really didn't agree with Red Lewis? Heinie thought that these people built up the United States. I say they're holding it back. The people who built up the United States are the heavy drinkers and the persistent lovers and the writers and the musicians. In other words, my boy, the artists. And if I discover, when I become an angel, that the other angels aren't artists, I'll really know that God is cruel. There must be a limit even to God's cruelty."

He took another long drink of his beer. "Ah, now it's a small town hotel. I may be wrong, yes, I may be wrong. But I never have been."

Suddenly he said, "Angoff, do you think they serve good drinks in Heaven?"

"In Heaven they serve Passover wine and seltzer."

He smiled. "That's not a bad drink for pregnant women. What about hell? Do they serve whiskey sours and Martinis and . . . what do they serve? You know about all such things."

"In hell they serve all the same drinks they serve here. But there's one difference."

"What's that?"

"In Heaven you don't have to pay, and in hell you do have to pay."

"Well," he said thoughtfully, "I don't know about that. If it's free, there must be a catch somewhere. Angoff, I want to ask you something?"

"Yes."

"You know I'm going to be an angel."

"I'm sure of it."

"Tell me, Angoff, who was the one great man who lived in my time? You'll outlive me by 50 years, but I want you to be objective in answering."

"In literature?"

"Of course. That's all that matters. Literature is king and queen and Pope and everything. Don't be a mealy-mouthed politician, Angoff. Whatever you say will be held against you. I'll quote you wherever I'm going."

"Dreiser," I said, though I wasn't sure why.

"A good answer, but you're wrong."

"Who was it?"

"O'Neill, Eugene O'Neill. One of the things I'm most sorry for in all my life is that I didn't go to his funeral."

I didn't know what to say.

"Even more so than my not going to Heinie's funeral. I should have gone, I really should have gone. It's been gnawing at me, Angoff, that I didn't go. Think of it, America's greatest playwright going to his grave, with only his wife accompanying him. Terrible, very terrible. . . . A man needs friends most then, don't you think?"

"Of course."

"Angoff, is there a Broadway in hell or heaven?"

"I think so."

"That makes me feel better. You know, Heinie and I used to have arguments about New York. He looked upon it as a Babylon, you know, all that talk. He hated New York. And that was why he never really could be as important as he wanted to be. He was a small town man. He had small town tastes. New York is the capital of the United States, and it always will be that. It's a lot more important than Washington. Tastes are fashioned here, manners are born here, everything has to pass through New York before it's important. I've said this to you before. It's the cities that build up civilizations, and the deserts that build up religions. This isn't my idea, I'm too old to fool you that way. But it's true, isn't it, eh?"

"I guess so."

Again silence. Then he turned to me and said, "I was reading a postcard I got from Scott Fitzgerald . . . he must have sent it to me many years ago. I got to thinking about the changed view of him now. It amazes me."

"What do you mean?"

"Well, what the critical boys say about him, especially those in the *New Yorker* crowd. They hail him as a genius. That poor novel by Budd Schulberg was worse than poor. Scott deserved something better than such slop by a poor writer, but the Mizener book is no better. Neither of them understands Scott. Scott was no great writer. He wrote about life he didn't know much about. *The Great Gatsby* is about the sort of life Scott would have liked to have lived. It's fictional fiction, that's what it is. Scott was nothing more than a somewhat glorified Richard Harding Davis. Very little more. That's where I agree somewhat with Heinie. Heinie shouldn't have praised *This Side of Paradise* as much as he did. It's a poorly written book, really little better than a series of superior comic strips, with hardly any characters. I imagine it will make little sense to people twenty years from now, because, well, simply because it's not literature. But it does have a vitality of sorts, or it did."

"They're talking about *Tender Is the Night* now," I said.

"Well," said Nathan. "I vaguely remember it. It made little sense to me, the little of it I could read. I know they talk about its beautiful writing. Just a little polished, that is all. Sometimes I think the twenties were a period distinguished by good writing by poor writers, and bad writing by good writers. I refer to Dreiser and O'Neill. Neither writes well, but both are great writers."

"And Willa Cather?"

"Yes, I know, you're a fan of hers. Well, she is good, and she is a writer. But I hope you will forgive an old man when he says he finds her dull. All her characters smell of Ivory soap, even the 'bad' women, and that's something I don't believe. Sin doesn't smell like soap, it smells like perfume—cheap perfume, perhaps, but perfume. Ah, I have a man who will confound what you're thinking about."

"What man?"

"Sean O'Casey. He should get the Nobel Prize, he's the best playwright in the world, since Shaw and O'Neill became angels. But the Nobel Prize Committee is full of politicians. They may not get around to the Irish till they've given prizes to the Pakistanis and the Punjabites and the Liberians and the rest. Then there is Sean's Communism. But he's no more a Communist than is the Pope. But, my boy, you were right about only one thing."

"What?"

"Eisenhower. I voted for him, and I was wrong, dead wrong. He's only a Coolidge in a military uniform."

I laughed.

"Mencken would have liked to have said that," said Nathan. "I'll tell him when I see him. Well, I'm getting tired. I think I'll turn in."

We walked over to the Royalton across the street. We were at the entrance. Nathan smiled and said, "Goodnight. And you ought to drink a little more beer. Good for you."

"Goodnight."

Robert Frost

O F ALL THE CONTEMPORARY AMERICAN POETS ROBERT FROST has always seemed to me to be profoundly European—in his basic attitude toward life (a combination of despair and trembling optimism), in his comfort in the old poetic forms, in his silent courage in a world that has never taken too friendly an attitude to poets. The first book of his I read, *North of Boston,* when I was barely out of Harvard, was a turning point in my life. Here was a man I could follow. Here was a man who understood what was troubling me. Here was a man who could talk to me across the miles of cold distance.

When I was on the *Mercury,* way back in the twenties, I pleaded with Mencken to ask Frost to submit poems to us. Mencken said, "I won't ask him. He should submit poems to us himself." I asked Mencken what he thought about Frost's poems.

Mencken said, "Oh, they're all right. I think Robinson is a better man. The trouble with Robinson is that he's not a salesman. In this world of sin and corruption one has to be a salesman to get ahead. Frost is a salesman. I hear he's also a vain man. I believe that. I sense it, and don't you tell me I'm talking like Blanche Knopf. I'm better than that, and you know it."

I protested as vigorously as I could. I said that Frost might be a

vain man, but that this could be forgiven in view of the harsh treatment he got at the hands of American editors when he first sent his
poems around. Mencken pooh-poohed me. "You're too enthusiastic,
Angoff. Keep your pants on. Robinson is just a better poet. When
you get older you'll agree with me." Alas, we never did print a poem
by Robert Frost.

As the years rolled on I did see him now and then at gatherings,
especially of the Poetry Society of America, of which I have been
a member for many years. Robert Frost was honorary president of
the Society. Often he came up to me and spoke in a cordial manner.
He spoke as if he had known me for years and we had been friends
over a long period of time. I was astonished. Once he asked me
about Mencken. "A strange man," said Frost, "a very strange man.
I think there are many Menckens, and most of them are unhappy."
I asked Frost what he meant. "I mean just that," he said. He did not
elaborate this statement.

Many years later I was doing research work for Meet the Press,
a radio-television panel program. For years I had been pleading
with Lawrence E. Spivak, the producer of the show, to put Robert
Frost on. Spivak had been having politicians on generally—United
States senators, congressmen, governors, income tax commissioners,
ambassadors, and so on. "How about having a decent man on, like
Robert Frost?" I said. "All right, I know how you feel about poets."
Spivak had the common attitude toward poets, that they were
"strange" but to be tolerated. "But," I continued, "a decent man
like Frost would add some dignity and quality to your program.
All right, put him on in the Christmas season." Spivak finally
agreed. I believe he was actually sympathetic to the idea right along.

I wrote an introduction to the Robert Frost program and he was
pleased, according to Spivak.

Months passed. Years passed. Then Meet the Press held a party
for its tenth anniversary on the air. The party was held at the
Sheraton Park Hotel in Washington. I was invited. It was a huge
affair. Some 750 people were present. I sat at a table with leading
television and radio personalities.

At the end of the party I went into the men's room. It was filled with some of the eminent guests. One of them I recognized immediately. I had never met him before, but I had seen his photograph in the newspapers many times. He was Senator Theodore Green of Rhode Island. God alone knows why I did it, for I was entirely unprovoked. I went up to him and said, "Senator, I want to tell you that you stand for the best in New England." The aged, undersized member of the Upper House of the United States Congress looked at me, and it was obvious that he was pleased. He didn't know that I was then a voter in New York, that I had not voted in Massachusetts for many years. But apparently he took no chances. A potential vote is a potential vote. Senator Green smiled and thanked me.

"Senator Green, how did you like the proceedings?" I asked.

"Fine, fine," he said.

"That's good," I said.

The Senator turned right and left, apparently to make sure nobody was listening. Then he said to me, "You know something?"

"What, Senator?"

"There was only one honest man on the platform, Robert Frost." He smiled.

Frost was the only poet on the platform. Among the other eminent men were Vice President Barkley, many United States Senators, even more United States Congressmen, at least one member of the United States Supreme Court, a few governors, and hordes of lesser officials.

The following day Spivak gave a lunch for Robert Frost. I was invited again. Mr. and Mrs. Spivak were present, also two people from NBC, a public relations man for the Democratic National Committee, and I. Frost ate very well. He downed two drinks—I believe they were martinis—with relish. He then excused himself to Mr. Spivak and asked if he might take me along to an adjoining room for a gabble.

As he stretched out on an easy chair, he looked like an aged, spreading, but powerful oak tree that had faced up against all sorts of inclement weather. "Last night was a night," he said in his slow, slightly hoarse voice.

"Yes," I said.

"Did you see the Vice President?"

"Yes."

"I like him, I do like him. I sometimes think he's in the wrong business, and I told him so, I did. He would make a good teacher and a good poet, maybe a good college president. Not those big ones that are factories. Yes, factories. Some of them, and I have taught at some, look like Times Square. No, you can't learn anything in Times Square. You only get to dislike people, and that's not learning, it's bad learning, and bad learning is not learning, you know."

"I like the Vice President, too," I said. "I wish he had told some more stories."

"Yes. He is a good story teller. People don't tell enough stories nowadays. Too busy for stories. People are too busy for stories. America was great when people told stories. I have a theory about Lincoln. He was what he was because he was a good story teller. And another thing. He wasn't solemn. Trees are never solemn. The sky is never solemn. It's angry sometimes, but not solemn. Only people are solemn. Animals are not solemn. They get angry now and then, and every intelligent creature in this world has a right to get angry. But not solemn. That's a sign of defeat. Yes, the Vice President is never solemn, and he knows how to tell stories. I wish the Democratic Party would take over story-telling, make that part of its platform, its whole platform." He smiled slowly . . . his well-known secretive smile that somehow filled the whole room with sunshine. He was proud of what he said.

"That would be a good idea, I mean a good platform," I said. "I like that."

He was pleased I agreed with him. He began, "The others—" and he made a wide sweep with his hands. "But I like to be among them. Maybe that's bad of me. My mother would not have liked that, I guess." Again that smile. "Well, I like to be around them. They're really not as evil as they would like the rest of us to think they are. No, they're not evil."

Spivak brought in some coffee for both of us. Spivak said, "Perhaps, Mr. Frost, you would like some whiskey instead."

"Yes," said Frost. "Some whiskey, but I like coffee, too. Whiskey and coffee. That will do, a fine combination. People like combinations now, don't they?" He stopped. Apparently he was searching for some pithy remark to make about combinations, but the remark wouldn't come.

He said, "Yes, the Vice President. You know, there's a little of the story teller in President Truman. I say a man who likes to play folk tunes is a man who likes to tell and hear stories. Small town men, both of them, the President and the Vice President. It's small town men who will keep the nation strong, and it's such men who will keep the Democratic Party alive. The same with preachers. In small towns people are more honest than in big towns. Too many people watching in small towns. In big cities, too many people rushing too much to watch their neighbors and the politicians. Yes, the same with preachers. Preachers are a sort of politicians, anyway." Once more that smile.

Then he said, "There was a preacher in our neighborhood. A good man, and I used to go to his church. He got $5,500 a year, or something like that. But he also got his house and a car, not a fancy car but a good serviceable car, and he got other things free or at reduced prices. He got many of his groceries free or at reduced prices, as I said, and the same with furniture. I thought he led a good life, a comfortable life. He was a good man. Then he got a call to a church in the Boston neighborhood, a very rich church. They gave him, I think, fifteen thousand dollars a year, that's a lot of money, eh, and they gave him a good car, much better than he got in Vermont, and he got other, what do you call them, fringe benefits, so that he was getting a total of maybe twenty thousand dollars a year, no, closer to thirty thousand. Well, he took the job, and he left us. We were sorry to have him go. Well, when I was in Boston not long after I went over to his church to hear him preach, and I could hardly wait for the end. In Vermont he used to preach against sin and selfishness and industrial evil and racial snobbishness, and he preached for Christian decency, which is all right, what a preacher should preach. Now, he was all smoothness, you know, he spoke with qualifications, nevertheless this and to-the-contrary-notwithstanding that. I don't remember exactly what he said, it made me so sick, but he sort of said that perhaps the South, in the segregation fight, had a reason for its stubbornness and that the North should practice Christian patience. You know the sort of cautious talk. I say this man became dishonest, and I went back to Vermont and I told the folks that we were well rid of him."

I asked him about various poets, in both America and England. He smiled, "Oh, sometimes I think I'm out of the running. They all seem to have so many secrets. I say, well, if you have secrets, you can keep them." He smiled at me. He was proud of the line about secrets. He continued. "Yes, they're secretive. The good ones and the bad ones, all secretive. Even the good ones I hardly understand. Sometimes I do, sometimes I don't. I really have to strain myself to like any of them, even a little. Poetry, like love, shouldn't be made so difficult. When it's difficult it doesn't last."

He seemed to be especially disturbed about John Ciardi. "John, maybe, has something. I used to think so, anyway. Maybe he still has. But he tries to do too many things. And he ought to be a little more at ease, quieter. Moving to New York and the New York magazines made him shrill. The New York noise gets into people. I don't like a place where people can't be quiet and absent-minded. A poet gets his best ideas when he's absent-minded. Nerves, nerves. I walk along Fifth Avenue, and I look at the poor trees. I can see them tremble with nervousness. Terrible. In Vermont trees tremble only when the wind comes to them, and then they really don't tremble. They sort of embrace the wind, in a hammer-lock, is that what wrestlers call it?"

"I don't know."

"Yes. Anyway, trees never tremble on a sunny day. Trees are never nervous. They don't take aspirin. But I'm not sure about those Fifth Avenue trees. They may have to. But the grass on Fifth Avenue. Sometimes, as I walk along the Avenue, I see a blade of grass between slabs of cement, and that blade is not nervous at all. It's astonishing how many of these solitary blades manage to get through a day and a night without getting trampled. A blade of grass can be very sturdy." He smiled a crackling slow smile. "I don't know. Maybe grass is meek, and the meek, we are promised, shall inherit the earth."

Suddenly he changed the subject. "I never met Mencken. I liked him, and I didn't like him. I don't mind a man with a sharp tongue, but I do mind a man with hardness in his heart.

"I know he didn't like poetry. That's all right. You know what I mean. Lincoln, I guess, didn't like poetry, such as the twist poets write, I call them twist poets, eh?"

I sensed he wanted me to approve his phrase. "That's a good phrase," I said. " 'Twist poets.' "

"But Lincoln had a poetic soul, and his Gettysburg address is poetry. Mencken has no poetic soul. Lincoln heard the music of words and he heard the music of nature and of life and of man. Mencken only hears the music of music. That's parochialism."

The last remark impressed me very much and I couldn't help exclaiming, "You got him just right."

"But he was amusing," he continued. "I mean sometimes."

Just then we were called back into the adjacent room, where some more people had come.

Sinclair Lewis

I ONCE SAID TO H. L. MENCKEN THAT IN MANY WAYS THE MOST successful of Lewis's novels was *Dodsworth*, and that Fran was far more likely to endure as a woman character than was even Leora Arrowsmith.

"You're crazy, Angoff," said Mencken. "Lewis's best book is *Elmer Gantry*, and the boys who have sneered at it will regret their comments. But what you say leads to me to tell you something. Poor Lewis has never been loved. The two women he married were dreadful. His first wife was a fake Bronx duchess, and his second was a hurricane. I must also add that women found him rather unappealing physically."

The final estrangement between Lewis and Mencken—it lasted the remainder of their lives—was due, in so far as I could make out, to an act of bad taste on the part of Lewis. Shortly after Mencken's marriage to Sara Haardt, Lewis invited them to spend a long weekend at his home in Vermont. The very first night that Mencken and his bride had closed the door to their room for the night, Lewis barged in on them, and let out a loud guffaw. Mencken was outraged—perhaps a little more so than was his wife who looked upon Lewis as something of a juvenile delinquent.

A few days later Mencken said to George Jean Nathan, "Did you ever hear of such a swinish thing?" Nathan said, "That's Red Lewis."

One day Lewis invited a group of us—Mencken, Nathan, Philip Goodman (a play producer), a dentist (whose name I don't remember: he was short, completely bald, and quite pleasant) and me—to come to his apartment in New York City, which I believe was, at the time, in the East Sixties. Lewis had been drinking, but he had not yet become insulting. As we went in Dorothy Thompson was holding forth about the world situation, especially about the then Prime Minister Neville Chamberlain. Lewis waited till she was through. Then he got on a chair and in his truly inimitable style delivered a speech on "British Rights in a World of Sin," that was so deadly a take-off on Mr. Chamberlain's oratory that we could hardly control ourselves with our laughter. Dorothy Thompson merely looked at her husband, stone serious, not saying a word. When Lewis was finished she said, "As a college boy prank, dear, you were funny, real funny, but that is all. You simply know nothing about world politics."

On the way home Goodman turned to Mencken and said, "Henry, did you see poor Red, how he was on the verge of crying? What a bitchy woman!"

"You talk like a cynic, Phil," said Mencken. "Didn't you know marriages are made in heaven?"

Not long after pretty much the same group went with Lewis to the same apartment to have dinner with him. He was sober and in good spirits. As we got to the door of his apartment Lewis put his ear to the door. We could all hear Dorothy Thompson talking at the top of her voice to an audience that had come to obtain enlightenment from her on some world issue. Lewis listened and listened. Then he turned to us and said, "It is talking again. Let's go to Lüchow's."

I was at Philip Goodman's house one night and the talk came around to Lewis. Lewis and Goodman, for a short time, were close friends—and then they parted for a reason that is still mysterious to me.

"Charlie," said Goodman, "did you ever notice how uncomfortable Lewis is at the Algonquin?"

"No, I haven't."

"He is. He doesn't like literary company, he doesn't like literary gossip. I honestly think he's most at home in the back room with a group of Elks or Masons. And maybe that's what Mencken likes about him. They're both essentially small-town men. Now Nathan, who's a snob of the worst sort, he's a metropolitan man. Am I being silly, or am I being profound, or is there little difference between the two?"

When Lewis got the Nobel Prize Mencken spread the rumor (made up entirely out of the proverbial whole cloth) that Upton Sinclair had cabled to Stockholm asking whether the Committee hadn't made a mistake because of the fact that *Sinclair* was part of the name of each writer. If the rumor reached Upton Sinclair he no doubt took it in good spirit, for he must have become used to Mencken's brand of humor across the many years of their friendship.

Lewis was generous in his praise of younger writers. Among those he singled out for praise was Thomas Wolfe, whose *Look Home-ward, Angel* he liked. Wolfe didn't think so highly of Lewis. "Lewis is no writer at all," I once heard him say.

In the middle Thirties I met a former mistress of Mussolini. They had known each other in Mussolini's Socialist days and had been deeply attached to each other for many years. She left him abruptly when she was convinced that he had betrayed Socialist principles and had embarked upon Fascism, which stood for everything that she abhorred. She was one of the best-informed and gentlest women I have ever met—and to this day I am amazed that she ever was captivated by the hooligan who led Italy to catastrophe.

She knew world literature very well. She knew American literature better than many university professors know it. I once heard her say, "American men lack tenderness. American writers lack it even more. Even your women writers lack it. Willa Cather is, emotionally, a calculating woman. Ellen Glasgow interests me more. Your Sinclair Lewis is wholly lacking in emotion. I mean he is sorry for people, he doesn't feel gentleness toward them, no tenderness. Dreiser is a little better. Only a little. But, really, Sister Carrie is not a real woman, as written by a man who understands women, and Jennie Gerhardt isn't either. Only a tender man can understand the tenderness in women as it is warped by life and by men and by the passing years. But, as I said, Lewis understands women least of all, except maybe Hemingway, who knows just nothing, nothing at all, about women, shockingly nothing."

For years I had the feeling that George Jean Nathan had not too high an opinion of Lewis as a fiction writer, but he wouldn't say anything in print, or personally. But once he let the cat out of the bag, so to speak. It was near the end of his life. We were talking about the absurd cult of Fitzgerald that had sprung up. Nathan laughed at the *Disenchanted*. "A disgraceful performance," he called it. "How it has been received is even more disgraceful." Then he added, "I knew Scott very well, as you know. I liked him personally. I helped him when I could. But he was hardly a great writer, not even a very good one. *The Great Gatsby* is written by a man who doesn't know Long Island life. Scott's ignorance is on every page. Scott was really little more than a glorified Richard Harding Davis. And Red Lewis, I'm afraid, is not much better. Neither of them knows the dark places of the human heart."

Lewis called me up one afternoon, in the late Twenties, and said, "Sorry, Charlie, my boy, to trouble you, but could you give me Cabell's home address? I'm supposed to know it, and I'm ashamed." I gave him the address. Then he said, "Say, Big Boy, this will interest you. Phil Goodman and I played a dirty trick on you. We called up the Harvard Club, right here, on West Forty-Fourth Street, and we asked the doorman to page you. He came back and said you were not there, which surprised us. So we asked him to page you again, and again he said you weren't in. So we asked him to page you every half hour till three in the afternoon. We told him to tell you that Walter Lippmann wanted to talk to you. How do you like that?" Before I could say anything, he burst out laughing. Then, abruptly, he said, "Thanks for the address," and hung up.

About two weeks after that he invited Phil Goodman and me to lunch at the Algonquin. He was an hour late, and when he arrived he was so drunk he could barely walk. Goodman took him to his own apartment. Late that night Lewis sobered up, and he was all apologies.

The labor novel that Lewis planned to do is one of the mysteries in his life. The late Benjamin Stolberg spent much time with him on it, giving him lessons in American labor history and American labor politicians. Stolberg was fond of Lewis and glad to help him. But he was not fooled by him. Not long after their "collaboration" began, Stolberg said to me, "Lewis will never do that novel. His mind wanders off as I talk to him. Why he persists puzzles me."

Oswald Garrison Villard and the Nation

I WAS AN EDITOR OF THE "NATION" FOR LESS THAN A YEAR, ONLY about eight months, in 1935, and was unhappy there. That was thirty-one years ago, and whatever personal ill-feeling I may have had, I believe, has disappeared. I was unhappy largely because I was disappointed. I had for years had a large respect, nay, an awe of that magazine and its editors. In Harvard, it, along with the *New Republic,* was my way-shower in the realms of politics and economics and the arts, especially literature. Carl Van Doren and Ludwig Lewisohn and "The Drifter" and Oswald Garrison Villard— these and others told me pretty much what I thought and what I argued for. I took them on faith.

Almost the first day I was on the *Nation*—I went there immediately after I left the *Mercury*—I was depressed by the tired feeling that seemed to pervade the office. I had expected a tenseness of concern for the problems of the world. Instead, I encountered a certain *Gemütlichkeit* that seemed to me more appropriate to the offices of the *Atlantic* or *Harper's* or some other such "capitalistic" magazine. Further, the editors appeared to be keeping "banker's hours."

On the *Mercury* I had been accustomed to coming to the office close to 9:00 A.M. That generally was the hour that Mencken arrived. I arrived at nine on my first day at the *Nation* and found present only the woman proofreader. I asked her where the staff was and she smiled. "Freda [Kirchwey]," she said, "usually comes in about eleven, maybe a bit earlier. Joe Krutch probably won't be in at all today. He seldom comes in. Peggy [Marshall] is out of town. Ordinarily she comes in half past ten. And . . ."

"So I guess I'm the early bird," I said.

"Earlier than that," she said.

"I don't suppose Raymond Gram Swing will be in much earlier," I said.

"Well, yes and no. He comes in once a week or maybe once in ten days from Washington. He comes in about ten-thirty, except when he returns to Washington; on those days he sometimes comes in earlier. I think he'll be in today. There's an editorial conference, or haven't they told you?"

"No, they haven't," I said. "I know there's one every week, but I thought it takes place in the middle of the week, or am I wrong?"

She smiled. "I know, I know. That's how it is."

"What do you mean?"

"I've been here a great many years, and . . . well, that's how it is. You get accustomed to it. The magazine comes out every week . . . so that's how it is. That's what really matters."

The editorial conferences were also tired and depressed me almost from the beginning. I had thought that they were prolonged and thoughtful and well-informed affairs, but it became clear quickly that they were nothing of the sort. The general question of India, for example, came up at one of the first conferences, and there was some banter—it was little more than that—between Dorothy Van Doren and Freda Kirchwey and Raymond Gram Swing. I got the impression that none of them had any special knowledge of the subject. Nevertheless, it was decided to have Dorothy Van Doren— or so I believe, after all these years—write the editorial, and all she said was that the Indian people had a right to self-determination, that Gandhi was a great spiritual leader, and that England should realize once and for all that the day of colonialism was at an end.

Oswald Garrison Villard dropped in now and then, merely to

say hello or to exchange a few remarks. He reminded me of New England worthies of the mid-nineteenth century whose portraits I used to see at the Harvard Union. At first he elicited great respect from me. He seemed so rugged of character. He was the personification of the *Nation*. The *Nation* was the oldest major liberal weekly in the United States, founded in 1865 by the great editor E. L. Godkin. It was the mouthpiece of great thinkers of the late nineteenth century. It was, for a while, one of the chief, if not the chief, spokesmen for Woodrow Wilson's New Freedom. During the 1920's it was a haven for nearly every progressive idea in the land—literary, economic, political, psychological. During a brief period it also gave space to proponents of "greater sexual freedom." Oswald Garrison Villard, who was the *Nation's* editor from 1918 to 1932 thus was a molder and shaker of opinion. The average circulation was only about 25,000, but it was an influential circulation. By 1935 he had relinquished his control of the magazine, but he still came to editorial conferences, and he had considerable moral force among the editors.

At one conference he said he was disappointed in Franklin Delano Roosevelt. I asked why. He said, in effect, "He isn't taking advantage of the times. We are living in a period of great moral bewilderment. The country is ready for bold steps, and he isn't being bold enough."

This puzzled me, and I asked him to be more specific. He said, "Roosevelt should nationalize all the public utilities, or most of them—the railroads and the telephones and the telegraph and the water works. What is needed now is boldness."

"OGV," said Freda Kirchwey, "you are expecting too much at this time. The logic of history doesn't permit this."

"What is the logic of history?" asked Villard. "I know only history."

No one seemed to know precisely what the logic of history was. I didn't, either, but suggested that perhaps it was a concept invented by German philosophers to justify their imperialistic ideas and their basic convictions of superiority to all other peoples: *Deutschland Über Alles*.

Villard, who had some German blood, jumped on me: "You

mustn't say that. We've had enough hatred of German people in this country. We mustn't hate anybody. If we didn't have all this hate, we wouldn't have had that abominable Versailles Treaty, and we wouldn't have Hitler, and maybe we wouldn't have Stalin."

This was the same meeting at which I prevailed upon the others to let me write an editorial taking Mayor LaGuardia gently to task for taking away the licenses from the street vendors of flowers. Some of my fellow editors thought I was silly to want to write such an editorial. But Freda Kirchwey and Villard, to my pleasant surprise, were for the editorial. Swing said nothing at all.

After a while I hardly participated in the editorial conferences, so disappointed was I. It was a weekly miracle that things did get written and did fill up the two or three pages generally allotted to the editorials.

My chief interest centered on Villard more and more. I don't know exactly why. He was sometimes so fuzzy, so ridden with political morals (he couldn't see why one nation should want to "steal" land from another, and he couldn't see how a diplomat could "lie without feeling moral compunctions") that at the beginning I was at times ill at ease in his presence. Occasionally he reminded me of an elementary school teacher who read to us, every Friday afternoon at exactly two o'clock, Kipling's poem "If." And always she told us, after reading the poem, "Guide your life by this poem and you'll come out a good and honorable person."

But I learned that there was much more to Villard than a certain innocence in the political realm. As a matter of fact, he was extremely well informed about *Realpolitik*. He knew about economic forces and religious forces and geographic forces in world politics; he knew the difference between personal morality and international morality; and he also knew American history. Actually, his inclination toward the moral interpretation of history stood him in good stead on several occasions, especially in one. He objected to the Russian dictatorship from the very beginning. He was a guiding figure on the *Nation* when the Czar was overthrown, and he was one of the first editors to welcome the Kerensky government. But he was one of the first editors to warn the world against the machinations of Stalin and Trotsky. To him they were both evil, except that one was more unscrupulous than the other; but, as he often said, "If Trotsky were in power he would be as abominable as Stalin. Trotsky is better educated, but he is no less immoral and cruel." Villard's major objection to the Soviets was a simple one. He said, "I am against every government anywhere any time that violates the Bill of Rights. A government that does not permit free speech and a free press and free assembly and genuine democratic government is my enemy."

Villard never fell for any form of fellow-traveling. He objected violently when his successors on the *Nation*—or some of them—in one way or another joined the United Front, as speakers, as article writers, as letterhead disciples. This took courage. These same editors called him an old fogey and "unrealistic," and he told them that if he was an old fogey, then they were juveniles.

Villard's regard for journalistic morality was profound and adamant. Perhaps nobody has done so much as he, as an individual, to wake up the American daily press to its professional responsibilities. His many articles and books on the subject are truly magnificent. Yet he had strange aberrations, even in the realm of morality. One morning I picked up my morning newspaper, and there I found a large advertisement telling the world that Oswald Garrison Villard found a certain cab company a mighty fine firm to do business with. I gasped. Surely this was a glaring example of "being taken in" by what Villard himself had called "the cunning pressures of American capitalism." I assumed that Villard was being paid for this shameful thing, and that made it still worse. I asked Villard directly to explain himself. He was not at all offended, and as I remember it he said the following: "First of all, I did not get paid for my endorsement. In fact, I sought out the company's advertising firm and asked them to permit me to say something nice about them. Because, well, because I think this company is really good. I use taxi cabs a good deal, and so many of the companies are so bad, their cabs are so dirty and the drivers so impolite, that it is a pleasure to use the cab of this company. I think I owe it to business morality to come out in public and say my say." I was surprised by this display of naiveté, but I said nothing more.

There was another time when Villard got into quite a state, at an editorial conference, over the "injustice of the tax structure." I thought he meant the injustice of the income tax structure on the lower levels, but he quickly disillusioned me. He objected to certain provisions of the income tax structure on the upper level, which was his level. Liberal that he claimed to be, he said that it was becoming pointless for him to study his investments, manipulating them here and there to increase his profits, "because Washington is taking away my profits more and more. And that is hurting business, keeping back money from the investment market; also it is hindering private enterprise." Shocked as I was by this, I was even more shocked by what he said shortly thereafter. At the time there was a movement in Washington to tax the income from certain state and municipal bonds, which had been tax exempt. Here, too, his argument was a moral one: "I have quite a number of government bonds. I get very little interest on them, less than 4 per cent. When I bought them I did so with the understanding, given by the United States—and the states and cities, of course—that these bonds would be tax free. If the government now taxes me, it will be breaking its word. That's immoral."

I would often come to the *Nation* office before nine in the morning, because I liked the quiet and could do some of my personal writing there. Several times Villard came down from his office on a higher floor in the Vesey Street building where the *Nation* was to look for some back issue of the magazine, where he wanted to check a reference. Slowly we became friendly, and he and I had lunch several times in a small restaurant on Church Street, not far from the *Nation* office. He was a very polite man, and also, in some respects, a humble man. He asked me what I thought of his articles on the Boston newspapers, which had appeared in the *Nation*. "You know Boston so much better than I do," he said. I assured him that while I probably knew the geographical city better than he did, he knew its newspapers and its general cultural picture phenomenally well. He was glad to hear me say that. He wondered whether he hadn't been a bit unjust to the Boston *Herald-Traveler*. "They're quite reactionary, as I said; that I don't take back. But they're otherwise quite good. I mean their news is often fair, on the international scene at least. Their editorials are stupid most of the time, but they're well written. Of course, there's no excuse for their kowtowing to the Catholic Church and the unspeakable Cardinal O'Connell, but they don't disgrace themselves quite as much as the Boston *Post*."

Several times he spoke about Woodrow Wilson. He apparently had known him very well and long admired him. Villard was one of the first champions of the New Freedom, but he had grave doubts about our entering the First World War, and he had even greater doubts about the Versailles Treaty. "A stubborn man," Villard often said, "a very stubborn man, even though most of the time he had a fine moral sense. He allowed himself to be hoodwinked by Clemenceau and Lloyd George, and once hoodwinked, so stubborn was he and so jealous of his own righteousness, he insisted on remaining hoodwinked. A tragedy, a great tragedy, that's what it was. He could be very sweet, friendly, courteous, but he carried grudges to his dying day. I saw him often when he ran for the presidency in 1912, and later, but then I differed with him and said so in print, and he would not answer my letters. After he left the presidency, when he was living in Washington, I tried to see him a few times. He was receiving visitors, but each time his wife or secretary would write me a note saying that the President was not receiving visitors. No, he never forgot, and he never could forgive criticism. But he was a great man, of that there is no doubt, and, I suppose, great men make big mistakes and have petty faults. I would love to write a biography of him, but I would first have to wait fifteen years or so in order to get a good perspective, and that's more than I can afford." He smiled. "I'm afraid I won't be here by then."

He was depressed about the future of newspapers in the United States. "They're amalgamating at a fast rate, and soon there will be big cities with only one newspaper, and that's obviously bad. I fear something else. The same chain will have single newspapers in various cities, and soon there will be a virtual monopoly in large sections of the United States. Everybody will be subjected to the same political policy, in these areas, and they will be subjected to the same columns. Actually, I assume there will be less and less local news, and that's bad, too. The local news will probably be covered by weeklies, and they, too, in time will come under some central chain. Even if they don't, they're bound to be bad. Local weeklies are less and less able to remain independent without large local advertising, and that means that the editor will kowtow to the local merchants. These merchants really won't be too much in need of the local weeklies, so they'll tell the publisher and editor of the local weekly, in effect, he runs the paper they want or they won't advertise. Of course, they won't be that crude, but they'll be saying this in another, more polite way.

"This means that there's a big chance coming for magazines, monthlies and quarterlies, especially monthlies. I don't see much chance for the liberal weeklies. The *Nation* and the *New Republic* are going to have hard times. *Time* and *Life* and *Newsweek* will take over the weekly market, and on a big scale. But they're silly and super-conservative magazines, more interested in income than in being great periodicals with an influence on the turn of events. The bigger their circulation will become, the less influence they will have. *Collier's* will die, and so will the *Saturday Evening Post*. The people are ready for some other form of inferior journalism. The *Atlantic* and *Harper's* have a real chance here, but I doubt they will take it up; they're edited by timid men. The radio? I don't see it as taking the place of the printed word. Nothing can take the place of it."

After I left the *Nation* Villard and I exchanged a few polite letters and then we did not get in touch with each other for a long time. When I returned to the *Mercury* for a brief stay, Villard got in touch with me over the telephone. He asked whether we'd be interested in any articles from him. He said he had some new material on John Brown, and I said we'd be interested in that. He sent the article in, and I liked it. But Lawrence E. Spivak, who was then editor and publisher and who had liked the idea of an article on John Brown in the first place, said he didn't like the finished article. He said it was poorly written and poorly organized. I said it was well written and well organized. But he insisted he was against it. His objections made no sense to me. I pleaded with him, but he remained adamant. So I wrote to Villard and told him the whole truth. I said I was very sorry. Villard called me on the telephone. He was shocked by my letter, though he said he understood my position. I said I hoped that this experience would not keep him from sending us another article soon. He said it would not. But I did not hear from him again for a long time.

Then, out of the proverbial blue, there arrived one morning an article by him, on Calvin Coolidge, an analysis and a commentary. It wasn't too good. It was too editorial in character, it needed more documentation, and there was somewhat too much sheer vituperation in it. I wrote a polite letter to Villard, telling him that we liked the article in essence, but that it needed some repairing, and I detailed the nature of the repairing. Almost by return mail I got a letter from him that said: "I have your letter. This is the end of our relationship." He signed the letter "Yours truly." I was very much disturbed. I called his office and asked to talk to him. His secretary waited a moment, then said, "Mr. Villard said he has nothing to say to you."

There was clearly nothing else for me to do except write a letter to him telling him that he was being childish, but I couldn't write such a letter to a man who was almost old enough to be my grandfather. Weeks and months passed by. I often thought of Villard— with gratitude for what he had taught me and with sorrow for the coldness that had come between us. His pride and joy, the *Nation,* was now but a shadow of what it had been under his editorship. Its influence had greatly declined. Few people referred to it. The intellectuals who had, in Villard's day, looked forward to it, waiting at newsstands Friday morning, were now reading the *New Leader* or *Partisan Review* or the *Saturday Review.* Its circulation had not dropped much. Some weeks, indeed, it had gone over 30,000, but it was a virtually inert circulation. It had lost much of its literary leadership and its political leadership. It was now a frail old lady of

America's Fleet Street—and many were not sure that it was a lady, in view of its flirtations with the extreme left.

More weeks and months passed by. I was on the way to Grand Central Station to take a train to Boston to visit my family, and I stopped off at a restaurant on Forty-second Street. Suddenly Villard appeared and asked if he might sit down at my table. I said of course. We exchanged some trivialities. I apologized to him that I had to leave soon to catch my train. Then he said, "I want to apologize, too. That last letter I wrote to you was very childish. Please forgive me."

Thomas Wolfe and the Opulent Manner

T HE OLD "AMERICAN MERCURY" HAD A DEPARTMENT CALLED THE "Check List of New Books," in which appeared brief reviews of new books that, for one reason or another, did not appear to merit more extended attention. Generally H. L. Mencken and I did all of them, but now and then a friend of Mencken's or a friend of mine would contribute a brief review. Most publishers sent their books to the New York office, really the central office of the *Mercury,* while a few sent them to Mencken's residence in Baltimore, and a certain number of others sent their books to both places.

The publisher Scribner's was then a bit erratic in this regard. Sometimes they sent books only to New York, while other times they sent them only to Baltimore, and still other times they sent them both to New York and Baltimore. I liked this last arrangement best. It meant that I could have whatever books I wanted. Mencken had left it to me, in the case of books that came only to New York, to send him whatever books I thought he was most interested in. In the case of books that I thought would interest him but that I also wanted, I of course sent the books to him—and I was left with the painful prospect of not having the books at all or paying for them.

Scribner's sent a copy of Thomas Wolfe's first novel, *Look*

Homeward, Angel, to New York and another to Baltimore. I had heard about the book through Philip Goodman, the play producer and long a close personal friend of Mencken's—perhaps, for a period of years, Mencken's most intimate friend. I had also heard about it from Ernest Boyd, the literary critic and husband of Madeleine Boyd, the literary agent, who had done so much to help Wolfe place his novel.

I read the book and was fascinated—so much so, in fact, that I called Mencken on the telephone and suggested that he do a long review of it in his department, "The Library."

"I have no more interest in novels," he said. "Besides, Phil Goodman has probably influenced you, and Phil has reached the stage where he likes flyspeckled novels by flyspeckled novelists."

I told Mencken I hadn't talked to Goodman about the book . . . that the book was really wonderful . . . a fresh talent . . .

"Keep your shirt on," counseled Mencken. "You shouldn't use the word *wonderful* about a first novel so freely. Further, my dear sir, as a man whose favorite drink is Manischewitz's Passover wine with seltzer, you are unfit to offer a valid aesthetic judgment. Have a few beers and a whiskey or so, and calm down. Do you really think it's good, Angoff?"

"Yes."

"Well, I'll give it to Sara. She's a Coca Cola fiend, and hence not much better than you, and I'll see what she says. Give my best regards to Cardinal O'Connell of Boston."

"He's dead."

"Through prayer you can reach him."

A week later I got a brief note from Sara—she later became Mrs. Mencken—in which she said that she liked the Wolfe novel very much, and that she was doing a "Check List" on it. I wrote back and said that she should try to get Mencken to allow her to do a longish review of the book, not necessarily in Mencken's department of "The Library," but in the "Check List" proper, and by a long one I meant only one of about 500 words; the usual length of our "Check List" reviews was seldom more than 250 words.

I got a letter from Mencken in which he admonished me not to "mislead an innocent girl," and he added that an ordinary "Check List" for the Wolfe novel was enough. He promised to read the book, which I am positive he never did.

This incident began a long mock-wrangle between Mencken and myself about Wolfe as a novelist. Though he never read this Wolfe book he denounced it as a wordy, sloppy piece of autobiography, and when he later was told that Wolfe did not dress like a Brooks Brothers product he really let me have it: "Remember, Angoff, no shlump has ever written anything worthwhile, and don't you bring up Walt Whitman, for he is vastly overrated. The same with girls and women. Girls and women with ink on their fingers and blouses that are unwashed never write good lyrics. It's God's will. You may have this information free, and I trust you will keep it confidential."

After Mencken left the *Mercury* and after a brief interval of another editor, I was put in charge of the magazine, and one of the first things I did was to get in touch with Wolfe's agent at the time. She was Elizabeth Nowell, who later edited his *Letters*. Miss Nowell suggested a dinner engagement, and the three of us met in an office on Fifth Avenue, somewhere in the mid-Forties.

I had heard about Wolfe's height, but I was astonished when I actually saw him for the first time. He was truly enormous, not merely in height but in sheer bulk. He obviously hadn't had a haircut for several weeks and his shirt had seen considerable wear and not too much washing. But there was something innocent and charming about his clear eyes and his almost pinkish skin.

"Let's eat anywhere you say, Mr. Wolfe," I said. "I got money. I'm on an expense account. None other than Alfred A. Knopf himself is paying for whatever we do tonight."

"I wish I were really hungry," Wolfe said. "I'm for screwing publishers."

"You said you like Jewish food," said Miss Nowell, "or maybe you said you haven't had it. Would you like to go to a Jewish restaurant? Angoff knows several downtown."

Wolfe agreed. He had some difficulty getting into the taxi, and immediately he said that we should have walked downtown. Since

I have flat feet and at the time didn't care much for walking, I protested. "I'll never make it," I said. "Have pity on a poor Boston boy."

"Now there is a town!" exclaimed Wolfe, and thereupon he began a harangue about the virtues and vices of Boston that lasted till we reached a certain Jewish-Rumanian restaurant on the lower East Side. He lambasted the Irish, he lambasted the Yankees, he lambasted State Street (the Boston Wall Street), and then he said, "But I love the stinking town. It's full of sin. What other town has an Old Howard Theatre, where the dirtiest burlesque is shown, and where the Harvard professors go?"

Wolfe told me to order for him. I ordered chopped chicken liver, mandel soup, boiled beef, with boiled potatoes and carrots and peas, *kichlach* (cookies), and tea. "You can have coffee," I told Wolfe, "but it will have to be black. This is a kosher place."

"Hell, that's all right," he said. "Brooklyn is full of these places. It doesn't bother me a bit."

The waitress had put "the usual" on the table before actually serving: a heaping pile of pumpernickel and rye bread, pickled tomatoes and onions, and a huge platter of sauerkraut. Wolfe went immediately after the bread. I apologised to him for the lack of butter: "Kosher, you know."

"Fine bread," he said, and continued eating slice after slice. Then he had a few tomatoes and a couple of tablespoonsful of sauerkraut. The waitress brought all of us plates of chicken liver. I thought the portions were generous, and just as I was digging into my portion I saw that Wolfe had finished his and was looking around rather sheepishly. "Would you like some more?" I asked him. He said that he would. The waitress looked at him; she had never before encountered such an appetite. She brought him a second helping, almost as big as the first one. He took a little more time with this portion, but he was through with it before I had finished mine.

Miss Nowell apparently didn't like chopped chicken liver, and she asked Wolfe if he would like her leftover. "No," he said shyly, then changed his mind: "I'll just taste it." He tasted it till he finished it.

He still was hungry, so he ate more bread. Then came the soup and after that the main dish, the boiled beef, plus boiled potatoes and carrots and peas. Wolfe finished the boiled beef and the boiled potatoes and carrots and peas in terrific haste. Nowell and I were still working on the first half of our boiled beef. Wolfe apparently was embarrassed, and kept still. I looked at him and said, "It's usual to have second helpings here."

Miss Nowell burst out laughing.

"Well, I see no reason why Mr. Wolfe can't have more boiled beef." I signaled to the waitress and told her to bring Wolfe another order of the same. She did. He finished it. The *kichlach* and the tea went off without hitch.

What did we talk about at the dinner? I don't recall precisely, but I do recall that it was chiefly about Boston and the sales of *Look Homeward, Angel.* Wolfe was bitterly disappointed at the way the book had gone. "Nobody's buying it," he said.

"Oh, no, Tom, it's doing very well," said Miss Nowell.

"Well, I still say it's not doing very well," said Wolfe.

We went out of the restaurant and walked a few blocks along Delancey Street. Wolfe kept on repeating one phrase as we walked, "I don't understand, I just don't understand." I asked him what he meant, after the first time he said the line. But he ignored me. He merely said, "I just don't understand how people can stand all this."

We passed a huge delicatessen store, and Wolfe stopped and admired the display of various kinds of processed meats. I had the feeling he wanted a pastrami or salami or tongue sandwich, and I didn't know how to suggest it to him without embarrassing him. Miss Nowell helped me out. "You want something here?" she asked him.

"Well, not now," he said. "Another time."

We went back to Miss Nowell's office, and there we talked "business." I told Wolfe how much I admired his work, and I asked him to give me something for the *Mercury.* "I can't pay much," I said, "but I promise to give you the best price I can possibly get for you. We're virtually bankrupt, but I'll do my best." Miss Nowell said complimentary things about me, and Wolfe said he would send me something.

Not long afterward Miss Nowell brought me a 25,000-word manuscript. She smiled. "This is Tom's idea of a short story," she said.

I gasped. "What shall I do?"

"First read it, and then we'll see what we can do."

I read it and liked it, but I thought it was verbose. The more I read it the more I thought it could be cut. Again I asked, "What shall I do?"

"Now," said Miss Nowell, "you know what problems Max Perkins had with Wolfe."

"Suppose I cut it, and show him the result," I said.

Miss Nowell smiled. "I want to be around when the result shows up."

I cut the script down to about eight thousand words. I read it and reread it, and I was rather proud of my job. I showed it to Miss Nowell. She liked it. But there was Wolfe to contend with. I sent him a copy, with a note that I thought was diplomatic. I told him that his original was powerful, but that the *Mercury* couldn't give that much space to a short story, that I had tried to keep the substance of his story, and I hoped that he would agree. He responded the very next day on the telephone. He called my work "an outrage," and demanded that I return the original at once. I said I would. But I didn't. Instead I called Miss Nowell and told her the substance of the conversation with Wolfe.

"You did the right thing in what you said, but don't do what you promised. He'll cool down. He'll call you in about a week and ask you what happened to the manuscript he asked you to return. That's when you have to tell him that you have been thinking over what he said, and that you agree with him, and that you would like to discuss his manuscript with him. That's when I hope you will call me in. I think I can help. I saw how Perkins worked with him." Wolfe called in a week. He said what Miss Nowell said he would say, and I said what Miss Nowell told me to say. The three of us met, and we wrangled over his script. He revealed a considerable diplomatic streak. He began by saying, "You did a mighty fine job of cutting, Mr. Angoff. But I wish you had allowed some of my favorite passages to remain." I asked him what his favorite passages were. By the time he was through pointing out these favorite passages, he had in effect asked me to print his story exactly as he had submitted it to me.

'But if I print the whole script, Mr. Wolfe," I said, "and that is really what you want me to do, I would pretty much have to devote the entire issue of the *Mercury* to the story."

'Why not do that?" he asked.

I was not prepared for that question. I looked at Miss Nowell. "Now, Tom, Mr. Angoff can't do that. You know that. A magazine is a magazine."

"I know, but why not print the whole story in a whole issue?" persisted Wolfe.

"You can't," said Miss Nowell.

Wolfe seemed bewildered. I was glad that I didn't have to answer his question, though he asked it of me first. I wasn't sure I could answer him. I had no reason why a whole issue of a magazine couldn't be given over to one feature.

"Well, there ought to be more. What Mr. Angoff has done is take the life out of my story," said Wolfe.

"Oh, no," said Miss Nowell. "He has merely pointed it up. The story remains. And I think he has done a fine job of editing."

"Yes, yes," said Wolfe, "but now it's not mine."

"It's all yours, Tom," said Miss Nowell. "Nobody else's."

The three of us struggled with the story for the next three weeks, meeting most of the time in Miss Nowell's apartment and the rest of the time, at night, in the *Mercury* offices in the Hecksher Building at the corner of Fifth Avenue and Fifty-seventh Street. Finally, Wolfe agreed to a compromise version, which was about a thousand words longer than I had in my original, edited version. It appeared under the title "Boom Town" in the May, 1934 issue of the Mercury.

But before it appeared Wolfe argued with me about the price. The *Mercury* then was in grave financial difficulties. Alfred A. Knopf, the publisher, was having troubles of his own with his publishing firm—as, I imagine, other publishing firms were. All of us on the magazine had taken big cuts in salary. I was the chief editor at the time and I was getting $55.00 a week. Our regular rate of payment at the time for a manuscript of Wolfe's length was $170, at the rate of two cents a word. With considerable trepidation I asked Knopf to let me pay Wolfe $250 for his story. Knopf hesitated, and I sympathized with him. I told him the Wolfe story was a very fine job and I argued that it would probably help us win back some of the readers we had lost during the last year of Mencken's regime—when the magazine (as Mencken's organ) refused to recognize the depression. . . . Mencken called it "sheer newspaper talk." Knopf finally agreed, and I sent Miss Nowell a check for $250. The next day she called and said that Wolfe refused to accept it. He wanted "at the very least" $750. I told Miss Nowell that was out of the question. I told her some of our troubles, and I further told her that $250, in our current circumstances, was really very generous. And I added, "I personally want that story very much." Miss Nowell said that she, as Wolfe's agent, understood, and she personally did not object and would continue to urge Wolfe to accept. I told her that I would go ahead and set the story and publish it. "Go ahead," she said. "I think Tom will cool off."

He did cool off. The story aroused considerable favorable talk. Harry Hansen selected it for inclusion in his *O. Henry Prize Stories, 1934*. Wolfe was pleased. He called me to tell me he was pleased. But he added, "I think both you and Hansen are crazy. My first version was the really good one."

I now think, as I have thought for many years, that Wolfe was right. My editing was an example of what editing should not be. A good editor should know when not to edit. A good editor should never forget that there are two basic styles of writing: the opulent and the parsimonious. Dreiser, Zola, Balzac, Melville wrote in the opulent manner. Edgar Saltus, Willa Cather, Hemingway wrote in the parsimonious manner. A good editor must never violate a writer's style. I violated Wolfe's style. My edited version of "Boom Town" is a piece of carpentry. It is neat and swift and polished. But it is not genuine Wolfe. His original had a flow and a richness and a thunderous impact that my version hasn't got. But doesn't Wolfe indulge in repetition? I used to think that he did, but I haven't been so sure for years. He builds, he seldom repeats, and even when he repeats he often enriches.

William Carlos Williams

YEARS AGO, WHEN I WAS EDITOR OF THE "AMERICAN MERCURY,"
Dr. William Carlos Williams sent in a half dozen poems. Three of
us read them. We all thought they were not his best work. We
were very sorry. We had high respect for him, and we wanted to
get him into the pages of the *Mercury*. We thought we would be
doing him an injustice by printing the poems he sent us. I was
especially sorry about the fix we were in, for I had for a long time
been drawn to his work. I offered to write to him as diplomatic a
letter as possible. I wrote that letter. I tried to make it especially
clear that we wanted very much to have him in the pages of the
Mercury. Almost by return mail I got a postcard reply from
Dr. Williams. Unfortunately, I lost the card. But I do remember the
general content of the card. He called me "a damn fool," and he
called the *Mercury* "a stupid magazine to which no decent person
would care to contribute." I replied that we still wanted very much
to have him in the magazine, and asked him to send us more poems
and any prose he wanted to have published. I told him that I liked
his book of sketches and stories, *In the American Grain*, very much.
He did not reply.

Some months later Weldon Kees, a poet of considerable power,
called me on the telephone. He had lived in Colorado, I believe, and

now was living in New York City. He wanted to see me. We met. He reminded me of some letters I had written him several years before. He had just begun to write poetry and was pleased by my polite handling of his poems. I hadn't accepted them, but I had shown an interest. He had been encouraged. He wanted to say thank you. I was pleased. Then he asked me if I knew Dr. William Carlos Williams. I told him about the above episode. Nevertheless, I offered to write a letter to Dr. Williams, introducing Weldon Kees. I asked Kees whether he wanted to take this chance. He said, "Sure." To my great surprise I got a very friendly card from Dr. Williams. Yes, he would be glad "to see anybody whom you like. As they say, a friend of yours is a friend of mine." I didn't quite know how to take this note. I decided to take it at face value.

Weldon Kees saw Dr. Williams. He told me about the meeting. "Say," said Kees, "he's a very good friend of yours. I thought you two had never met."

"We never had," I said.

"That's funny," said Kees. "He spoke as if you two had known each other for years."

"No, I had never met him," I insisted. "Did he say anything about that unpleasant. . . ."

"Oh yes, sort of. He said you two had had some words. He was sorry that he had made a fool of himself."

When the *Literary Review,* of which Dr. Clarence R. Decker and I are co-editors, was founded, I approached Dr. Williams for a contribution or two to the first issue. I thought I would have some trouble. So I began by pointing out to him that Fairleigh Dickinson University, sponsor of the magazine, was situated in Rutherford, New Jersey (that is, the mother campus was), that he was a Rutherfordian, and we wanted to do him honor by featuring him in the first issue.

"Why, sure, Charlie," he said, smiling somewhat shyly. "You don't have to give me that spiel. Sure, I'll be glad to appear in the first issue. Hell, you don't have to give me all that spiel. Hell, no."

I thought he blushed as he said all this. I had the feeling that his innermost being, for some vague reason, was not too happy with his blustering good fellowship. It was the first time that I met him. I had called him on the telephone, and he asked me to come over. His wife met me at the door, and she, too, was friendly. I had the feeling that Flossie, his wife, was the business person at 9 Ridge Road, that she sort of ran him. Compared to her husband she was firm. Dr. Williams appeared to be shy. Almost pleadingly he said to his wife, "Won't you give Charlie a drink?" Then he turned to me and said, "I like bourbon, do you? As a matter of fact, all the whiskeys are pretty good." I asked for a bourbon high-ball.

He let me have virtually anything he had available on hand. One of the truly fine things he gave us was a sketch of his mother. It is one of his most memorable prose pieces.

I suggested to Dr. Sammartino that he give Dr. Williams an honorary degree. I did this through Dr. Decker, the vice-president. Dr. Williams was enormously pleased. Somewhat later I saw him and said how nice it was for him to accept the honorary degree and I said the obvious thing, "By accepting it you did the University honor."

"Hell, no," he said, "they honored me. I was just thrilled to get it. Hell, I'm a Rutherfordian, don't you ever forget it." He smiled. "I was wondering how much longer I would have to wait. You know I'm not a well man."

I learned later how unwell he was. He had had a severe heart attack some years before. Now and then, I was told, he had little strokes that laid him low for a while, but fortunately, he eventually got out of them, without any outward permanent damage. Somebody told me that one day he would have one stroke too many and that would be the end. I asked my informant if Dr. Williams knew that. "Sure he does. He told me about it."

I was associated with the Writer's Conference at Wagner College, on Staten Island, in New York City for four years. The third year it occurred to me that it would be a good idea if Dr. Williams would come over to address the students. For some strange reason I forgot, for the moment, that he was an unwell man, and called his house. His wife answered. I told her why I called. "Oh," she said, "but

Bill is sick. He's been in bed for the past couple of days. I mean. . . ." She stopped, and I overheard her talking to somebody, though I couldn't hear the exact words passed. The next voice I heard was that of Dr. Williams. "Hello," he said.

I was embarrassed. I said, "I'm sorry. I didn't know. I mean. . . ."

"Don't apologize, Charlie," he said. "A little sickness between friends is nothing. What was it you wanted?"

I told him, and again apologized.

"Never mind the apologizing," he said. "I'll be glad to come over. Only there is one condition." I heard him laugh. "Only one condition," he repeated. "Are you sitting down?"

"Yes, why?"

"Good, the one condition is that you get me a bottle of Wilson's whiskey. It doesn't have to be Wilson's, but I just happened to think of it. It's as good as any."

I hesitated. Wagner College is a Lutheran-sponsored college, and I had heard some stories about some of its preacher trustees. They had the reputation of being "strict." The rule apparently was that drinking was absolutely forbidden on campus, but that professors could "indulge" outside the campus, "with moderation, of course." The catch was that the conference was housed at a girls' dormitory on campus, and obviously getting a bottle of whiskey on campus and in a girls' dormitory was "out of order."

"Well?" asked Dr. Williams.

"I don't know," I said. "That really is a problem. You see, we are staying at a dormitory, and drinking is forbidden, and . . . I just don't know what to say."

He laughed. Then he said, "That is my condition."

I hesitated, then I said, "All right. I promise I'll get you the bottle of whiskey. It's entirely illegal, and I don't know how I'll manage it. I just don't really know. But I'll get it for you."

"Good boy," said Dr. Williams. "Good boy."

I solved my problem by merely telling Gorham Munson, the director, what I planned to do. Gorham smiled. "Oh, get the whiskey. It's, let us say, illegally legal. Nothing will happen."

I got the whiskey. I got a room for Dr. Williams in the girls' dormitory. He asked me to fill a half tumbler with straight whiskey —no "adulterants" such as water or soda or ginger ale. He took it down almost in one gulp. I marveled at him. His face became flushed and for a few moments I was worried. Then he said, "Now, let me get at your students."

He was magnificent in his talk before the students. He spoke to them in the open on a portico facing New York harbor. He was on his feet for almost an hour and a half. His voice was strong. He spoke cogently, poetically, brilliantly. He discussed the essence of poetry. He gave examples of good poetry and of bad poetry. He answered questions—quickly, politely, but incisively. He received a long and obviously sincere ovation.

I invited him to dinner after his talk. "I hope you're hungry," I said. "I am, but a little drink would help me along," he said.

I managed to sneak down a drink for him. He ate a fine dinner and his conversation was lively.

I put him back in the automobile about nine o'clock. I apologized for the late hour. "Not at all," he said. "I loved it."

Without his knowing I had brought down the remainder of the bottle of whiskey, and as he made himself comfortable in the automobile I gave him what was left of the bottle.

"You're a sweetheart, Charlie," he said. "Just a sweetheart. I was wondering what was going to happen to the bottle. I think I'll take another drink before I go off to bed."

Not long after I had a poem in the *Arizona Quarterly*. It was entitled "Silence." Shortly after it was published I got a letter from Dr. Williams telling me how much he had liked it. A colleague on the faculty of Fairleigh Dickinson University, a few days later, told me that he had talked about the poem at length one night when several people were visiting the Williamses. I wrote Dr. Williams a note thanking him for his note. He wrote back and said he had long been an admirer of my work, and he added, "After all, you and I are the most frequent contributors to little magazines in the country. We must stick together."

News reached the East that Weldon Kees had committed suicide.

I had not heard from him for a long time. He had left New York City for the Pacific Coast and had sent me only occasional cards or brief notes. Once he had asked me to send him whatever writings I came across that had to do with suicide. I did send him some pieces. I put no especial importance to his request. I was only helping out a friend.

When the news of his suicide reached me this request of his came back to my mind—and now it made a grisly sort of sense.

A few days later I was at Dr. Williams' home, and I brought up the matter of Kees's suicide. "It puzzles me," I said. "It puzzles me and it pains me, you know what I mean."

Dr. Williams looked at me, his eyes became bright, he turned his head, then he faced me and said, "I don't understand it, I really don't. All he had to do is kiss his wife or wait for the sunset."

I went to Dr. Williams' funeral. I was heartsick. Chiefly because his own wishes about funerals had not been followed. In a poem called "Tract" he had suggested that no flowers be placed on a man's coffin, but something he really cared for, old clothes, or a book, or something else he cherished.

Dr. Williams' own coffin was covered with flowers. There were no old clothes, no book. But then it occurred to me that he would not have been angry. He was a man of outbursts, some of them violent—as when he denounced Robert Frost as "an old fogey"— but if one waited a few minutes he would take back what he had said. He was a true democrat. He loved Rutherford and he loved people and he loved small towns and he loved America and he was disturbed by God's mysterious plans—but whenever serious doubts assailed him he kissed his wife and he waited for the sunset—and he was happy again.

Ernest Boyd

Ernest Boyd had one of the strangest faces. He looked, as Mencken once said, like the twin brother of Jesus Christ, but when his eyes began to twinkle he also looked like Lucifer. This contradiction probably reflected a contradiction in his make-up: he was calm and indifferent and kindly, and he was also in a constant state of turmoil, very much involved in the literary world of his time, and cruelly biting in his comments. He liked it in the United States—he had come from Ireland as consul in Baltimore, and had decided to give up diplomacy and remain in this country—and yet he was unhappy. His domestic life was not ideal, his writing assignments were often petty, and he seldom had the job that made full use of his editorial talents. But if his marriage had been happier, and if he had had better assignments and better jobs, he would probably still have been unhappy. There was something about this country that offended him. "So many things seem to be so unreal here," he once told a visiting Englishwoman within my hearing. "One day you see a building that seems set for permanence, and in a week you see the wrecking crew breaking it up. And the men are immortal today and forgotten tomorrow."

Alas, Boyd himself is now virtually forgotten. But I have a feeling that he will be referred to often in the literary histories and critical works twenty-five years and fifty years from now. Was he a great critic? Probably not. Was he a systematic critic, did he stand for any specific theory of criticism? Definitely not. Did he influence the literary trends of his time? Very unlikely. Did he influence other critics? Very little, if at all. And yet as I go over his writings in my mind, and study the notes of my meetings with him, I am astonished at how wise and sharp and "right" his critical judgments often were. But, I guess, what draws me to him as a memory—and what drew me to him as a man—was his inner being as it revealed itself in his silences, in his gentle sneers, in his ill-hidden sighs. He was one of the most amoral men I have ever known. He seemed to be completely indifferent to the pressures of any overt or implied code of living, save what he called "honor," which sometimes conflicted with at least half of the Ten Commandments and a good deal more of the laws on the statute books.

And he lived by his "principles" to the very end. He died in 1946, at the age of fifty-nine, but as a writer of consequence he had been dead for a decade before that. He was in financial straits for more than ten years. He borrowed money from friends and acquaintances. He knew he would probably never be able to pay them back, and they probably knew it, too. He went lower and lower on the economic ladder. His friends became fewer and fewer in number. Some remained longer than did others. Philip Goodman helped him out as long as he could. Mencken helped him out with money, with suggestions of jobs, with recommendations for free-lance editorial work. Boyd accepted a free-lance assignment now and then, but his urge for work of any kind became weaker. His desire for alcohol became stronger. Mencken became disgusted. Then came the time when Boyd wrote Mencken a letter in Baltimore, asking for a "loan" of ten dollars, and Mencken wrote back that he didn't have it. They never met again after that. But each was troubled. Boyd said little about the incident. He found it difficult to say anything. Mencken had befriended him in Baltimore, Mencken had introduced him to writers in New York, Mencken had gotten Boyd a big assignment from Alfred A. Knopf to edit the complete works of Guy De Maupassant. Boyd could hardly blame Mencken for getting tired of giving him "loans." And yet Boyd had hoped that Mencken would not do what he did. Mencken, who was a good deal of a Babbitt, was offended by Boyd's persistent unemployment and by his drinking. To me and to others he would say, "I'm sorry for Boyd, but it's damn annoying to pay for his lunches whenever we meet, and then to top it off with giving him a ten-dollar bill. I don't like people who don't pay their way, especially when they're perfectly able to. There are plenty of jobs around. Besides, getting drunk during the week, in the day-time, is no way for a civilized man to live." These comments eventually reached Boyd, and they lowered his morale still more.

He never "surrendered" to any religion or moral code that was generally accepted. This was one of the things about him that called forth the admiration of George Jean Nathan, who continued to see him and help him financially almost to the very end. Nathan liked writers, especially those who got into difficulties with women, or who drank excessively. Particularly (till near the end of his life) was he fond of writers who were complete hedonists and religious infidels and non-submissive to "the morality of the herd."

Nathan often spoke to me about his admiration for Boyd. It was, indeed, through his insistence that Boyd became a co-editor of *The American Spectator,* which Nathan founded. The other editors, Eugene O'Neill, Theodore Dreiser, and James Branch Cabell, were not too happy about Boyd being with them. Nathan was outraged by Mencken's final letter to Boyd. By that time Nathan himself was barely on speaking terms with Mencken. I asked Nathan how he explained Mencken's action. "It's quite easy," Nathan said. "Mencken is a Prussian, inflexible, and he's a Babbitt. Besides, he has an idea that Boyd doesn't think too much of his learning, so I guess they all add up to what he did."

As for Boyd's amorality, Nathan said, "That's probably something else about Boyd that Menck can't stand, no matter what he says to the contrary. Mencken cannot get it out of his mind that anybody who doesn't pay his bills can't be much of a writer, and he also, deep down, has respect for people who go to church, and he dislikes people who leave their own churches. I know, Menck left the Lutheran Church he was brought up in. He didn't leave it formally, but he just stopped going. He boasts of it, I know. But I think that secretly he feels guilty about doing that. You wait and see, Menck will end up by going back to the Lutheran Church, or maybe he'll join up with the Catholics."

"The Catholics?" I asked, surprised.

"You wait and see. But Boyd never will go back to the Catholic Church. Of that I'm positive."

Nathan was right. Boyd never did go back. He was a non-believer till the end. The irony of Nathan's remarks, however, is that it was he, Nathan, who joined the Catholic Church, and Mencken remained a non-believer till his death.

I saw a good deal of Boyd over a stretch of about twenty years, particularly toward the end. He would come up to the *American Mercury* office, but more often I would see him at his favorite saloon, Pete's Tavern in downtown New York where O. Henry used to sit and try to wash away his memories. Pete's Tavern is a wonderful, raffish place, with old mirrors surrounded by fancy woodwork, large, simple, wooden tables, and the whole atmosphere is that of ease and financial modesty.

In the early 1940's one could get a fair lunch at Pete's Tavern for less than $1.00, and the beer was ten cents a glass, and a Martini was fifty cents. Boyd would go there about ten-thirty or eleven in the morning and stay on through lunch till three or so in the afternoon. Sometimes he would pay for his own meal and drinks, but sometimes (more often, I fear) others would pay for him, and generally there were people who were glad to do so.

Boyd had a favorite corner not far from the Irving Place entrance. He would generally begin his stay by drinking a few beers and munching the bits of cheese and the pretzels that came with the beer. Toward noon several people from the neighborhood would come in. Then, a bit later, literary folk or theatrical folk from lower downtown or further uptown would show up "for the atmosphere." One or two of them would recognize Boyd and walk over to his table to say hello, but he would greet them with such graciousness that they remained—and that was how Boyd sometimes got his free lunches and drinks. With his conversation he more than paid for them.

He was really at his best at these times. Whatever inhibitions he may ever have had pretty much left him. He felt he owed nobody anything. He didn't have to meet any deadline. There was no special reason for his going "home," which was a somewhat impoverished two-room apartment, where, on occasion, he would have a female companion. One or two of these companions probably credited herself with having won Boyd's love. But that, very likely, was an overgenerous appraisal of Boyd's attitude. He was attracted to raffish young women, especially Jewish and Russian and Greek and Turkish ones. I suppose it is fair to say that he especially liked Jewish women. "I imagine," he once said, "this side of hell there's no warmer and more comfortable place in the world than the lovely valley between a Jewish girl's breasts. I wouldn't mind having what I just told you, Angoff, on my tombstone. It's pretty nearly the only thing I know that's true."

It was at Pete's Tavern that I learned most of what I knew of Boyd, and that wasn't very much, for he was not given to discussing his personal life. Apparently he was on intimate terms with George Moore and George Bernard Shaw and several of the Abbey Theatre men and women, including Sean O'Casey and AE and Lady Gregory and Dr. Oliver St. John Gogarty. How well he knew James Joyce I was not sure. Boyd, I felt, sometimes "elaborated" his "facts." Sometimes he spoke of Joyce as if the two were close friends, and other times he spoke of him as if they were little more than acquaintances. He was in the diplomatic service for a while, but apparently his heart was never really in it. At bottom, I guess, he was a gypsy, one who loved to travel among all manners of people, who was as carefree and morally untrammeled as are so many gypsies, but who at the same time yearned for the company of literary men. Literature to him was one of man's noblest occupations, perhaps the very noblest. As well as I could make out, he had little interest in any of the other arts. He was first and last a reading and writing man. He was fond of the great English and Irish writers of his day. But his real love was for the French writers, for the men who chose their words carefully, who were clear, who cared little for the conventions of the socially dominant group. He admired Shaw, but he loved Flaubert. He admired Katherine Mansfield, but he loved De Mauppasant. He admitted that Paul Valery had little to say, "but how well he says it!" he would add. He admitted that D. H. Lawrence had "importance of some sort or other, and I do like him for sneering at middle-class morality, but how fuzzy he is!" Next to the French he seemed to admire most the Spanish and Italian writers, and the Germans and Russians he appeared to put last.

But Europe as a whole, French, Russian, Spanish, German, and Italian and all other peoples, fascinated him. The temper of the Continent was to him a truly civilized one. "The Europeans," he once said to me, "accept reality, they don't fight it, the way Americans do. They don't divide the human body into two halves, above the belt and below the belt. To Europeans it is all one, and they know that people make love not with an organ but with a personality, a vision, a dream. To them love is more than a physiological exercise, though it is all of that, but it is more. The whole business of pornography is alien to Europeans. Oh, they know that some things are dirty, but they are dirty not because dirty things, like sex organs, are involved. They are dirty because there is nothing else in pornography but sex organs. Sex organs in themselves are not dirty to Europeans. They are just there, like the nose, the foot, the ear. Europeans don't go into a tizzy because they see a human breast or a vagina. These in themselves don't mean any more than does a finger or an ear. But to Americans it is different. Do you follow me?"

"Yes."

"Well, the same with their writers. They accepted and still accept reality. Now consider Andre Gide. I think he's basically second-class, but he's European. Say what you will about *The Counterfeiters,* it is a European book. To the Europeans homosexuals are people, there are quite a number of them in the world, and therefore one should write about them if one feels like it. Nothing more. In America, the attitude is different. Here homosexuals are dirty, dangerous people; in Europe they are just people, with special behavior problems, that's all."

The relative quiet of Europe also appealed to him—and Europe, to him, I have thought, did not include England, and it did not include Ireland. Though a born Irishman he never did feel entirely at home there. He liked the back-biting among the writers, he liked the general malice-mongering—and this, he said, made him "a 100 per cent Irishman"—but he did not like what he called "the slavery to the Catholic Church and the general hold the Church has over the country. Too many priests, too many nuns, too many churches, and you can almost feel the heavy hand of the Church in everything. Individual priests and nuns are fine, hedonistic, sometimes even atheistical folk, but the organization is hard and scheming and repressive and quite uncivilized. A man like De Valera represents the Irish at their worst, he's only part Irish in his blood, but he does, and that's the miracle, represent a great deal of what is terrible in Ireland. Especially his piety. Irish Catholics, I mean the hierarchy, are the worst Catholics in the world. They take their nonsense seriously, which even the Italian Catholics don't do. The Italian Catholics have never taken Catholicism too seriously. It's a show to them, and quite profitable. After all, all those nuns and priests and officials coming from all over the world, have to spend money in Rome and elsewhere in Italy. Of course, before 1870 the Vatican got hold of some of this money, and since then the Vatican has been sore because the Italians, the Italian business men, have taken most of it. Anyway, religion is a fine business for the Italians, but the religion itself they just laugh at, politely, of course. Any Italian of any culture will tell you with shame when a son of his has gone into the priesthood, or a daughter has gone to study for nunhood. Even the Spanish don't take their religion as seriously as do the Irish bishops and archbishops. Spain is the worst country in the world, as far as fanaticism in religion goes. They believe with all their hearts. And what burns them up is that so many of their bishops and archbishops and even Cardinals come from Jewish stock, you know, the Marranos, the Jews who professed Catholicism outwardly to save their skins but practiced Judaism secretly."

Of all European countries Boyd clearly loved France the most. He loved the French attitude toward their politicians. "Ah, France is a country where a politician really is held in contempt. You should hear the dirty stories the French tell about the President of the Republic. Right in the open, too. And French Senators are just nothing at all. Members of the Chamber of Deputies are held in somewhat higher respect, but not much. I guess Members of the Chamber get less money from the government, steal less, so the French people like them a little more, but only a little."

Boyd's books dealt almost entirely with European literature. There was his massive edition of the complete stories of Guy De Maupassant that he did for Knopf, there was his *Studies in Ten Literatures,* and there was his *Essays in Irish Literature.* These books are now pretty much forgotten, but one hazards the guess that they will be revived, at least in the critical writings of students, years from now. They are filled with many insights, and they are graciously written.

Boyd occasionally wrote about American works and their authors, and one could almost always detect a sneer in him when he did— especially when he dealt with contemporary writers. Try as hard as he would in his study of Mencken, called simply *H. L. Mencken,* he revealed a considerable disrespect for him—for his learning, for his writing, even for him personally. It was Boyd who was the first major writer to point out that Mencken totally misunderstood Nietzsche, who was his alleged idol. Mencken said, among other wrong things, that Nietzsche was a believer in the efficacy of liquor to the human being, whereas Nietzsche was a total non-drinker, and indeed urged others not to drink. He was, from Mencken's point of view, that most horrible of all people, a Prohibitionist. Boyd also pointed out that Nietzsche was not at all the great admirer of the German people that Mencken thought. Nietzsche had a great deal to say in criticism of the Germans, whom he called poltroons and *lumpen.*

Boyd was a co-editor of *The American Spectator,* but deep down, I always felt, he had little regard for the attainments of any of his colleagues, with the possible exception of Nathan, whom he probably liked more as a man than as a critic. Toward the end of his life, he talked rather freely about his colleagues on the *Spectator* and about other American writers. I once asked him if it was true,

as had been freely reported around town, that he had called Henry
Seidel Canby "the man with the face like an arm-pit." Henry Canby
had been a professor of English at Yale, had been literary editor of
the *New York Evening Post* and at the time of my conversation with
Boyd, was editor of the *Saturday Review of Literature* and chairman
of the Book-of-the-Month Club selection committee.

"Yes, it's true," said Boyd. "I did call him that. But I also said
other things about him. He had the face of a tired vagina. Yes, I
know that's low-down talk. Sometimes I think, when I look in the
mirror, that I, too, have the face of a tired vagina. Most men do,
as they get older. But with most men, at least intelligent men, there
is something in their eyes and in their character as it shines through
their eyes and as it expresses itself in the mouths and in the cheeks,
there is something that makes you forget their looks, that sort of
cleans them up. But not so with Canby."

"Why do you dislike him so much?" I asked. "After all, I understand he was a pretty good professor at Yale, and he has said some
fine things about Emerson and Thoreau and others, and he has
written a pretty good book, *Studies in Classic American Literature,*
and . . ."

"Now, now, Angoff, you're pulling my leg, and you must never
do that to a man like me who's *in extremis,"* said Boyd, as he smiled.

"I only meant," I began. . . .

"Canby is really quite dreadful," said Boyd. "He's not only bad
in himself; he reflects, if I may use a terrible academic word, the
badness of so much American criticism. He's polite, he's ignorant
about all the things in literature that matter. Well, let's say it this
way. I can't imagine any real writer who would want to spend any
time with him, say, on a girl party, or even on a picnic. Worse, I
can't imagine any woman wanting to commit sin with him. Now
don't laugh. I mean that. A good writer is a good sinner, and women,
all of them, love good sinners. And a critic is a writer. I'm not at all
sure that the old distinction between creative writing and non-
creative writing holds. By the way, in Europe no such distinction is
made. A writer is a writer. A writer has to use his imagination, even
and especially when he's writing history or biography or anything.

George Nathan is right when he sneers at the distinction. Now, where was I?"

"Canby."

"Good God, yes. I am sure he's not the good teacher you say he is, and I bet you made that up, just trying to be polite and fair and all that, now didn't you make it up? Who ever told you Canby is a good teacher?"

I smiled. "Oh, I heard . . ."

"That's what I thought. You heard. Canby has to be a bad teacher, he just has to be, because he's not excited about literature, he's not excited about anything, and a man who's not excited is a bad teacher. That is an axiom, right?"

"Right."

"His criticism is cold soup. Now tell me, do you remember anything exciting, refreshing, even true that he has ever written? I've been trying to make sense out of what he wrote on Emerson and Thoreau and Emily Dickinson, but I can't. I don't mind so much his dullness and obtuseness about Emerson, because he was just a fraud, a preaching fraud, who talked in riddles, because he had nothing to say. He's so bad, so ungrammatical, so hollow, so mystical, which means hollow, that I'm amazed he has not yet founded a religion. Hell, he's no worse than Mary Baker Eddy. As a matter of fact, the two have much in common, always talking about love, and I bet neither was much of a lover. And, you know, that's why I don't like Freud and Ellis."

"Havelock Ellis?"

"Yes."

"But why?"

"Because he's such a neuter in sex matters. He and Olive Shreiner never really had a good time in bed, neither of them liked bed much or at all, she was a little or a lot lesbianish, and yet he had the effrontery to write on *The Psychology of Sex*. I've looked into it, and it smells. It makes me feel I'm in a drugstore, not in a bedroom smelling of woman. A man like that just can't have anything important to say about sex. He can't. He may be scientific, whatever that is, but he's way off."

"But what about Freud?" I asked.

"He's closer to what goes on in bed, much closer. Chiefly because he's a Jew, and Jews are more honest than Christians, and Ellis is a Christian no matter what he says. But Freud is a good deal of a prude, there's no record, I mean, of his having anything to do with a woman not his wife, and that's bad. A normal man gets tired of his wife and goes out hunting. Surely he hunts plenty before he gets married, and Freud didn't. No, the only people who really know anything about sex are good writers, because good writers are basically immoral."

"But don't you have to have marriage, on account of children and . . .?" I asked.

"Maybe you do, maybe you don't. I'm not so sure a man has to know that this or that boy or girl is his. A child is a child. And I sometimes think one of the worst things for children is the so-called normal home, which is really a battlefield, where father and mother specialize in hating each other before their children. Going into the same woman night after night is a boring experience."

"Why is it boring only for men? What about women?" I asked, trying to draw him out.

"The reason is simple. Women have no imagination, so they don't get bored. A man is a man, and that's all that matters to them. A man is also a guarantee of financial and social security, and that's all most women want anyway. Those women who have imagination and want more out of the bedroom and out of life are not very good to sleep with. That's the real tragedy of life, and that's why I'm an atheist."

"I thought you were an agnostic?" I said. "Mencken told me . . ."

"Mencken doesn't know the difference between an agnostic and an atheist. He calls himself a sort of combination agnostic-atheist. But he knows little about religion. He may not go to church, but he believes in churches and pastors and all that stuff. I'm an atheist, and I can prove atheism."

"How?"

"It's easy. Any world where a third-rater like FDR can be President of the United States, where a man like Nicholas Murray Butler can be president of Columbia University, where Henry Seidel Canby can be considered a man of letters, where women lose their bloom by the time they're thirty, where men get impotent just when they begin really to enjoy sex, where there are colds and dandruff and poverty, where a good man like me has to be where I am right now, such a world is not run by any god, it's run by a devil, or it's just run by nobody and nothing. No god could be that stupid, that cruel. If he is that stupid, that cruel, then he's no god. So anybody who says he's an agnostic because he doesn't know whether there is or there isn't a god, I say that such a man is a liar. He knows very well that there is no god. But you see, it's only in America that all this god-business is taken seriously. In Europe nobody, no intelligent person, takes religion seriously, not even intelligent priests. Being a priest is just a job, like selling a fake cure for pimples or piles, or selling some fake stock."

"Why didn't you ever become a priest, since you say you don't really have to believe to be a priest?" I asked.

"You have something there," Boyd said. "You surely have something there. It's one of the worst mistakes of my life. A Catholic priest is the best of all. Few Catholic priests take their religion as seriously as do most Protestant ministers. You see, Catholicism is so superstitious that you simply say you believe and you don't have to worry about it ever again. You don't have to do any thinking. But the Protestants are in a bad way. They claim that their religion is rational so they have to watch out constantly that miracles and customs stand up to reason. And that's difficult. How can anybody make sense out of Jesus and the miracles and communion and all that stuff, and most Protestants believe that, and the intelligent ones among them are always asking questions. That means headaches for the ministers, and that's tough. A Catholic has no such worries, he tells whoever is asking a question that he's being irreligious, that he shouldn't ask questions, that he should believe, and so on. Besides, Protestant ministers get married, and that's bad."

I was surprised. "Why?"

"Because a minister has to stay married to the same woman all his life, and that's a hardship obviously. Ever hear of a Protestant

minister divorcing his wife? It's worth his job, more, it's worth his
position in the community. And he can't go out with another woman.
Oh, he can, but it's hard. Too many people know him, besides he
has inhibitions."

"What sort of inhibitions?"

"The sort of inhibitions that every man of the cloth has. You see,
any man who becomes any sort of minister isn't entirely normal, to
begin with. Very few normal people, really normal, have even
thought of entering into the ministry. It's no place for a real man.
So they have inhibitions. But there are fewer of them among
Catholics. Most Catholic priests are cynical. They can't marry, but
that doesn't mean they can't have housekeepers. I know, most
housekeepers of priests are along in years, but remember that an
elderly woman can still be good in bed, sometimes much more
comfortable than a younger one. And younger women come to the
priest's house for all sorts of questions. Then, again, he has no
worry about making a living. He's set for life, with mighty fine food.
Very few Catholic priests look underfed, and no Catholic priest is
a Prohibitionist. Look at Spellman, the Archbishop here. Look at
his round, piggish face, very content, not a worry. So it's a good
life. A very good life."

Boyd's attitude toward women was a combination of respect,
bewilderment, love, and indifference. For marriage as an institution
he had little more than contempt. "Marriage is simply impossible.
It's fine for most women, because they are dull, deep down. Those
that aren't either are Ph.D.'s, and they are revolting as women, or
they're prostitutes, and that's not so good either. There are some
in between, very few of them, and they're the best, I guess. Unfortunately, there are not enough of them to go around. So I suppose
men have to share these good women. I see nothing wrong in that.
Victor Hugo and Sainte Beuve shared one woman. She happened to have been Hugo's wife, but I don't think that makes so
very much difference."

While Boyd thought little of marriage, he thought almost as little
of divorce. He looked upon it as foolish. He preferred adultery to
divorce. As he said, "Adultery is much more sanitary, less trouble-

some than multiple matrimony." His own excursions in the realm of the female sex were sometimes mysterious. He did not always bring his companion of the evening to a gathering of writers. When he did I somehow had the feeling that she really was not a "companion" but a sort of acquaintance. His real "companions" he more or less kept to himself. Not that he was in any way ashamed of them. He was attached to them, in his own way. But, I guess, he wasn't too sure that American writers would appreciate what he was doing. For, deep down, he looked upon most American writers as prudes and Puritans, people who were afraid to follow their truest instincts in the world of sex.

He was, as I have said, a raffish man through and through. I often imagined that he would have been most at home in the company of Rabelais—of that section of the medieval world that outwardly conformed to the customs of the Catholic Church but that actually was quite pagan and entirely free in its talk and very free in its actions. I once heard Boyd say, "Never sneer at a Cardinal with a mistress. There you had a perfect companionship: a man of learning and genuine honesty and a real atheist, a cynical atheist, the best sort, and you also had a woman who appreciated quality in a man, and didn't care much for the morals of the world."

In his last days, as I have said, he spent most of his day-light hours in some saloon, generally Pete's Tavern. He looked rather seedy and pathetic. It was clear that he wasn't well. He would cough rather persistently, and now and then he would say a word or two in self-pity—"Editors don't want learning and real writing now, they want flash, well . . ."—but most of the time he did not refer to his own status. He accepted whatever fate had allotted to him. He got much pleasure out of his surroundings and out of his stray friends. He felt at home here—certainly more so than at Twenty-One or Coq d'Or. Perhaps he would have preferred Lüchow's, with its large hall and chamber orchestra and huge tables and heaping dishes of food and large steins of beer and fine glasses of wine—especially the back of Lüchow's, "where people who can read and write go." Perhaps. But it didn't matter too much.

My last encounter with him was over the telephone. He had sent me at the *Mercury* two and a half pages of reminiscences about George Bernard Shaw. There was almost nothing in them and I had to return the manuscript, much as I didn't want to. I wrote him as diplomatic a letter as I could. He called up from Pete's Tavern and asked whether he could do anything to make the manuscript acceptable.

I hardly knew what to say. "Well, Boyd, it's really not yet a manuscript. I mean, you have to say more, much more, fatten it up. All you have there is a sort of sketch or an outline of an article."

"But it's good material, isn't it?"

"Well, not what you have there now. I'm sure what's in your mind, your memory is very good, and all you have to do is get it on paper."

"Of course, of course. But I'm a little strapped now for money, you know. I expect a check from a publisher for whom I did some work, should have come in this morning, but you know the mail."

"Sure. Would you like . . ."

"Yes, in a way, just for a day or two. I'll put one of the men here on the phone, and you tell him that I'm good for the money, lunch, a drink, you know, he's a new man here, you know."

"Of course, I will," I said.

He died a few days later.

I still cannot get rid of the feeling that I should not have returned the manuscript, but accepted it, sent him a check, and put the whole transaction down to "profit and loss." If anybody deserved that kind of white lie, he deserved it. Perhaps such a white lie would have added a little self-respect to his last days on earth.

Dorothy Thompson:
Kansan in Westchester

Across the years I have encountered many men and women who were their own worst enemies. They had talent, they had perception, they had graciousness, they had the capacity for friendship, but they all ended up sorrowful and pathetic wanderers. Perhaps their chief misfortune lay in the fact that they wanted to be what God apparently did not want them to be.

One such person, I believe, was Dorothy Thompson. I first met her through H. L. Mencken, who introduced her to me in the lobby of the Algonquin Hotel in New York City. This was some time in the middle twenties, a little before she and Sinclair Lewis were married. Mencken was polite in his best Baltimore manner. Dorothy Thompson appeared shy, despite the bluster in her voice, as she greeted Mencken. Before the two parted, she was talking like a Kansas milk maid, or the way I imagine a Kansas milk maid speaks: soft, sincere, a bit hesitant of voice. The bloom of young womanhood was all over her. The phrase "milk fed" passed through my mind. She was then only a newspaper woman and an occasional magazine writer, and I had read only a few pieces by her, and not been overly impressed. The American newspaper world, especially the New York City newspaper world, had many newspaper women, who each wrote what they wrote, frequented speakeasies, sometimes drank too much, thumped the bar for "another Martini," and then had to be helped home by a male newspaper man—sometimes to her apartment or to his own. I didn't know that Dorothy Thompson did all this. She probably didn't. The look in her eyes not only was a kindly one, but also a shrewd and knowing one. But she did belong to the league, so to speak.

"How do you like her?" asked Mencken.

"I think she's nice," I said.

"That's no way to describe a grown woman. No grown women are nice."

"I like her," I ventured again.

Mencken smiled. "I don't know her too well myself. But I've heard about her. She frightens me. I don't like women who don't concentrate on their main job, snaring a husband. I think she's had one, but lost him. When a woman loses a man, it's her fault, all the time. Remember that."

A few months later I heard that she had married Lewis. "Poor Red," was Mencken's comment. "His first wife, Gracie, told Red she was a better writer, and Dorothy will tell him she's a better man than he is. She looks like Hindenburg as a young man."

The comparison made me laugh.

"Poor Red," repeated Mencken. "Men who marry more than one woman always make the same mistake. The only difference is the woman's name."

"I still like her," I said.

"You're stubborn," Mencken said.

About the same time there was an international uproar in the journalistic world. Dreiser and Dorothy Thompson charged each other with stealing each other's facts in reporting the general situation in Russia. Apparently Dreiser and Lewis came to blows in some European restaurant—I believe it was in Vienna.

Mencken was outraged. "Imagine a woman getting a man into that kind of mess. I told you Lewis's wife was a man-eater."

"This is the first I heard you call her that, a man-eater," I said.

"I just made it up," Mencken said, smiling. "But she shouldn't have done that."

"Done what?"

Again Mencken smiled. "Hell, I don't know. If she didn't steal Dreiser's stuff, then she was too close to him anyway. I don't know what happened. But two American writers of the stature of Dreiser and Lewis shouldn't be battling in public—and over what a woman did or didn't do!"

For a long time afterward, Mencken tried to make peace between Lewis and Dreiser, but I don't think he succeeded. Once Mencken told me that one of the things that worried him was that the British— "the damn limeys"—would take the Lewis-Dreiser battle "as a further bit of evidence that the Americans have no literary culture."

The battle probably became intensified when Lewis was awarded the Nobel Prize—the first American writer to be so honored. Dreiser, I was told, had let it be known, through friendly channels, that he should have had it.

Lewis and Dorothy Thompson took a picture together on the boat that was to take them to Stockholm. Mencken was in the office of the *Mercury* the morning that picture appeared in the newspaper. "A mighty fine picture," he said. "I suspect Red Lewis is about 25 per cent sober. But I don't like that woman with him."

"I think she looks rather pleasant," I said.

"Time will teach you better," Mencken said.

It was not long afterward that Dorothy Thompson became a columnist for the *Herald Tribune* and for two or three hundred other newspapers. She lectured all over the country on national and international affairs. She issued statements to the press—about literally dozens of topics, political, economic, cultural. She was given all sorts of awards and honorary degrees. She became sufficiently important for writers and cartoonists to satirize her. She was portrayed as giving advice to the Pope, to the President of the United States, to the King of Sweden, to the Emperor of Ethiopia, to the President of the New York Stock Exchange, to the President of Harvard University. She became the Woman of the Year. She became the Woman of the Decade. She became the woman of the Twentieth Century.

For about five years she was perhaps the most sought after lecturer in the United States. She was now the mother of a boy,

Michael, but it was reported that she did most of her mothering by long distance telephone and through the United States mail. In view of her speaking schedule she couldn't have done otherwise. Occasionally she would write to Mencken from some distant city. A polite man, he always answered her at some length, but after he signed the letters he would exclaim, "Ignorant bitch," "Shrieking hurricane," or simply, "Poor Red Lewis, stuck with that."

Lewis was stuck only legally. It wasn't long after the birth of Michael that Lewis began to wander off by himself. I fear he wasn't too good a father, and he probably wasn't too good a husband, but Dorothy, from all reports (made by Nathan and Philip Goodman, who was very intimate with Lewis) was not an ideal wife, either. Were they merely bad for each other? I doubt it. They were probably just bad for marriage. They wanted the pleasures of marriage without paying the price for it. And neither, probably, was psychologically capable of being a full-time parent.

Mencken's dislike of Dorothy Thompson increased when she began to write about Hindenburg and Hitler. She argued that the general was inept and unfit for his massive job. She argued that probably no military man could possibly be good for Germany in the thirties. The times called for a statesman on the grand scale. She thought Hitler was a clown and wouldn't last long. As I recall it, she said he wouldn't last longer than six months. When it became clear that Hitler was in for a long time she denounced the German people, and she was particularly violent about the Nazi atrocities against the Jews. Since Mencken was a Germanophile—he sometimes spoke and wrote as if the German people could do no wrong for any extended period of time—he was offended by Dorothy Thompson's writings. He was now in a strange position, for Sinclair Lewis agreed with his wife's political views, while he disliked her personally. So Mencken took it out on Dorothy Thompson by mumbling in the *Mercury* office what a horrible woman she was, and by writing editorials and book reviews in the *American Mercury* and columns in the Baltimore *Sun* arguing that the whole world was against Germany, that the real culprit in the world mess was Great Britain, whom he referred to generally as Perfidious Albion. Sometimes he also blamed France, "land of the frogs." Dorothy Thompson apparently was not unmindful of what Mencken was doing, since she would write in newspapers and magazines, and say from the lecture platform, that the world must never forget that England was the Mother of Parliaments and France everybody's second homeland.

On the surface Lewis and Dorothy Thompson still were man and wife. They occupied the same apartment in the New York East Side, and they also had a home in Westchester. But each was seldom in either place, and they were together hardly ever. In the five years of her eminence I saw her only three or four times. Once I went to a huge party she gave in her New York apartment, and I was one of probably 150 invited guests. She had become quite stout of body, but her eyes were still bright and young. Mencken, Nathan and I went together. Mencken's comment was, "Noisy, but I'm glad, because nobody heard what anybody else was saying. The drinks were superb. Did Dorothy say anything to you, George? She only said hello to me."

Nathan answered, "She said hardly any more to me. She did introduce me to a young woman who wanted to become an actress."

"I had no such luck," said Mencken, and added, "You mean she was fifteen or sixteen?"

"About that," said Nathan.

Mencken referred to Nathan's attraction to girls in their early teens.

Neither asked me, but I volunteered the thought, "She looks sad to me. I don't think she's happy."

"Angoff has a crush on Dorothy," said Mencken. "He likes big noisy women."

"I still like her, though what she writes seems rather pontifical. She'd be more right if she didn't scream." I was sorry I said this, because I instantly recalled the silent debate Mencken and Dorothy were having about Germany and Hitler. I was also beginning to have arguments with Mencken about Hitler. I urged that the *Mercury* print articles against the Nazi book burnings, and Mencken objected on the ground that Hitler wouldn't last long and, besides, "These book burnings are exaggerated by the reporters."

Another time Philip Goodman took me to the Lewis-Thompson home in New York. It was one of the few times, I guess, when they were together. Only about ten people were present. Lewis was standing on a chair and was holding forth in the manner of Prime Minister Neville Chamberlain, who at the time was predicting "peace in our time" in his negotiations with Hitler. Lewis was hysterically funny. He was a superb mimic. We all laughed. But Dorothy said, "No, no, Red. You may be a good writer, but again I must tell you, you do not understand politics." Lewis was crestfallen, and the guests were embarrassed. I had the feeling that Dorothy knew she had done something unpardonable for a wife, but she didn't know what to do about it at the moment. I said so to Goodman as we walked home.

Goodman hesitated, then said, "Well, you're probably right. She's no fool, but she lacks the instincts of a woman. She's an opponent in a household. A perfect example of what a career has done to a woman."

Naïvely, I said, "I hope she apologizes."

"It makes no difference whether she does or not. Such things cannot be apologized for."

The next time I saw her I was with the late Benjamin Stolberg. He wanted me to be present at an interview he was having with Lewis about a projected novel about American labor that Lewis was planning. Lewis had hired Stolberg to "fill him in" about the forces and personalities in the labor movement. Ben and I went to a small town in Westchester, where Lewis had his country home. A maid greeted us, and added that Lewis was not present and she had no idea where he went or when he would return. We went into the house, and soon Dorothy greeted us. It was late afternoon and she offered us drinks. Stolberg was angry, and Dorothy did what she could to calm him down. "Ben," she pleaded, "please don't be that way. You know Red. He is that way sometimes. I didn't know myself he had gone until Irene, the maid, told me. She says he left early this morning. He left no note, no message, nothing."

Ben went out for a while. He was gone a half hour. Dorothy and

I were alone. It was clear that she had been drinking before Ben and I had arrived. It was also clear that she was disturbed about something—and she had plenty of reason to be disturbed about her career as well as about her husband. Some of the weeklies and dailies had begun to question her omniscience, and it was rumored that some newspapers had cut out her column.

"How is Freda?" she asked. She referred to Freda Kirchwey, who was a colleague of mine on the editorial board of the *Nation*.

"Oh, you know I feel that she somehow always makes important issues seem trivial, and she dramatizes trivial issues. I suppose what I'm saying is that she rubs me the wrong way; I mean the way her mind works annoys me. Perhaps what I mean is that all issues to her are what they were to her in Barnard where she revolted, I believe, against the ruling forbidding students to wear what they called bloomers in those days."

Dorothy smiled. Then she said, "Well, the poor woman . . ." She did not elaborate. She had another drink.

"I wish I hadn't gone to the *Nation*," I said.

"Yes. But it's as good as any of them. I believe that the day of serious magazines, even bad ones, is going out. Democracy is being too successful. Bad women's magazines—and, in a sense, all women's magazines are bad—will take over. And since there are more silly women than silly men, it's going to be terrible. A silly woman can do more harm than a silly man. A silly woman is belligerent. Silly men get drunk, and in any case they hardly bother anybody." She smiled. "My lecture audiences should hear me now. But they won't mind if they did, that is, the few audiences that are left. It's hard to talk to these assembled women. They're so stupid and so pretentious. I'd rather talk to a bunch more honest. Mencken should hear me now!"

"He might agree with you on this."

"He's a Prussian through and through, your former boss is."

"Are you working on a book now?" I asked.

"No. I'm in the same doldrums Red is," she answered in the only reference she made to him. "Michael is a joy."

Dorothy now took a long drink—a double Martini, it seemed to me, and I was worried for her. She was silent for a few moments, as she caressed the drink. Then she said, "Are you religious?"

"Oh, I don't know. I'm a Jew, but as for the amount of religion I subscribe to, I don't know. But I am a Jew."

"Have you known many rabbis?"

"Oh, yes, definitely. I wish I knew what they know. I mean of Jewish traditions, customs, religion, you know."

"I'm glad. I've been thinking a lot about religious people lately and about religion. I guess it's age. Listen." She stopped, and her mind seemed to be far away. Then she said, "You think I come from Kansas or some such place, don't you?"

"Why yes, don't you? Mencken led me to believe that."

"Oh, Mencken," she said. "He's full of misinformation. That's his stock in trade. He comes from Kansas. He's really a Middle Westerner. He never did understand the East—cities, big cities. He's not even a Baltimorean. No, I was born in New York, and I am a New Yorker. I just can't understand why people look upon me as a Kansan. Do you?"

"I don't understand either."

"Do I look like a Kansan?"

"I wouldn't say that."

"Well, I guess I do look like a Kansan, a drunken Kansan. I looked into the mirror this morning, the bathroom mirror, and I do look like a Kansan, and I say this without any disrespect to Kansans. Really, I mean it. A Kansan in Westchester!"

George E. Sokolsky

FOUR OR FIVE TIMES A YEAR I WOULD MEET SOKOLSKY ON THE street, or he would call me on the telephone, and always there was a strange combination of coolness and a desire to be friendly on both our parts. This went on for years, though there were long stretches of time when we did not see each other or talk to each other. I had not seen him or heard from him for almost six months when I read about his death. I was more than sorry; I had the feeling that he had been unhappy on many levels for a long time before he died, and that, sudden as his death reportedly was, he probably welcomed it in the few seconds of knowledge that he had before he lapsed into total unconsciousness.

How do I know this? Well, I don't actually know it; he never said so to me. But I had a hunch that as he was getting older he realized more and more that his life, in a profound sense, was pretty much a failure. Towards the end, I am quite sure, he had little respect for most of the men on the Hearst chain, for whom he wrote his column, and I also believe that his column was a spiritual burden to him.

About six months before he died, I had occasion to call him on the telephone. Most of the time he used to call me. I called him because at the time I was doing research for "Meet the Press," a TV-Radio panel program, and for a while the producer, Lawrence

E. Spivak, thought of having Sokolsky on a program. Spivak suggested I "sound out" Sokolsky, get his attitude toward a man, Dr. Fred Schwartz, leader of a vague anti-Communist movement about whom Sokolsky had written. I had read Sokolsky's columns on Schwartz, and was pleased. Sokolsky thought that Dr. Schwartz was in some respects a dubious man, that his movement was silly, and he deplored the fact that so many of his friends were backing Dr. Schwartz. Especially was he put out by Eugene Lyons, who wrote glowingly about Dr. Schwartz.

I said to Spivak, "For once I must say that Sokolsky is on the right side, I mean on my side, and that surprises me, because he and I disagree about so many things. I'm beginning to get worried. If Sokolsky is on my side, then I must be wrong. On the other hand, Eugene Lyons is on the other side; so I must be right."

"You're prejudiced, Charlie," said Spivak. "You don't like Lyons; so you talk that way."

"Well, I can get along from New Year to the last day in December without missing Lyons' writings. That's true. But Sokolsky— what's got into him?"

"Well, you have them both wrong," said Spivak diplomatically. "I know how you feel about Lyons, but talk to Sokolsky more, and you'll see you have him wrong."

"Wrong about what?" I asked.

Sokolsky kept me on the telephone for a half hour. I don't remember our talk word for word, of course, but I do remember its essence and many of the phrases. He called Dr. Schwartz a "Galitizianer"—in the social hierarchy of Jews (not taken seriously by any intelligent Jew) perhaps the "lowest" type of Jew. He called him a demagogue, a rabble rouser, a no-goodnick, "a meshoomed" (convert). I reminded Sokolsky that Dr. Schwartz did not himself convert from Judaism to Christianity; it was his father who converted. "Well," said Sokolsky, "that's nonsense. He could have unconverted himself. Because his father made a dumb mistake is no reason why the son should continue it."

I asked Sokolsky why Lyons had so much faith in Dr. Schwartz. "Oh, hell," Sokolsky said, "Gene is the only Jew I know of who really has no Jewish humor. He has a goy *kopf*, I sometimes think. How can any Jew with any humor have anything good to say about Dr. Schwartz? How can he? Besides, what the hell is this Dr. Schwartz jackass doing in the United States anyway? Why doesn't he stick to Australia? He's been doing very well here, financially and in every other way; so he should become a citizen. Not that I want him to be one—he's no addition—but what's he doing here anyway?"

"George," I said, "I hear you're going to leave columning and become a rabbi."

He laughed. "Well, maybe I will, maybe I will. I may go the way you've gone."

"What do you mean?"

"I mean a Jew is a Jew."

I reminded him that he had been printing translations of Jewish prayers in his column in the *Journal-American,* the New York Hearst evening newspaper.

"Sure," he said. "They're very good, don't you think?"

"Of course. Remember, George, we talked about all this years ago?"

"I remember, Charlie. I remember very well. I've been thinking about it a lot recently. It was at the Cafe Royal on Second Avenue."

".Right. You remember."

"Why should I forget? But remember, Charlie, that I never went wholly away. Not like some other guys you and I know."

"For instance?"

"Never mind. Did you know I go to Central Synagogue on Lexington Avenue?"

"Of course, I did."

"How?"

"George, don't you know I'm the section leader of the Jewish Underground in New York City, midtown section?"

"All right, all right. Do you know what I've been wondering about lately?"

"What, George?"

"Well, I've been thinking about doing something to help some organization, I forget the name, in their attempts to convert Christians to being Jews. Well, I guess I don't mean convert. I suppose I'm still sort of opposed to that. I mean, I guess, telling the *goyim* more about what Judaism is. It's amazing how little they really know. They're filled with the nonsense about Judaism being the religion of duty and law, and Christianity being the religion of love and pity. Hell, this is all wrong. But their priests and ministers fill them with this nonsense. We have to diseducate them and then educate them again right from the beginning."

"Remember, George, we talked about this at the Cafe Royal?"

"I know. I know. There's been a lot of things happening since then."

"Ever see Westbrook Pegler?" I interrupted.

"Oh, Charlie, that's a dirty question. I think you got him wrong. He overstated, he was angry, but there was something not bad inside of him—still is there. I wish I knew what got him all twisted up. I wish I knew. You know, Charlie, that's what the problem is, the real problem, on the individual level, on the national level, on the international level. We get twisted up, and we don't know why or how or when. I was plenty twisted, you're plenty twisted. Gene Lyons is all twisted up. That's the problem. It's a problem of values. We all know what's true and good and beautiful, and we all, or most of us most of the time, turn the other way, do silly things, say silly things, talk silly things; and then when we get older and see how silly we've been, it's too late, and we get bitter or we get soft, and we wonder how it all happened. That's the problem, the real problem."

"I think you're talking real sense for the first time in your life, George," I said.

"You're joking, but *you* may be telling the truth the first time in your life. You know what I've been thinking about, Charlie, seriously, you know what?"

"What?"

"We got more Jews in New York City than ever before, more Jews than any city has ever had in all human history, but the city is less Jewish—do you feel this way?"

"What do you mean?"

"Oh, hell, Charlie, you know. There used to be Second Avenue and the Cafe Royal and the Yiddish theatres and Yiddish restaurants and Yiddish clubs and Jewish affairs, and you could be a Jew, a real Jew. Now, it's gone. The intellectuals are reading *Commentary*, and those intellectuals are not intellectual Jews. They're phonies, who are interested in Faulkner, not in Sholom Aleichem, in Kierkegaard, not in Maimonides. Hell, there's more real Jewishness in the *Forward* than in a thousand *Commentarys*. The salvation for Jewish Americans lies in becoming more Jewish, and this way they'll also become better Americans. Oh, hell, I just don't know, I just don't know. I go to Central Synagogue. It's Reform. It's all right. I'm not happy with the Orthodox or with the Conservatives, and I'm not altogether happy with the Reform. There's something missing all around. But I don't know what to suggest."

"You sure are thinking a lot about the Jews and Judaism now."

"I'm thinking about nothing else, Charlie."

"Do the Hearst boys know?"

"Sure they know, Charlie, you got the Hearst people wrong. They don't bother me at all. Well, it's good talking to you. It took a cunning *shlemiel*, no, he's worse than that—it took Fred Schwartz to get us to have a *shmoos*."

When I took over the editorship of the *American Mercury*, early in 1934, George Sokolsky wrote to me that he wanted to see me to discuss some articles. I had heard about him vaguely from various people. Many of them said that if anybody knew the Orient it was he. It was reported that he had been in China a long time, married a Chinese girl, and was a hard-headed reporter. I inquired of somebody at the Simon and Schuster office, and was told that they were negotiating with him about a book on the Orient, and I was assured that "George knows China and Japan, too, as nobody else knows it."

When Sokolsky came up to the office I was astonished by his size. He was truly huge. But I was disconcerted by his eyes; they seemed to be sizing me up and I had the feeling that he wanted to make sure I was the sort of man he could do business with. Altogether I didn't like him. But I brushed aside my personal prejudice based upon only a few minutes of talk, and I recalled the good reports I had about him. So we agreed that he should do an article on the talk about a coming Russo-Japanese-American conflict. He was eager to do it, and the more he talked the more did I see in what he said an article that might cause discussion. At the time many of the people in my circle of friends said that there would in all probability be a conflict between the United States and Japan, and that Russia would be on whatever side suited her interests. I printed the article, entitled "The Russo-Japanese War Myth," in the May, 1934 issue of the *Mercury*. I don't believe we got a single letter from anybody for or against it; but some of my friends said that Sokolsky had sold me a piece of rubbish.

Bad as this article was, and time has proved it to be utter nonsense, the second article he wrote was probably even worse, and why I printed it I don't recall. As I re-read it today I blush. It leads off the July, 1934 issue of the *Mercury,* and is entitled, "America Drifts Toward Fascism." In it Sokolsky argues that the New Deal, in some mysterious, nefarious way, is the father of American fascism, and he implies that some form of fascism is definitely on the way in the United States. I was vaguely uncomfortable about this thesis, but I didn't know enough about politics to state my discomfort in intelligible sentences. I should have rejected the article on the mere ground of my vague discomfort—in editing, it is a pretty good rule to reject if in doubt—but instead I showed it to some experts who told me to print it. I learned much later that some of these "experts" were either Communists or fellow-travelers who, I imagine, were eager for fascism to come here in order that Communism could take over. Fascism would unsettle the whole American scheme and violently disturb the people, and the country would be ripe for the Communists. This is the sort of diseased thinking that was prevalent in certain alleged intellectual circles then.

Sokolsky suggested other articles, but I said no. I simply didn't trust him any more. My vague dislike of him had become intensified. I began to have the feeling that he really knew much less than his admirers claimed. I also had the feeling that he was, in some way, unprincipled. But he interested me as a human being. I had never before met such a man. So, when he invited me to visit him at his home, in an apartment in Abingdon Square, New York City, I went. He tried again to have me tell him to do more articles for me. I told him that his ideas were being "done" by others; that the ideas were "not for us"; that we were "full up with material"; and so on. Smart as he was, he apparently didn't realize what I was telling him. He continued to try to impress me with his knowledge of world affairs and with his "intuition" about events and people. He smiled at my "intuitions." He called me naïve. He said that the New Deal was "un-American" in that it denied private initiative to work its miracles; that FDR was "power hungry"; that Harry Hopkins and Harold Ickes were "typical pro-Fascist maneuverers." I laughed at all this. I said that I simply could not see America going Fascist. He called my attention to the contention of the New York *Daily News* that there probably wouldn't be any free elections in the United States for much longer. I said that I had heard about this and that I thought it was ridiculous.

"Well," said Sokolsky, "that only shows once more that you don't understand the American people. Say what you will about the *Daily News,* and it's a much better newspaper than your kind seem to think, say what you will about that paper, it does keep its pulse on the American people, and you just can't pooh-pooh what they say."

"I pooh-pooh it," I said.

"Why?"

"Well, for a very simple reason. I think that the spirit of the Declaration of Independence and of the authors of the Constitution and of Abraham Lincoln's Emancipation Proclamation is still too powerful in this country to permit any kind of fascism or Communism. The American people just won't stand for it. There will be many who will try to become Fascist leaders, but they just won't succeed. They'll come close, perhaps, but in the end they will fail."

"You're an optimist."

"I suppose so."

"And a sentimentalist, too."

"Maybe."

Sokolsky spoke at length about Japan and China. He again told me that the likelihood of a war between the United States and Japan was "remote." He also thought that Russia would never go to war with Japan, because "there's no economic reason for such a war. The extra room that the Japs need for their rising population they'll get in China and in Formosa."

But Sokolsky spoke most of all about Jews, Jewish traditions, Jewish customs, Jewish prayers—and about Jews in general. He knew Yiddish very well, and also a little Hebrew. I asked him directly how he squared his intense interest in his Jewish background with the fact that he had married a Chinese girl. He said:

"I don't mind at all your asking me, if you are worried on that score. To me there's no contradiction whatever. I keep my customs and she keeps her customs, and our son is enriched thereby. I speak about her in the present. She's dead, as you know, but she's alive here in this apartment, her spirit is alive. You see, I have pictures of her all over. That's where I go along with the traditionalists. I believe in immortality, in the immortality of the spirit. Of this there's no doubt whatever; there can be no doubt. Neurosis? None whatever. You didn't say it, but others have; they said that with such an inter-racial, inter-faith marriage there's bound to be neurosis; that in this way I assure, with my son, a life-long customer for the psychiatrist. That's nonsense. He's a better human being for this—much better. But he's missing something, of course."

"What's he missing?"

"Well, he's missing what you and I had. The old, genuine, religious feeling—the old, genuine Jewishness. That's where Orthodoxy has it all over Conservatism and Reform. Intellectually I'm Reform, I suppose, but emotionally I'm Orthodox, and so are all of us."

"You could be right," I said. He continued:

"And you know, Charlie, we Jews really are chosen—I mean in some strange, mysterious way. I don't mean in any racial way. We're not superior intellectually to others. I know of plenty of Jewish dopes, and so do you. I suppose what I mean is that we're chosen to have some special attitude toward life; maybe history chose us for that; maybe events have forced this on us, but the Jewish attitude is something special. Sholom Aleichem knew this. Peretz knew this; all the great Jewish writers knew this, and still know it; and you know it and I know it. Jewish humor is like no other humor. Would a *goy* ever say, 'Thank God, I am starving to death painlessly'? Would a *goy* say, 'I am starving to death three times a day'? It's a grizly kind of humor, but it's common among Jews. Yes, I know, they're full of this kind of humor because otherwise they couldn't stand their persecution by the *goyim*. But I have a theory that the Jews had this same kind of humor when they had their own land. I'm sure of it. And when they'll get their country back, they'll still have this kind of humor. By the way, I'm absolutely sure the Jews will get their country back."

"Why?"

"Because they're stubborn, the most stubborn people known to all human history."

One evening, as we were in the midst of talking, he suggested that we go to the Cafe Royal. "Maybe we'll see Trotsky there," he said.

After we were in the cafe for a while he said, "Well, Trotsky isn't here tonight."

"What do you suppose he's doing now?" I asked.

Sokolsky wasn't ready for this kind of question. "Well," he said, "I suppose he's sulking over Stalin."

"No," I said, "that's where I have it over you. I know what Trotsky is doing now. He's writing a book."

Sokolsky smiled. "You're right. When a Jew has time he's writing a book or reading a book, or wishes he had written a book or was reading one. You're right. You know something, Charlie? I don't like German Jews."

"Why?"

He replied: "It would never occur to a German Jew to start a cafe like this. The first thing a German Jew would do is to start a sort of German cafe, and admit a few Jews, and he would be happy if the men and women in such a cafe spent their time talking mostly about German things and maybe making a little fun of Jews, especially Russian Jews. And all the German Jews would be like German army lieutenants and they would be overly polite to each other, and they would make fun of America. God, they're an awful people—German Jews. No wonder Karl Marx was anti-Semitic. He saw so many German Jews. Hell, even the God of the German Jews is not like a Jewish God. He's a God who speaks German and sneers at Russian Jews. I said before that I'm probably a Reform Jew now, but one of the many things I don't like about Reform is that it is so much a German-Jewish movement."

"Why don't you start an anti-German-Jewish movement?"

Sokolsky saw no humor in this suggestion. His mind seemed suddenly to have wandered off. Then he said, "You're a Democrat."

I replied: "Oh, most of the time, I guess. I'm an independent, but I do vote most of the time for the Democratic ticket when they don't put crooks up for office and the Republicans haven't any better candidates. I believe in these two parties. I have never voted the Socialist ticket. At this moment I feel proud of this. It makes me feel very realistic, loaded with *Realpolitik*."

He saw no humor in this remark either. He said, "I don't think I like FDR. The Republicans are more American."

"You talk like a Hearst writer now, George."

He got angry. I could see it in his eyes. "Hearst, Hearst, hell, Charlie, Hearst has done a lot of good things. I wouldn't mind writing for the Hearst people."

"I would," I said, 'I'd mind very much. I still like the story about the young man who wrote that he was playing the piano in a whorehouse instead of working for Hearst, because he didn't want his mother to be ashamed of him."

Sokolsky was solemn, "That's a dirty story," he said. I could feel one of his legs trembling . . . I hadn't known he had that kind of nervousness, . . . now he began to tap the table with his fingers, . . . we each finished our tea and cake and I ordered another round . . . Sokolsky paid no attention, and he was surprised that I had ordered again.

"FDR could be a dangerous man," Sokolsky said.

"Rubbish," I snapped.

"It's liberals like you who don't see dangers in people like FDR."

"There's no danger in him. I don't agree with everything he's done. I used to think he could have done more. But now I think he did about as much as possible for the time in our history."

"Well, I don't know. There's one good thing about you—you don't take all that *New Masses* stuff seriously. They're for FDR, but I suppose they have reasons of their own. Commies always have secret reasons."

"The *New Masses* people call me a social fascist, a capitalist lick spittle, because I said something nice about Trotsky in one of my pieces in the *Mercury*. They'll never forgive Trotsky, because Stalin will never forgive anybody who's better than he is; and all I'm saying is that I'd rather spend a few hours with Trotsky than with Stalin, who strikes me as a gangster, an illiterate gangster. Trotsky is a literate man, with a fine critical head. Too bad he's a Communist, but he knows things."

"I have a theory he's not a Communist really. No Jew can long remain a Communist, that is, an Orthodox Communist. Trotsky is closer to Kerensky than to Stalin or even Lenin. But you're wrong about FDR. The man has a lust for power."

"I don't believe it."

"Don't."

This fundamental disagreement is what ostensibly stopped the development of our relationship. But there were deeper reasons. He sensed that I really didn't like him personally as well as his ideas, and that I was seeing him out of sheer curiosity. I had a vague feeling that he represented a growing breed of men, a breed that I feared would increase in this public-relations world—men of considerable native intelligence and sensitivity but without much character, men who were willing to do almost anything in order to "get ahead," because, so cynical were they that they believed that only in this way could they reach "success." Some of them did reach success, but I doubt that a single one of them had much respect for himself, at least not in the deepest recesses of his heart. In their climb up the shaky ladder of success, they often married wives who were even more "immoral" than they were. Perhaps unconsciously these men married these women because they thought they would make good hostesses and, in general, "good fronts" for them: "A woman can do a lot for a man by just being gracious and charming." These women were, in large number, originally secretaries in business offices where their employers were obsessed by the same false system of values as were their future husbands. Like attracted like. And all went well for years, with the woman often remaining in her "immoral" morass, but the man growing more and more unhappy to the consternation of the woman by his side. Now and then, very rarely, indeed, both man and wife realized that they had sold out their souls and somehow redeemed themselves by way of resigning from their old lives and devoting themselves to doing "good works." But more often, perhaps, it happened differently—that is, the resignation. Both husband and wife resigned themselves to being "immoral," or the man noted his obtuse wife and was fearful that if he married again, he would probably marry the same woman under another name—bad habit dulls perception. Besides, he was too old to go through the enormous wear and tear of a new marriage. He decided that it was better to live with the devil you know than with the devil you don't know. Hence he simply decided to stick it out with his woman, suffer in silence, and seek solace in drink or in occasional dalliance with a buyer or an office girl or a colleague's wife who has a roving eye.

Sokolsky, to me, to some degree, belonged to all these categories of "immoral" men who were eager for "success." His reputation as a reporter was not very high. He had hardly any style. He had hardly any ideas that well-read men could respect. But he did know how to make the unwary reader think that he was being enlightened by reading Sokolsky. He sensed that the newspaper reading public was bewildered by all the "facts" in the newspapers and magazines and on the radio, that it wanted guidance. He knew enough about real values to be astonished by the sensational success of Westbrook Pegler. He took the logical step when, I imagine, he said to himself, "If such as those, especially Pegler, can get away with it, then I can." He was more inclined toward "liberal" views, but, I imagine, he saw that it would be better business to take an in-between stand—be a liberal-conservative, or a conservative-radical, preach Republicanism with a heart, and espouse Democracy but with caution for "realities."

Somehow he sold himself to the very same newspaper that published Walter Lippman, the New York *Herald Tribune*. Apparently the readers of the *Tribune* wanted more than Sokolsky could give them. So Sokolsky switched to the Hearst press, and there he found his ideal audience—men and women who looked for "common sense," devoid of all "wild-eyed ideas," and all this stated in simple words and short sentences with occasional references to philosophers and doctrines that they had never heard of, but that somehow gave them, the readers, a feeling that what they were reading was sound and solid and right from Mt. Sinai. The fact that Sokolsky was Jewish, in some strange way, was pleasing to the Hearst readers. Jews were shrewd; every non-Jew knows that, of course; and so what Sokolsky said was "doubly true." Now and then Sokolsky came out for inter-faith discussions; he talked before Catholic groups and Protestant groups, and not too many Jewish groups. This, too, was just fine. It showed how tolerant and broadminded Sokolsky was. The newspapers of the hinterland bought Sokolsky's column, and he became famous—a real "success."

He yearned to be a book writer, a real *lamden* (scholar), as he once told me. He wrote on politics, on labor, and on the Jews. His study of *The American Way of Life* was so superficial and so uncritical of the contemporary political and economic scene that Fulton Ousler, editor of *Liberty,* wrote a glowing Introduction to it. Sokolsky's naïveté (unconscious or deliberate) is revealed by his unqualified remark, "It is to the interest of the whole American people to defend advertising because advertising serves them." In his book, *Labor's Fight for Power* (1955) he accepted almost *in toto* the line of the National Association of Manufacturers.

Sokolsky discussed the Jewish "problem" at length in *We Jews* (1935). Sokolsky was hardly a profound student of Jewish history or philosophy or literature or psychology. But many of his instincts were sound, and he did have some sharp intuitions for the "polite anti-Semitism" one meets so often in "higher" intellectual and social circles in metropolitan America and in small-town America, too, it is feared. Has the Jew an equal chance with the non-Jew even in the *"goldene medine"* America is? Of course not, says Sokolsky: "We Jews have to be a superior people to live happily. We cannot risk the faults that other folks enjoy." And he added the obvious, "All Jews have to suffer for the sins of a single Jew."

Sokolsky knew what some Jews take a lifetime to learn: "The Jewish Jew does not suffer from discrimination as much as the others who try to pass."

He was a Zionist and he believed in the centrality of religion to the Jews though he himself was hardly an observant Jew. He said: "No matter how he rationalizes his position, the Jew is dominated by a religious force which alone gives him form and content, tradition, and hope. Should Judaism as a religion disappear, the Jews as a race and a nationality would disappear." The Jew needs a spiritual home: "That home can only be Palestine, . . . there dwells their God, and only in their God are they united."

Sokolsky wrote this in 1935, twenty-seven years before he died. For about twenty of the years that remained to him he was far more interested in defending the Republican Party and the principles of the National Association of Manufacturers than in discussing Jewish affairs. The establishment of the State of Israel in 1947 naturally re-awakened his interest, but then he went back to praising the ideas of Senator Robert Taft.

He became a huge success on the Hearst chain; but as he got older, I believe, he became more "honest" and he knew how hollow his success was. Bewildered, he "went back" to his roots, Judaism. One reason was that it was becoming fashionable for Jews to "go back." But perhaps a deeper reason was that Sokolsky felt more at home among Jewish values such as he had learned as a young boy. He began to read carefully the English translations of the prayers, and to his astonishment they were "really good." He told his readers how good they were. He printed them in his columns.

I believe that slowly he would have left his Hearst columning. He had all the money he needed. He was very sick—heart trouble, diabetes, rheumatism. He was in the late sixties. He wanted to end up with some semblance of self-respect. I represented to him a certain aspect of his Jewish past. He could talk to me, "take guff" from me. He had nothing to fear from me. I was not the "success" he was. "Talking to you, Charlie," he once said to me, "is like going to a Jewish religious service or Talmud class way down on the East Side or in one of the more conservative of the Conservative synagogues."

"I take that as a compliment," I said.

"I mean it as such," he said.

I was not at all surprised that Sokolsky apparently had requested to be buried from a synagogue. But his ghost, I believe, was not altogether happy. He was "back home," but not quite all the way in.

Oliver St. John Gogarty

O NE OF THE FEW GENUINE WRITERS I HAVE EVER KNOWN, WHO
lived the literary life because it was the only life that made sense
to him, who was, indeed, the very personification of the writer, was
the late Dr. Oliver St. John Gogarty, the model, it is said, of Buck
Mulligan in James Joyce's *Ulysses*. I knew him about five years, and
in that time saw him only occasionally, but on one occasion we saw
each other every day for two weeks, eating together, walking
together, and always talking. The place was the Writers' Conference
of the University of New Hampshire, in Durham, New Hampshire.

He was already in his middle seventies then. But he walked erect—
indeed, from a distance, he looked like the legendary German
lieutenant out for a brisk stroll. He had a Mephistophelian face,
which became even more devilish toward the end of his life. His
eyes, when he was silent, were determined, looking ever forward,
his nose was a trifle hooked, which added to the aura of sheer evil,
and his jaw jutted out a little and was a trifle lopsided, and this, too,
stamped him as, at least, Lucifer's trusted emissary on earth.

But when he held forth—which was whenever he was in the
company of friends and the friends had enough sense to let him talk
on and on and to supply him with proper liquid refreshments (chiefly
beer, toward the end) and long cigars—his face would become like

that of a tomboy. His eyes would dance with mischief, his mouth would wait upon his eyes, and both would wait upon his tongue—for there would pour from him such talk as has seldom come from any writer of our time—gay, malicious, bitter, contradictory, kindly, lyrical, bawdy, tender, lusty, hilarious, vile, scandalously unfair, profoundly considerate, scurrilous, untrue, deeply perceptive, and irresistibly fascinating. Insofar as I knew him, I should say he was a man of few, if any, deep personal loyalties. One day he would laud someone to high heaven as a true friend of many years, and a week later he would denounce him in terms fit only for a segregation-ist agitator. He wrote some lovely lyrics about women—I incline to think these will keep his memory green for a long time—but in conversation at cocktail time he could talk about women, some of them friends of long standing, with the sharp and vile tongue of a drunken fishwife. Four letter words were too tame for him: he would use the phrases describing commonplace physiological acts to make himself clear, and being a physician he knew whereof he spoke. And yet, even when he was his most malicious and most devastating he would end his tirades with a smile spread all over his face—almost like that of the proverbial little boy caught with his hand in the cookie jar—and the smile seemed to say, "Good, eh? Of course, I didn't mean it literally, I simply think the phrase is rather fetching, and I'm sure you'll forgive me for whatever I've done to damage anybody's reputation."

By profession he was a physician and surgeon, and I understand a very good one. He had eminent personages for his patients, among them an American ambassador to an ancient European country. The ambassador was an immensely wealthy man, "with a tremen-dous amount of Irish blood," Dr. Gogarty told me, "yet it didn't seem to do him any good. He loved money like an English lord, he would shake all over with delight when he told me how he was received by royalty, and he could barely read a sentence of English without using his stubby thumb. He had a throat infection and his throat was a mess, probably because he drank so much champagne, which as you must know, is a terrible drink. Well, when I looked down his filthy throat, I would think of his mind, which was no doubt just as messy. Now, listen to this. He thought Eamon DeValera was a statesman. Think of that! That humbug a statesman!" Dr. Gogarty had no use for DeValera. He saw no reason for him to call himself an Irishman. "He belongs in Puerto Rico, or some such place, but not in Ireland. We have enough humbugs without him." *Humbug* was a favorite word of Dr. Gogarty's.

Like so many other doctors who were also writers (Anton Chekhov is the classic example) Dr. Gogarty had grave doubts about the efficacy of medicine. "It's not a science at all, not yet, and it's not an art either. You'd be surprised what mistakes of diagnosis are discovered at autopsy. I never go to a doctor if I can help it. I doctor myself, and at least I suffer from my own mistakes." He doctored himself quite a bit near the end, and his self-therapy, I imagine, would hardly win the approbation of the medical faculty. In New Hampshire I once came upon him, in his room, lying on the floor with his feet straight and his arms at his sides. The room was dark, the blinds had been pulled down. I asked him what was up. He merely mumbled, "Quiet. Sit down and wait." I sat down and waited for about fifteen minutes. Then he leaped up, with the agility of a man thirty years his junior, and said, slapping his chest, "Now I feel better." I asked him to explain what he had been doing. He said, "Listen to this carefully, it will increase your life span. Lie down on the floor every day for twenty minutes or so. Be sure the room is dark. Lie in the direction of the magnetic needle, and the earth's magnetism will go through your body and invigorate you." I asked him how one can tell quickly the direction of the magnetic needle. He looked at me, smiled and said, "Oh, whichever way you lie is the direction of the magnetic needle."

He had doubts about American faucet water. Once he told me there was too much chlorine in it, another time he told me there wasn't enough chlorine. In New Hampshire he would walk long distances to get bottles of carbonated water, which he said was very beneficial. He said, "The bubbles in the water expand the arteries, and that's good for circulation." I said, "But the bubbles disappear in the stomach. There are no bubbles by the time the carbonated water reaches the arteries." He looked at me and smiled and said,

"But I like it. What I have just said makes just as much sense as a good deal of what you read in medical journals. These journals are ninety per cent humbug."

He thought refined sugar was a curse to civilization, and he also wasn't too sure about all the milk-drinking that went on in America. "Human milk is good, mother's milk for babies. But cow's milk I'm not so sure about. It's too active, it speeds up human growth, makes the human body grow too fast, and that's probably behind a great many of our nervous ailments." When I told him I liked ice cream he was horrified. But I talked so enthusiastically about the ice cream made by the agricultural department of the University of New Hampshire that he finally consented to try some, "for scientific reasons." He loved it, and thereafter had two huge scoops of ice cream every afternoon for a whole week.

He loved walking, and sometimes I would accompany him. He walked briskly, and did not pay too much attention to the traffic. Since I have flat feet I did not feel quite comfortable on these walks. I would suggest that we rest now and then, but he would sneer at my suggestion. One afternoon we had walked so much I began to wonder about his motives. "Are you trying to kill me?" He laughed and said, "I just thought we'd take a walk to Boston." The distance from Durham, N.H., to Boston is about thirty miles. We turned back.

He was violent in his views about coffee, and I do not recall seeing him drink it. His theory was that the high incidence of heart disease in America was due to the excessive coffee drinking. He claimed that coffee was sheer poison to the heart muscles and especially to the aorta, the large artery that leads to the heart. He thought it was a disgrace that the medical profession didn't warn people about the grave effects of coffee drinking.

His opinion of medical schools was hardly flattering. He thought that medical education was largely a racket, that students were made to spend too much time in book study. "Whatever there is to be taught in medicine," he maintained, "can be taught in two years. Students should be made to spend more time in the offices of good general practitioners, that's where you learn more about ailments— or the absence of them—than anywhere else. The medical profession is making a swindle out of medicine, making a sort of Jesuitism out of it. You know the Jesuits keep their slaves in the seminary for fourteen years. That's nonsense, too. But, it's the time you spend in a general practitioner's office that really counts. And, by the way, a good doctor knows when not to medicate a patient. Most ailments are in the head, psychosomatic, or else they're economic and financial, and medicine is of no use there, anyway." He often reminded me of a remark by an eminent physician—I believe it was Sir William Osler—who said, "A young doctor has fifty medicines for one disease, an old doctor has one medicine for fifty diseases, and a great doctor has no medicines for any disease." He also told me the remark attributed to the great French physician, Pare, "God does the curing, and the physician pockets the fee."

Despite all these remarks, Dr. Gogarty was proud to be a physician and surgeon. Yet, I had the impression that his heart was really in his writing, and the abiding heartbreak in his life was that he did not win the respect and admiration that he craved from both the critics and the general public. That respect and admiration he richly deserved—for he was a lyric writer of genuine beauty, a fine writer of short fiction, and one of the most gifted essayists of our time, possessing what was probably a genius for getting down on paper the grandeur and the glory of a by-gone era. He was also a classicist of wide learning and delicate perception, and one of his disappointments with his long stay in the United States was that so few of our critics, and virtually none of our reviewers, know Latin or Greek. He said that without a thorough grounding in these two languages and in classical civilization as a whole no one could possibly write criticism that was worth reading. That was one of his many complaints about H. L. Mencken. He called him "an ignoramus, a humbug, a mere circus clown, and not always funny, either."

He had a sharp tongue, as everybody knew who was in his company for longer than five minutes, but it is astonishing how few people recall his large-heartedness. He had no respect for virtually all the noisemakers in the realm of American poetry today, but he did have the highest respect for some of the quieter ones, particularly Robert Hillyer and Witter Bynner. For William Butler Yeats, of course, he had an awesome admiration. At a meeting of the Poetry Society of America I once heard him tell of his discovery that Yeats was mortally ill—a series of examinations clearly indicated that Yeats was suffering from cardiac arterio-sclerosis and at Yeats' insistence that he be told the truth, Dr. Gogarty did tell him . . . and when Dr. Gogarty related this incident, his voice shook at the recollection, and he lowered his head. When I saw Dr. Gogarty for the last time, one day before he was stricken and carried off to the hospital, where he died, I asked him to let me see his notes for that talk at the Poetry Society, for publication in *The Literary Review*— I had seen a sheaf of notes in front of him. "Oh, that," he said. "I threw them away. I did bring notes. I always bring notes to a lecture, but I never pay attention to them. I do it only to give the atmosphere of scholarship."

Yeats was the subject of a bitter battle between Gogarty and a prize-winning poet, who was a professor of English and a friend of mine. There was a writers' conference, at which the three of us were present. I came upon the poet and Dr. Gogarty one morning, in the men's room, that most democratic of all places, and heard them shouting at each other while they were shaving. Apparently the prize poet had said that in his opinion Yeats was an inferior poet and that it was disgraceful that he had been given the Nobel Prize in literature. Whereupon Dr. Gogarty turned to him and asked him to repeat his remark. The poet did, and Dr. Gogarty said, "And you're a professor of English. What a pity that the professors of English have no professional practices committee as does the medical profession. What a pity." The poet sneered and said, "You Irishmen all stick together." Dr. Gogarty replied at once with: "This proves that you know no more about the Irish than about poetry."

Like all of us, Dr. Gogarty was many-sided, presenting one side of himself at one time and another at another time. He probably did change a bit more abruptly than is true of most of us. One's view of him thus depends upon what side of himself he chose to present on a particular occasion. In this brief memoir, naturally, I offer only a portrait of him as I knew him, and make no claim to present the whole man. He would at times talk glowingly of high social func-

tions, and I imagine one side of him did like them. But I believe
he was more drawn to lowlier functions and people. There was
something basically raffish about him, he liked the high jinks of
policemen and bartenders and soldiers and sailors and women of
democratic sexual habits. He never felt quite at ease in his dinner
jacket. He once referred to it as "another form of censorship." He
liked the company of poets, both bad and good ("even bad poets
have good pretensions, and that's a blessing in a world where there
is so much humbug"), and he was grateful to the Poetry Society of
America for many things, but he once told me that "poets' parties
should be held in basements, with not too many clothes on either the
men or the women, and the repast should be a sort of free lunch,
like they used to have in saloons." As a matter of fact, I saw him
now and then wandering on Third Avenue in New York City when
the Elevated was still up and the many saloons on the avenue were
even more "saloonish" than they are now, gloomy, damp, and
homey, where one could nurse a beer for an hour without any
interruptions, where one could listen in on high and free talk, without feeling one was intruding . . . I always had the feeling that
Dr. Gogarty liked that very much . . . People sometimes didn't
find Dr. Gogarty at his home, he didn't always answer mail or his
telephone . . . I think I know where he was then . . .

That last time I saw him, at an academic colleague's house—in
what grand and glorious form he was! He talked and talked, and
his eyes twinkled, and his index finger punctuated every malicious
phrase, as when, time and again, he called an eminent literary lady,
"rancid and unpleasant" . . . and then decided to dispose of her
merely with "rancid" . . . and he let us know that this man and
that man were "humbugs" . . . but he also spoke of Yeats and of
AE and of Lord Dunsany with affection and high regard . . . and
then he sent a dagger into the reputation of one of the ladies
involved in the Irish Renaissance . . . but he quickly came back
to his loves . . . and then he stood up, erect, this seventy-nine year-
old man, one day before he was stricken, and recited poem after
poem, including a bawdy and lusty bit of verse entitled "On First
Looking into Kraft-Ebbing's *Psychopathica Sexualis*"—in the man-

ner, of course, of Keats' "On First Looking into Chapman's Homer." I can still hear the roll of his voice, and I can still see the young and gay and grandly irresponsible gleam in his eyes and also that index finger pointing at us and at all New York and at the whole world . . . A few hours afterward, alas, he collapsed on the streets of New York and three days later he was gone.

Robert P. Tristram Coffin

H E WAS NOT A GREAT POET. HE WAS NOT ALWAYS A GOOD POET.
He wrote too much. He was a compulsive poet, rather than a discriminating one. But he was one of the most prolific and most
colorful poets in the last fifty years. I used to be in close contact
with him at the Writers' Conference at the University of New
Hampshire, held every August for some twenty years at Durham,
New Hampshire. He was a founding faculty member of the conference. I didn't come on the scene till the summer of 1949, and we
met every summer thereafter for the next six years. He died in
January, 1955.

I had never met him before I went to Durham, though I had
bought several of his poems when I was an editor of the *American
Mercury*. He was very polite and amenable to suggestions. Sometimes he would send in some poems that I liked except for a line
here or there. I used to write to him suggesting he do some rewriting.
He always complied graciously.

I was disappointed when I first met him. He seemed so cold and
so offish. I had expected a bit more cordiality. But my wife and
daughter, who had come along with me, found him more friendly.
I was puzzled. I asked my wife what she thought.

"He's afraid of you," she said, smiling.

"Of me?"

"Yes, of you."

Since my wife sometimes talks in riddles, I said nothing.

The first summer, I thought, Coffin was not merely offish, but even rude. One night it rained, and we all were to go to a public lecture at a nearby university building. Coffin offered rides to others. I thought he deliberately snubbed me. I said so to my wife. She said, "Maybe he's absent-minded. I don't think he means anything bad."

The next year, as soon as we came to Durham, Coffin came to our two rooms (the three of us generally occupied two adjacent rooms) and said, "I'm at your service. If you want me to drive you to the center of town for groceries or anything at all, or if you want to just take a ride around, you need only call on me, and I'll be your chauffeur."

I was astonished.

"See," said my wife triumphantly.

I didn't understand what had happened. I asked my wife to enlighten me.

"It's very simple. You went over with a bang last year. So Coffin said to himself, if we can't fight him, we'll join him. Not like that, not just like that, but something like it. Anyway, he was just hesitant and a little afraid. From now on he's our bosom friend. Wait and see."

He was our bosom friend—up to a point. He helped us in many ways: he gave us rides when it was raining or when we wanted to go to Portsmouth, some five miles away. He brought our daughter odd toys that he had picked up in Maine, his home state. And he became quite intimate with me. He invited me into his room whenever he brought cheese and crackers from one of his favorite places on the outskirts of Durham. And I was asked to join the others in the midnight get-togethers. These get-togethers were rather pleasant. Everybody became a bit high—we pitched in for a bottle of whiskey or gin—and everybody spoke a bit more freely than otherwise. The group also indulged in singing such old favorites as "Alouetta" and "Alice Blue Gown" and "Love Nest."

But there was one time when Coffin had had more than his usual share of liquor—a good deal more. His face became red, and he began, as the saying goes, to pick on me. He wanted to know why I had worked so long on the *Nation*. I protested that I worked there only a few months. This didn't satisfy Coffin, who said, "One day is too long." Then he wanted to know why I didn't grow a mustache. I said I didn't like it. He said, "That's a defect in your character."

I was responsible for getting Dr. Oliver St. John Gogarty to be a member of the faculty. Coffin tried to make friends with him, but Dr. Gogarty was cold towards him. Indeed, he was cold toward almost everybody. He was polite to me, but I had the feeling that this was merely out of gratitude for getting him the job. At the time he was in need of money.

One day I asked Dr. Gogarty what he thought of Coffin. He smiled and said, "He is the only empty coffin I have seen outside of a coffin factory."

Apparently this compliment was one that Dr. Gogarty had dropped here and there in Durham. Since Coffin was well known in Durham, news of the compliment reached him quickly, and he and Dr. Gogarty never talked to each other again.

Coffin disliked T. S. Eliot and William Butler Yeats profoundly. Not merely personally, but also their poetry. I could understand his dislike of Eliot's poetry, for I am not too fond of it myself. But I couldn't understand how any poet of any talent could fail to see the sheer genius in Yeats' work. I said so to Coffin. He said, "He's superstitious. He believes in all sorts of gremlins and gurus and the rest of it."

"But that is irrelevant to his poetry."

"It's in his poetry, too."

Later I learned from a close friend of Coffin, Herschel Brickell, that Coffin once tried to see Yeats, but that Yeats refused to see him. "Bob Coffin has never forgotten it," said Brickell.

Coffin was bitter about the neglect he suffered from the New Critics. They almost never discussed him, and when they did they generally sneered at him. One of the things that made him happy toward the end of his life was that a graduate student was doing a Ph.D. thesis on him. "I may tell him some of the truth," he said. We all said it was wonderful news.

Coffin was silent. "They should have done it long ago," he snarled, as he rolled his cigarette. He was one of the last to roll his own.

"Yes, of course, but they're doing it now," said one of us.

"Yes, I ought to be glad, I ought to be. But when is a man glad when he ought to be?"

This was one of the few bitter remarks I ever heard from Coffin. Generally he was an extrovert, a loud optimist.

He was, to repeat, a compulsive poet. He wrote almost literally in every spare moment. He wrote between classes. He wrote just before taking his mid-day nap. He wrote before falling asleep. Sometimes he wrote between courses in a restaurant.

I asked him once to explain his method of work . . . why he wrote at such odd hours and so persistently.

"It's very simple," he said. "I write because I don't feel right if I don't write, and I write all the time because I never feel right when I'm not writing. But I've learned something else. That is, that the best writing I do is always done in the time I steal from my sleep, from my social engagements, in other words, the writing I do on the run, so to speak. I think that this is true for all writers. What is re-written is cold and intellectual. What rushes out is spontaneous and good and all that's worth putting down on paper. I mean, of course, poetry and fiction and other such good things. All non-fiction is mere drudgery, and doesn't count in the long run."

"But what about the great histories and the great biographies?" I asked.

He looked at me and smiled. Then he said, "The only biography and history that has any value is largely fictional."

The matter of Pulitzer Prizes came up. Coffin had got one for Poetry in 1936. He said, "These Pulitzer Prize things are jokes. It all depends on the committee making the selection. If it's a stupid committee they make a stupid choice, if it's a wise committee, they make a good choice, as when they chose me. It's all luck whether a stupid committee is appointed or a wise committee. In the long run it all means nothing."

I thought, privately, that Coffin was a folk-poet, little better than a second-rate Carl Sandburg. Of course, I didn't say so to him, but I was always interested to know what he thought of his own work in the innermost recesses of his mind.

Once, at the home of a rich widow, in the outskirts of Durham, Coffin became quite intoxicated—he always carried his liquor well, but it was obvious when he had more than was good for him—and he said, "My friends and enemies and colleagues, I wish you would ask me something."

No one asked him.

Again he said, "Ask me something."

Again no one asked him.

Then he said, "In that case I will tell you. I'm as good as Frost, as good as Sandburg, as good as Vachel Lindsay of blessed memory. The only two poets I do not claim to be superior to are Walt Whitman and Emily Dickinson, and, in all frankness, I'm not sure about Emily Dickinson."

One of us, a person of tact, said, "Bob, you are one of the great. Of that there is no doubt."

"Something else," said Coffin. "I am proud to be counted with Longfellow and Whittier and Lowell, especially Longfellow. Know why?"

"Why?" asked the same person.

"Longfellow was a Bowdoin man, that's why. Bowdoin forever! I propose a toast, a good long one to Henry Wadsworth Longfellow, America's greatest poet."

James Michael Curley: Boston's Falstaff

EMOTIONALLY SPEAKING, I GUESS IT WOULD BE CORRECT TO SAY that to people of my generation Boston has had only two mayors: John F. (Honey) Fitzgerald and James Michael Curley. When I first became conscious of political matters—which was just before the First World War—"Honey Fitz" meant two things to me: he sang "Sweet Adeline" and he owned a large cigar factory, one of whose branches was in the Boston slums, where I lived. My father liked him because he had a round face and he smiled often, and he had heard that the mayor was "good to the Jews." I would go sometimes to School Street, where City Hall is, and look up to the second floor, in hopes of seeing Mayor Fitzgerald. I don't think I ever did see him, but I told my friends that "I saw someone who looked like him." That was enough to give me status.

James Michael Curley followed Honey Fitz in City Hall. He had the face of a man who seemed to have laughter in him—and playfulness and forgiveness. I had the feeling that he was never angry, that women liked him, that children liked him. When I was fourteen, fifteen at the most, I was walking down the main stairs of the Copley Square central branch of the Boston Public Library. I was big for my age, and I guess I looked like a young voter. Mayor Curley was walking up the stairs, with his entourage. I moved aside. He smiled at me and said, "Fine day, sir." "Yes, it is," I whispered with delight.

Later I heard a bit about his "past"—that he had served time in the Charles Street jail, which was not far from the slum tenement where my family lived. Apparently Curley had taken a civil service examination for a friend who wanted to be a letter carrier. The friend was a bit vague intellectually, and Curley sat in for him. Was it legal? Of course, not. Moral? Well, I didn't know.

I was not so non-commital when rumors began to spread that Curley had "sticky fingers"—that, in short, he didn't get poor when a substantial contract was let out for the paving of streets or the erection of schools and hospitals. Nobody seemed to be able to prove anything concrete, but it did seem odd that a man who was earning, I believe, $15,000 a year as mayor could live in a huge and lavish home in Jamaica Plain, have several servants and cars and "live regally," as the phrase went. I was suspicious, but I still was willing to wait for solid evidence.

Shortly after the United States entered World War One I got a job as a messenger boy at Porter's Market on Summer Street. It was not far from the South Station, less than two blocks, actually. In addition to my duties as messenger I also had to sweep the front of the store, fill the bins with this or that vegetable, see to it that the meat show cases were clean, and so on. One afternoon, as I was sorting out paper bags in back of the store, I saw a tall man and a woman walking slowly in the front part of the store, looking at the meats and the fowl and the vegetables. The face was familiar. I asked a fellow employee who the man was, and he answered, "Curley."

"Mayor Curley?"

"That's him and his Mrs. all right."

Immediately I picked up a handful of string beans and some heads of cabbage, and walked down the front of the store, hoping that the bins for string beans and cabbage would need replenishing. Fortunately, they did. I was close to the mayor and his wife. The mayor was dressed in a blue overcoat (it was late Fall), and he wore his felt hat a bit on the side, which gave him a slightly roguish appearance, and I liked that. His wife was perhaps ten years younger, and she was beautiful—perfectly white skin, a delicate nose, and warm, black eyes. She bent down now and then to snap a wax bean or examine a cucumber, and she would look at her husband, say, "I think we need some, James," and he would answer, "As you wish, Mary. They do look good."

I told my parents and my six brothers and sisters how close I had been to Mayor Curley and his wife, that I had heard them talk.

My brothers and sisters said, "Really?"

My father merely said, "By me he's not such a diamond."

"You mean the things you hear?" I said.

"What else?"

"But do you know for sure?" I pleaded.

"What do I know about what goes on in city hall or anywhere?" said my father. "All I know is that all his millions come from somewhere, not just from his wages. You don't have to know everything to be sure about something."

It was hard for me to answer my father. But I still liked Mayor Curley and his wife. However, I thought it best not to discuss him at home any more that evening. My father was right, yet he wasn't right.

Shortly I was promoted from being a mere messenger and cleaner-upper to a helper on the wagon. Porter's Market had a wagon and one of the clerks doubled as the driver. He would generally leave the store about four o'clock in the afternoon, make his deliveries on Beacon Street and Commonwealth Avenue and Newbury Street and other streets in the Beacon Hill section, and then he would return the wagon and horse to the stable. Sometimes, for very good customers, he would also deliver in Brookline and Brighton and Chestnut Hill and Jamaica Plain. I'd pick up a basket of provisions, run up the back stairway, make my delivery, and run back to the wagon.

One late afternoon my superior on the wagon said, "How would you like to make a delivery at the Curleys?"

"Mayor Curley?"

"Yah, we got some meat and lobsters to deliver."

I was in the proverbial seventh heaven. I hoped that the Mayor would be there. Alas, he wasn't. Only a kitchen woman was there, and she grabbed my package, mumbled, "About time," and let me know that I had better leave at once. I was disappointed. Still I was in Mayor Curley's home. The next time I made a delivery, Mrs. Curley happened to be in the kitchen. She smiled at me, and said, "Would you like a cup of coffee? It's very cold." I hesitated, and then said, "No, thank you, thanks just the same. I have more deliveries to make." And I was off, and I felt like kicking myself. A couple of weeks later I made another delivery at the Curley home, and to my great delight and amazement, the mayor himself opened the back door. I handed him the package, and was about to run off, but he stopped me. "Why don't you come in?" he said. "I was having a bite. You might join me. I'd like that."

He gave me a cup of coffee, a piece of cake, and he added, "Want any bread? I sometime like it better than cake." I said the cake was fine.

I was enormously attracted by his baritone voice and by the kindliness of his eyes. "I'm all alone," he said, "and I'm glad you stopped by." He asked me what school I was going to. I told him English High. "A fine school," he said, "very fine."

"Plan to go to college?" he asked.

"I hope so."

"Good. I couldn't go to college, but I always read. Shakespeare especially. Aye, there was a man, one in a million, one in ten million."

About a year later three of the employees of Porter's Market started a market of their own. They called it Rawson's Market, after one of the men, Pearly Rawson, who had worked for Porter longer than had the other two. I joined the new firm.

The Curleys came to the new store. I was now promoted to the job of counterman, with my chief duties at the fruit and vegetable counter, but I was also expected to take care of customers at the meat counter and the fish counter.

Once Mayor Curley came to Rawson's Market with his wife. He left his wife up front, looking over various vegetables, and he went into the back of the store, which was partitioned off and invisible to those up front. I liked the back. It was secluded and it was there that one of the police officers on the beat would come, take off his jacket, smoke a pipe, and take a slug of whiskey from a small flask that he carried on him. It was Prohibition time. At first I was shocked by this lawlessness on the part of an officer of the law, but then I was intrigued. I had learned my first major lesson in cynicism about laws and public morals.

When Mayor Curley came in the back, I happened to be opening a crate of strawberries. He greeted me. He took off his overcoat. He took from it a small flask. He helped himself to a drink. He wiped his mouth with his hand. He offered me a drink, but I refused politely. He sat down on a box, and he sighed, "What a world, what a world!" Andy Drew, one of the owners, came in the back to smoke a pipe. He greeted the mayor.

"Ah, I should have been in some other business," said Mayor Curley. "A worm is eating at my soul."

Andy Drew and I said nothing. I knew that I should leave and get about my business. Fortunately Mayor Curley said, "Remember to pursue your education, Charlie. Education is an eye opener." I took that as a request to stay on. Then Mayor Curley got up, took a dramatic stand, and recited speech after speech by Falstaff from *Henry IV, Part I*. His declamation mounted and mounted . . . and soon he was saying those great words of Falstaff's about honor: "Can honor set a leg? No. Or an arm? No. Or take away the grief of a wound? No. Honor hath no skill in surgery then? No. What is honor? A word . . ." I was thrilled. And then Mayor Curley came to Hotspur's great lines:

> O gentlemen, the time of life is short!
> To spend that shortness basely were too long,
> If life did ride upon a dial's point,
> Still ending at the arrival of an hour.

Curley went on and on, speech upon speech . . . and my delight knew no bounds. I actually felt goose pimples run up and down my back.

Now Mayor Curley suddenly stopped. He took another swig from his flask and began to chew furiously on a piece of gum. He looked at Andy Drew and then at me, smiling. He put on his overcoat, and he said, "Back to the world of make believe. Shakespeare is the real world. Out there . . . but we have no choice."

Joshua Liebman and Peace of Mind

O NE DAY IN JUNE, 1948, I WAS AT THE SOMERSET HOTEL IN Boston, attending a reunion of my class. A whisper spread through the celebrants that Rabbi Dr. Joshua Loth Liebman had just died there. The cause, it was reported, was a severe heart attack due to high blood pressure. He was only in his forties. Many of my class-mates knew who Dr. Liebman was. Indeed, there were not many readers in the United States who did not know who he was, for he had written one of the all-time best-sellers in the history of American publishing, *Peace of Mind*. My classmates said pretty much what was running through my mind: the author of *Peace of Mind* had just died of high blood pressure!

I was not altogether surprised by Dr. Liebman's death, but I was saddened, nevertheless. His whole life suddenly leaped into nothing-ness, and his few months of glory became a mockery. A bubble exploded. A mountain shriveled. I had first heard of him from a Jewish student at Radcliffe College. Brought up in a somewhat non-Jewish Jewish home she had taken little interest in Jewish affairs. But friends of hers got her interested in the Hillel group at Harvard, which also served Radcliffe, and it was through her attendance at Hillel meetings that she had first heard of Rabbi Liebman of Temple Israel in Boston. Rabbi Liebman had succeeded Rabbi

Harry Levy, who had made Temple Israel one of the leading Reform temples in American Judaism—at least that was what Boston Reform Jews said, particularly those who belonged to Temple Israel.

Following Rabbi Levy was not easy, but Dr. Liebman was so powerful a speaker that he immediately impressed his congregants. But he wasn't satisfied. Apparently he felt that his temple had not done enough to interest the young Jews of the Boston area— especially the many Jewish students in the many institutions of higher learning in Eastern Massachusetts. Rabbi Liebman instituted special programs, including religious services, for these students, and they found them to their taste, so much so, in fact, that they literally flocked to Temple Israel to hear him. He was a Reform rabbi, but he was something more. He was a liberal in his politics, he was enormously interested in psychology, and he had the notion that psychology—especially psychoanalysis and psychiatry—had much to give to pastoral Judaism. Rabbi Liebman's preachings on this favorite theme of his were at first tentative and exploratory, since no other rabbi, at least in his community, had ever before attempted to make this connection, between religion and psychiatry, on so large a scale. He sensed that he was being received with more than tolerance. Indeed, his mail became huge and a large number of his correspondents asked him to give them more and more of the same.

The result was that he became, quickly, a radio celebrity, and soon his fame spread to the non-Jewish world. My young friend told me about him. "He's like no other rabbi I have ever heard before," she said. "He makes Judaism interesting, really interesting, and he knows lots of things outside of Judaism, you know what I mean. Even our professors listen to him on the radio, some even go to Temple Israel to hear him." My sisters in Boston had written to me about Dr. Liebman, and they agreed.

My young friend became a devotee of Rabbi Liebman, and apparently she suggested that he bring together his speeches into a book. Whether or not he had thought of doing so himself I don't know, but her suggestion certainly interested him. It wasn't long before Dr. Liebman did collect his speeches and sermons and added several fresh chapters, into what he hoped would be a publishable book. He brought the manuscript to a publisher whom I knew.

"Did you look at it?" I asked.

He smiled.

"Well, did you, or didn't you?"

"Yes, I glanced at it. I don't think it's much, but don't let me prejudice you, as if I could."

I read the script and was appalled by the dreadful writing. I had heard him, finally, on the radio, some weeks after my young friend had spoken to me about him and I was impressed by his delivery: it was clear and effective, and it was obvious that Dr. Liebman had put in considerable preparation. I didn't pay too much attention to the sentence structure, but if anybody had asked me about it, I probably would have guessed that it was all right. But as I read it in black and white, it certainly wasn't all right. I was also offended by the poverty of the thinking. I said all this to the publisher in a memorandum, though I did point out that one of the chapters, "Grief," if expanded and rewritten, might have a chance with a magazine. I added, "But as a full-length book, this script simply is impossible. It's illiterate, it's hollow, it's adolescent."

The publisher was not surprised. He thought pretty much as I did about the book. But he decided to get the opinion of a mutual friend, the late Lowell Brentano, of the Brentano book-sellers and book-publishing family. Lowell was the very personification of kindness and gentleness, but he also had a sharp eye for publishable books. He came to see me after he read the Liebman script and he hemmed and hawed and finally said, "Rabbi Liebman must be a very fine man. I can see it. But this manuscript really needs some work."

"How much work?" I asked.

"Well, it really has to be rewritten completely."

"Will it sell then?"

"Who knows? But I doubt it."

Nevertheless Lowell took the script to three publishers, for two of which he was a scout, and they turned it down quickly. I think it was Lowell who then took the script to Simon and Schuster in the company of the author, but it is possible that Dr. Liebman himself took the script to Simon and Schuster. I don't remember exactly what happened. But I do remember that Dr. Liebman later came to see me. The publisher had written to him that I had "liked" the chapter on Grief, which wasn't exactly what I said, and Dr. Liebman was so heartened by the one "positive" comment about his manuscript that he wanted to thank me. I was embarrassed, because he spoke as if I liked his whole book.

Dr. Liebman spent more than an hour with me. I was both attracted and repelled by him. I had expected to see a tall man, and here in front of me was a rather short man, with pudgy fingers . . . much too neatly dressed . . . I had the feeling he had just come from a barber-shop where he had received "the works" . . . he had a puffy chin and bulbous cheeks . . . his eye lids were red . . . and his eyes seldom focused on me. Now and then he tapped my desk with his fingers, and then he folded his hands. He asked me what I thought of Simon and Schuster as a possible publisher for his book, and I said they were a good house, if they took his book they would probably do very well by it. His face lit up. I immediately added, "This is no guarantee. I am not saying they will take it. I'm only saying that they're very good promoters. They really give a book a big push, and keep on pushing it as long as they think it has a chance."

About three weeks later I got a letter from Dr. Liebman, telling me that "Simon and Schuster appear to be interested in my book." I imagined that the publisher had written him a polite note in answer to a question from him. I couldn't believe that they would ever publish his book, certainly not as it was. More than a month went by, when I got still another letter from Dr. Liebman. This time he told me "they were definitely interested. But they agree with you and Mr. Brentano, that the book needs a little polishing. They said they will write to me again." I asked Lowell Brentano what he made out of Dr. Liebman's latest letter, which I had shown to him. "Well, Charlie," said Lowell, "I must say that this means they really are interested."

"In what you and I saw?"

"Well, maybe not that, but in the idea."

"What idea? There's no idea there, Lowell, not a single idea. Liebman is merely telling people to buck up and be brave and face reality and all that."

"Well, yes, that is so, but I guess the boys at Simon and Schuster think they can do something with it. I must say that the script does need some work."

"Some work, Lowell? It needs a complete rewrite."

"I agree with you, Charlie, it's not a contribution to literature or psychology or any other science. But I suppose Simon and Schuster smell some good business in it. They know publishing. I have to give it to them on that score. I wouldn't publish the book, if I still had control of Brentano's. I admit that. But they know what they're doing."

Then I got a third letter from Dr. Liebman. This time he was jubilant. "Simon and Schuster have a man who says he wants to polish up my book a bit, and I am thrilled. I really am thrilled. I feel I have a chance to do some good with this book."

A week later Lowell told me that Simon and Schuster had got Henry Morton Robinson, I believe, to rewrite the book completely. Lowell impressed upon me that "even Robinson feels that the book is a little weak on content, but he feels with some rewriting it could sell very well. I don't know. I confess, Charlie, I'm sort of puzzled by the whole thing, and I would be glad to see what Robinson does. I really would be interested, very much so."

About two months later Liebman wrote to Brentano, that he had signed a contract with Simon and Schuster for the publication of his book. He said nothing about Robinson. But Brentano told me that Robinson had made "a very good deal" with Liebman and Simon and Schuster. I never did learn exactly what the deal was.

When the book finally came out Brentano and I agreed that it resembled the original only remotely. I volunteered the thought that about the only thing of Liebman's that remained was his name and some of his organization. The book caught on at once, and was a phenomenal best-seller.

I never heard from Rabbi Liebman by mail again. He now became

a national celebrity, lecturing on virtually everything. I did, however, hear vague rumors that he was ill . . . he had some nervous
ailment, some said he had high blood pressure, some said he had
domestic problems.

A year passed and I was in Boston, visiting relatives. I also visited
an old high-school friend, who was a professor of medicine. He
invited me for cocktails at the Harvard Club. We went to the basement, where it was quieter, and we conversed. Suddenly Dr. Liebman came to our table. My friend invited him to have a cocktail.
Dr. Liebman politely refused: he had an appointment. But he did
sit down for a few moments. He turned to me, just as he was about
to leave, and said, "Mr. Angoff, you never really liked my book,
did you?"

"Oh," I hemmed and hawed, "I never said this to you, Dr.
Liebman."

"No, you didn't," he said.

He became a bit stern. "Why are you afraid to tell me exactly
what you think, Mr. Angoff?"

"Since you insist, I will tell you that I did not like the book, and
still don't like it."

"Why? Is it cheap in your eyes?"

"I just don't like it."

He left us.

My medical friend looked at me. He said, "That little man can
use some peace of mind himself."

Louis Weitzenkorn

T HE TWENTIES AND THIRTIES, AMONG OTHER THINGS, WERE THE
years of great newspapers. They were also the years of the myth
of newspaper men as great men. Those years were also the years
when columnists were beginning to be influential. Future historians
will probably look upon the columnists of those days as the only
columnists of real stature and import in the shaping of some aspects
of American life. No one has quite taken the place of F.P.A. and
his Conning Tower column in the old New York *World*. It was a
repository of much that was charming and beautifully light in the
literature of the time. No one has taken the place of Heywood
Broun and his column, "It Seems to Me." Broun was the Addison
and Steele of Newspaper Row. His touch, perhaps, was not as light,
but he appeared to be almost as nimble. The Chicago newspapers,
especially the *Tribune,* had their columnists, and so did the Boston
papers and the Cleveland papers. Some of the latter had almost as
much influence as did the New York columnists. Philip Hale, who
first conducted a column for the Boston *Journal* and later for the
Boston *Herald,* had more than local celebrity.

The reporters with by-lines also had eminence. There was Henry
Pringle and Herbert Asbury and Dudley Nichols and Frank Ward
O'Malley—all men of much talent. And there were the occasional

columnists, the Sunday columnists, and the now-and-then essayists. They, too, were recognized as they walked along Fifth Avenue.

But few of them were as happy and content as their admirers imagined. Nearly all of them—surely those who had not reached their forties—were eager to get out of newspaper work and into magazine work or book writing. Many of them tried to break into the *Atlantic Monthly* or *Harper's* or the *Century* or the *Forum*. They had difficulties, for these publications were still inclined to be stuffy and to prefer an opaque article by Paul Elmer More or a trivial essay (couched in ponderous phrases) by Agnes Repplier to something alive and contemporary by, say, Stanley Walker or Stewart Holbrook. These people found a home in the pages of the *American Mercury*. But some couldn't find a home there either—they didn't write well enough or their subject matter was not suitable. One such man was Louis Weitzenkorn, who in many ways reflected the Era of the Newspaper Man Myth. He reflected its yearnings and its hurts and its joys and its disappointments and its bewilderments. He was for some years Sunday editor of the New York *World*, but he also occasionally wrote a column on Sundays.

I had seen his name in the Sunday *World* often and did not think too highly of his writings. They seemed to be full of an ill-hidden self-pity, and his sheer feeling for words was not too good. I had seen his play *Five-Star Final*, a cheap portrayal of tabloid journalism, by a man who was, perhaps, not much superior to the values he was portraying. I had little desire to see him.

I was editor of the *American Spectator* for a few months. It was a dismal period in my life. I had hoped to make something exemplary out of the magazine but I quickly learned that the publisher, who had taken over from Nathan and his group, had values that were diametrically opposed to mine. So I struggled on, hardly knowing what would happen to the magazine or to me. Fortunately, I did not have too much difficulty in getting material for the magazine. I could not pay more than about two cents a word, but people did send in manuscripts—people of the order of Mark Van Doren, Harold E. Stearns, Clifton Fadiman, and George Jean Nathan. One morning, I got a letter from Louis Weitzenkorn in which he said,

"I take off my hat to you for publishing a magazine as alive as the *Spectator*. Why can't we meet?"

Before I had a chance to answer his letter he called me at the office and then began a relationship that lasted for about five years. I didn't like him on sight, but I did like some of the things he revealed about a world I knew little about—the world of Hollywood and Broadway and the fancy hotels in between and the fancy women all along the line and the writers who didn't like what they wrote but were angry when they were criticised for doing the very things they were ashamed of. My impressions of Weitzenkorn were many, scattered, and cumulative.

I was astonished by his small size and by his belligerence of tone to his wife, who was Viennese and was some twenty years younger than he and had a very appealing accent. I was with him less than ten minutes when he asked me what I thought of Maxwell Anderson. I was a bit startled. I didn't expect to be grilled so soon. I said, "Oh, I liked *What Price Glory?*, and I liked *Saturday's Children*."

Weitzenkorn broke in: *"What Price Glory?* was largely Laurence Stalling's, and *Saturday's Children* was written by a girl friend of Anderson's. It's her play."

I said nothing.

"You didn't know that, did you?"

"No, I didn't."

"Oh, Louis," broke in Ilse, his wife, "you have no proof of that. You only heard it."

He looked sharply at her. He said, "You don't know a damn thing about that. So keep quiet."

"But you really don't know for sure, Louis," she insisted.

"Shut up," he said. "I said shut up."

Ilse looked at me, smiled, and kept quiet the rest of the evening.

Ilse was Weitzenkorn's fourth wife, I believe. By his first wife he had two children, one boy, whose name I don't recall, and another boy, Joseph. Weitzenkorn had left his first wife not long after the birth of the second child. These facts may not be exactly in line with the truth, for Weitzenkorn told various stories about his marriages and his offspring. But I believe they are substantially correct.

One evening Ilse told this story, "Listen to this, Charles. Louis was in rehearsal for some play that almost went on Broadway. And you know, Louis. He was on the stage, running around. A young boy came to him and said, 'My name is Billy.' I think he said Billy. Anyway, Louis looked at him and said, 'Get the hell out of here.' And the boy said, 'But I'm Billy, your son. My mother told me. I'm your son.' So Louis looked at him, and he quiets down, and he says, 'Hello, Billy.' And Billy stands there, and he walks away. Isn't that awful?"

I could hardly believe my ears.

"What's the boy doing now?" I asked.

"I don't know," said Ilse. "Louis doesn't know. Nobody knows. Louis never saw Billy again. Isn't it awful?"

Louis said nothing, except, "Oh, it was long ago."

One evening Weitzenkorn had James Waterman Wise at his apartment, which at the time was in lower Manhattan. He asked me over. I was eager to come over, chiefly to meet Rabbi Stephen Wise's son. I met him. He was as tall as his father, perhaps taller. He looked like his father. But unlike his father he spoke loudly and belligerently in favor of the extreme left, though he himself was not a member of the Communist party or even in its best graces all the time. I thought he was naïve about the Communist set-up in America as well as in Russia, and he spoke about such "social-fascist" magazines as the *Nation* and the *New Republic*. I tried to argue with him, but he quickly put me down as "a capitalist lick-spittle."

Louis at first was polite to young Wise. We had dinner at Albert's Restaurant. Then we went back to Louis' apartment. He began to drink. In an hour he became boisterous. He said to young Wise, "You, Jimmy, ought to know, that I have no respect for your father. He's a professional Jew."

Jimmy was understandably offended. It was at once clear he adored his father. "What do you mean by 'professional Jew'?" he asked. "My father is a good Jew, and that's all. He fights for Jewish causes. What's wrong with that?"

"Nothing," said Louis, who seemed to be a bit embarrassed even in his drunkenness. "Nothing. Only he's a professional Jew. That's clear, isn't it?"

"No, it isn't," said Jimmy. "Do you mean he's doing it for money, defending the Jews, preaching about them because of the money there's in it for him?"

Louis hesitated. "Well, in a way," he finally said.

Jimmy exploded, "You're a bastard," and he stalked out.

There was a silence in the room. Three or four other people were present.

Louis took a long drink direct from the bottle. "A sensitive bastard," he said.

Louis went occasionally to whore houses. I asked him why he did it. "Well," he said, "Charlie, you're naïve. I do it for protection."

"Protection from what? Aren't you afraid you'll get infected?"

"I thought that's what you were thinking about. Listen to me, brother, Real, professional whores are clean. They have to be to stay in business, to stay alive. They're cleaner than wives, a damn sight cleaner than amateurs from the Bronx or anywhere else."

"I still want to know why you go to whore houses."

"Well, it's a long story, but I'll make it short. My second wife, or maybe it was my third, how the hell should I know, was a real wonder of a woman. I used to almost faint wanting her. And she'd make me wait and wait. Women are cruel, whether they're frigid or nymphos. She finally left me, but that's another matter. Well, I told an old friend of mine, you won't know his name, he was just a reporter, but one of the wisest men I've ever known, I told him about the hold this bitch had on me. I really loved her. This friend of mine said, 'I know how you feel. There's only one way to lick it. As soon as you feel the love feeling coming on, just hop over to a cat house, and then the yearning is all over, and your woman is just another woman.' And you know what? It worked. That's how I got to going to whore houses. Now I guess, I just go for the hell of it.

Some of the girls are all right. At least they don't nag you like wives. They lay you, and that's that. But, then again, I guess, it doesn't work for everybody. It didn't always work for me, either, but that's another matter."

I got tired of him after a few months, but he moved into the Marie Antoinette Hotel, at the corner of Broadway and 66th Street where I lived at the time. It was difficult for me to evade him. He tried to seduce one of the telephone operators. She was a divorcee, with two children, and far from pretty or intelligent. I asked him why he was so eager. He smiled, "Oh, just to make Archie (a bell-boy, whose real name was not Archie) sore. And you know why I want to make Archie sore? Because he lied to me about what a bouquet cost. I sent him out to get some flowers and he lied. Know how I found out? I asked the florist."

Louis always denounced Hollywood for its cheapness. He had been there for several years off and on, but apparently had never achieved the highest salary paid to writers. "I'll be damned if I'll write drivel," he said.

Then he got an offer to go to Hollywood for $700 a week, for a period of ten weeks, merely to doctor up an inferior picture. He went. I was embarrassed to ask him why he went. Somebody else did ask him. "Well," said Louis, "I need the money, and maybe they'll give me more work." Actually, Louis didn't need the money. He had told me so many times. What is worse, he temporarily abandoned work on a play in order to go to Hollywood.

Five Star Final was the only play of Louis' that had any appreciable run on Broadway. Another play, whose title I don't remember, ran for only a few days to terrible reviews. Louis insisted that *Five Star Final,* as a newspaper play, was superior to *Front Page* by Ben Hecht and Charles MacArthur. This was so ridiculous that when he first said it to me I couldn't control a smile.

He claimed that daily journalism was sinking rapidly as a profession. "The boys print too many handouts," he said. "A reporter digs and digs."

"Was it really so wonderful on the old *World?*" I asked.

"Hell no. It's all a lot of hogwash. Make believe. The reporters and the editorial writers all wanted to quit. Only the columnists wanted to stay on. There's nothing so dead as yesterday morning's newspaper and yesterday morning's by-line. Hell, Maxwell Anderson quit, and Laurence Stalling quit and Dudley Nichols quit and Henry Pringle and I quit. We all wanted to write novels and plays and stories and books. This newspaper-romance stuff is all fantasy. I don't believe any first-rate writer ever wanted to be on a newspaper for more than a few years. Plays and novels, that's what they really wanted to write. Some of them made it, some didn't."

Louis didn't. His clothing was set aflame by a gas jet in his father's home in Wilkes Barre, Pennsylvania. Some of those who knew him best said it was "unintentional suicide."

Thomas Beer

I CAME TO NEW YORK THE END OF JANUARY, 1925. ONE OF THE first places I went was to the New York Public Library, at Fifth Avenue and Forty-second street. I had arrived on a Saturday afternoon, and the following afternoon I sought out the newspaper room, which at the time was hard by the Forty-second street entrance, and it was a wonderfully raffish place, pretty much like the newspaper room at the Central Branch, in Copley Square, of the Boston Public Library. That is, it was filled with vagrants, both sober and otherwise, who generally had newspapers in front of them, but they themselves were often sound asleep, some of them audibly so. I went to the newspaper room to read the Boston papers, of course. They seemed so much more interesting, now that I was many miles away from Boston.

Then I looked at the New York newspapers. I was especially interested in the book sections. I was immediately impressed by the vast amount of notice, both publicity and comments, given to a book that apparently would soon be published, *The Mauve Decade*, by Thomas Beer, who had written *Stephen Crane* some two years before. I had heard of Crane only vaguely at Harvard; the dominating personality at Harvard still was Emerson, who had died nearly fifty years before. One of my professors dismissed Crane with a sneer, so I had made up my mind to read Crane and Beer's study of him, but somehow I had not come around to doing so. Now I decided definitely to read works by Crane and Beer's book on him, and also to read this new work that some of the reviewers said was even better than *Stephen Crane*. The review in the New York *Sun* (I'm not sure whether it was by Ernest Boyd or Van Wyck Brooks) was the most glowing of all.

I liked Crane's short stories, especially "Blue Hotel Room," and I also liked *Maggie, A Girl of the Streets,* but I had my doubts about *The Red Badge of Courage*. I had the feeling that Crane didn't know the mind of the soldier. This was presumptuous on my part, for I didn't know it either. Crane at least had been with soldiers in Cuba; the closest I came to soldiers was to listen to what we later called "subway commandos," way back in 1917, plead with young men to join the colors against Kaiser Wilhelm. But I liked least of all Beer's book on Crane. I suspected that Beer was more interested in showing off his style than in telling us about Crane—and I also had the feeling that his book was really a blown-up article. Beer apparently hadn't done enough research. He didn't know too much about Crane's preacher father; he didn't know too much about Crane's early struggles to place his fiction with magazines and book publishers; he didn't know too much about Cora, who became Crane's wife; and he didn't know too much about Crane's last days.

The Mauve Decade, which dealt with American life in 1890–1900, seemed to me to be entirely meretricious and remarkably uninformative. My opinion was so at variance with that of nearly all the critics that I determined to read the book again soon. Meanwhile I wanted to discuss it with someone. At the time I was working on *The American Mercury* and was in daily communication with H. L. Mencken. But I hesitated, because I didn't know how Mencken felt about Beer's book and I didn't know how friendly Mencken was with him; but most of all, I guess, because the publisher of *The American Mercury,* Alfred A. Knopf, was also Beer's publisher.

My curiosity got the better of my caution and one afternoon, while Mencken was having me test various Scotches which his bootlegger had just sold him ("So help me, Mr. Mencken, these bottles come either from Canada or Bermuda, real, genuine stuff, so help me, I wouldn't fool a fine gentleman like you"), I asked him, "I was wondering what you think about Stephen Crane."

"Well," said Mencken, "Tom Beer is trying to build him up into an immortal, and that will boomerang. Crane is no Dreiser, certainly not. He's no Sinclair Lewis. But he stirred up the animals with his *Maggie, A Girl of the Streets,* and some of his short stories are quite good. He certainly made the life of the moralists uncomfortable, and that is to his credit. I guess his Presbyterian preacher father was plenty outraged. Think of it, the buzzard had seventeen or maybe it was eighteen or nineteen children. His poor wife never got dressed, and she never menstruated. Well, he may have had the right idea at that. All women over seventeen who are not pregnant are nuisances."

"I like *Maggie,* too," I ventured.

"I bet they never taught you about Crane at Harvard," said Mencken. "Are they still pounding away at Emerson at that dump?"

"I'm afraid so," I said.

"Well, Crane is better than Emerson. For that matter, anybody is. Emerson was a Rotarian, the first and the worst."

Then I asked Mencken what he thought about *The Mauve Decade.* Mencken hesitated, smiled to himself, then said, "Did you ever meet Tom Beer?"

"No, I haven't."

"I didn't think you had."

"I don't understand."

"If you had met him, Angoff, you would have the answer to your question. He writes the way he looks. He's suave, but lifeless. He wears brown clothes all the time, at least so it seems to me, and he writes a kind of thin, brownish, offensive language, sometimes tricky, never male, and I mean that. Some people can be offensive, but they're offensive in a masculine manner. Babbitts are that way. But Beer is different. I put no stock in the Freud pish-posh, and I don't think Tom is allergic to girls, though I have no evidence that he's jumped any of them. George Nathan thinks he's a bit of a homosexual, but George jumps to conclusions. I guess, though, what I dislike most of all is his trickiness. How does *The Mauve Decade* begin? 'Emerson enjoyed a bath at 10 a.m., and the President of France at that very moment signed a secret treaty with Afghanistan.' Now, that's cute, but it's cheap, tricky. It's all right for a sports writer to write this way, but not for a man who pretends to be writing literature. But there's something else I don't like about the book."

"What's that?"

"Well, I think Tom just doesn't know the decade he's writing about. He makes out of it a somewhat doilyish party, with some of the elderly goats pinching the maids in the shade. It was nothing of the sort. It was a raucous, immoral, thieving decade, with more illegitimate children than ever heard of in all history. Tom misses this. He never should have written that book. Any more than I should write a study of nunneries, or the spiritual life in them."

I forgot about Beer. Then I wrote an article on Boston for the *Mercury*. It appeared in the December, 1925 issue and was called "Boston Twilight." It was a brash article taking Boston to task for its lack of culture. It had all the marks of youthful belligerence and impatience and a vast lack of historical perspective. Perhaps this is being unfair to myself, but I certainly would not write such an article now. To my surprise it brought forth many favorable letters, and some of Knopf's authors, when they came to Knopf's office, asked to be introduced to me. Thus I met, for the first time, Professor Charles A. Beard, Elinor Wylie, Willa Cather, and Joseph Hergesheimer.

Then, late one morning, a somewhat stocky man, dressed in a brown suit, with his thinning brown hair combed straight back, shyly came to my office, and asked if I was Charles Angoff. I said yes, and he immediately introduced himself: "I'm Tom Beer. I'm glad to meet you." He said polite things about my article, and then talked at length about Mrs. Jack Gardner, who owned a celebrated collection of paintings in Boston, ran a celebrated salon there, and was a close friend of the eminent art critic Bernard Berenson. I told Beer that I had passed Mrs. Gardner's palace several times and had always hoped that the time would come when I would see the inside of her palace.

"Oh, I can arrange that," he said slowly.

"Thank you."

"But first," he said, "you must come to my house and spend a week-end with us, my sister and myself."

He lived in Yonkers. I said I would be delighted to come.

I got no invitation from him, I mean a specific invitation for a specific time. He did, however, write me a note—which I've somehow lost—in which he said some strange things about the Old Howard in Boston. The Old Howard was a celebrated burlesque house, which was frequented by adolescent boys, Harvard professors, and (so the legend ran) also by ministers of the gospel, who camouflaged their faces so as not to be recognized. I had gone there several times. The "hot shows" put on there were innocent enough when compared to what one can read in *Lolita* and in the works of, say, Philip Roth, Mary McCarthy, Saul Bellow, and Mickey Spillane, but for those days they were "quite rough."

It was clear to me that Beer knew little about the place. He said he had gone there once and was astonished that Boston permitted the place to be kept open. Then he referred to "its cramped quarters." This sounded strange to me, for the Old Howard had a splendid spaciousness.

I thanked Beer politely. I did not hear from him again for many weeks. Meanwhile I had read some of his "Egg stories" in the *Saturday Evening Post,* and thought them pleasantly harmless.

Then he showed up in my office as suddenly and as unannounced as he had the first time. This was almost six months since the first time we met. He seemed just as shy. He had little to say. He said that the weather was fine in Yonkers now. He said he did not like New York City. He asked me what I was writing. I told him I was puttering around with some short stories and poems. "Good, good," he said. I was waiting for him to invite me to his home. He said nothing on this score.

About a month later I got a post card from him, from somewhere in the West. I have lost the card, but I do remember what was on it, besides his signature. It was one word: "Greetings."

The man puzzled me. I asked George Jean Nathan what he knew

of him, what he thought of him. "I should call him an incomplete eunuch," said Nathan, smiling. "Of course, I don't mean this literally. Not that I'm sure he isn't a eunuch, but as a writer he is certainly that."

More time passed. I left the *Mercury*. I was on another magazine. It was two years now since I last heard from Beer. I wondered about him occasionally, but less and less. Then I got a brief note from him. It said something to this effect: "The flowers here are just superb. You must come over some time." I didn't answer.

Several weeks later I got another note from him. He had read something of mine in *The American Spectator*. He said he liked the article, but apparently what caught his attention was the word "mayhem" in it. I do not remember what the article was about, and how I used the word. In moving from one place to another I have lost the issue of the *Spectator* containing my article. I thanked Beer in a brief note.

More weeks passed. Then we accidentally met on Fifth Avenue. He was dressed in the same brown suit (or so it seemed to me) he had on when I first saw him. I was merely taking a walk, and so was he. He suggested that we go into a Schrafft's restaurant and have some ice cream and coffee. We spent more than two hours there.

Beer spoke chiefly about Cora, the wife of Stephen Crane. He had picked up some correspondence of hers, with Crane himself and with Crane's friends. Beer said that he was fascinated by the letters, but from what he said I didn't get any notion what was in them. "A troubled woman, a troubled woman," he kept on saying, but I didn't know what she was troubled about. I asked him directly what was in the letters. He merely looked at me, and continued his vague talk.

Suddenly he asked me, "Do you ever intend to go back to Boston?"

This startled me, for a reason I didn't understand.

"Oh, I don't know," I said. "I visit the place. My brothers and sisters are still there."

He ignored this information.

"I like Yonkers better," he volunteered.

I didn't know what to say to this.

"Have you ever been to Yonkers?" he asked.

"No."

"A wonderful place. You must come out some time. I have a theory," he added.

I looked at him. He looked at me. I got the notion that he was waiting for me to say something. All I could think of saying was, "What is your theory?"

His face lit up. "My theory is that Yonkers is much older than Manhattan. I mean people lived there long before people lived in Manhattan. I don't mean Englishmen or Dutchmen. I mean Indians, and others, or whoever was here before it became Yonkers, you understand."

I said I understood, though, of course, I didn't.

He stood up, and we parted. His last words were, "I'll have you come to my home in Yonkers very soon. You really must."

A few weeks later, I read in the *Times* that he had died. He was not quite fifty years of age.

The past few weeks I have asked a half dozen Ph.D.'s in American literature if they had ever read anything by Thomas Beer. Not a single one recognized the name. Somehow this made me sad.

Vincent Lawrence

HE IS ALMOST TOTALLY UNKNOWN TODAY, AND THAT'S THE tragedy of Vincent Lawrence and of so many other young men of talent who went out to Hollywood "just to make some money to write really good stuff." I have just looked at various reference books, and his name does not appear in them. I looked, in all truth, to get the titles of some of the plays he had on Broadway—plays that led some critics, including George Jean Nathan, to say that he had a bright future. Alas, his future always remained a future.

I do remember one of his plays. I remember it very well. It was called *Washington Heights*. An old friend of Mencken's, Philip Goodman, had invited Mencken, James M. Cain, and myself to his apartment on East Tenth Street. He had told us that he wanted to read two plays to us. We heard one play and told him that it didn't have a chance on Broadway. Later it was produced on Broadway under the title, *Another Language*. The author was Rose Franken. It was an immediate and huge success. As a result of it Miss Franken, for years, ran a series about its heroine, Claudia, in one of the mass circulation woman's magazines.

Goodman then read another play. It was called *Washington Heights*. The author was Vincent Lawrence. He had written about a half dozen plays, which had been put on Broadway. Nearly all the critics said that the first act or the first two acts were good, but that Lawrence had "third-act trouble." I don't remember the titles of the plays or what they were about. Lawrence had now written a new play. His former producers apparently were not interested. So he took his play (or his agent sent it) to Philip Goodman, who was not a full-time producer . . . he produced now and then, if he was profoundly interested. Goodman was very much interested in *Washington Heights*. But, since Broadway is so very much of a gamble, he wanted the opinions of people he trusted.

Mencken, Cain, and I told him that *Washington Heights* was wonderful, and I believe we predicted for it a huge success, critically and commercially. Vincent Lawrence at the time was deeply involved in a scenario in Hollywood. Goodman told him he would produce *Washington Heights*. Lawrence at once arranged matters in Hollywood so that he could come to New York to watch the rehearsals.

That's when I saw him for the first time. The New York rehearsals, I believe, lasted for almost a month. During that time I saw a good deal of him, either at Goodman's house or at Lawrence's hotel, the Pierre, in Upper Fifth Avenue. He was very happy that Goodman was going to produce his new play. "I really am glad, Charlie," he said the first time we met at Goodman's house. "It's my best, my very best."

Somehow—I don't remember how—I got to talking about certain aspects of metaphysics and epistemology. I pointed out the distinction that Kant made between *noumenon* and *phenomenon*. Since I had known the distinction since my college days I looked upon my exposition as more or less routine. But to Lawrence what I said was immensely revealing and fresh.

"I'll be god-damn," he said, "I'll be good and holy god-damn, I never thought of it that way. I thought that what I know I know, and it's out there, really real, you know what I mean. Now you go and upset me. You really upset me, Charlie."

Goodman was unimpressed by my learning. "Vince, that's a lot of hogwash. They teach the Harvards all this stuff to make them think they know more than you and I know. I never went to college because I wouldn't accept this nonsense. I told this to the president of the University of Pennsylvania, and he said that he didn't want skeptics like me."

"I thought you never went to college, I mean you never even applied," said Lawrence.

"You're being technical, my boy, plain technical," said Goodman. "I applied because my father wanted me to. I didn't want to. You know what I was thinking of? You really want to know, both of you?"

"Yes. Tell us," said Lawrence.

"Well, I said to myself, I said, if Spinoza could get along in the world without going to the University of Pennsylvania or even to Harvard, then I can do the same. After all, Spinoza was one of my ancestors."

I looked at Goodman in astonishment. "I thought Spinoza was not married."

"I thought you'd say that," said Goodman. "That's an old bit of misinformation that is spread in dumps like Harvard. Spinoza was married to a very fine Jewish girl, you'll be glad to hear this, Charlie, I know how you feel about Jewish girls, the best, and you may be right, they have wonderful breasts, so he, I mean Spinoza was married to this girl, and they had several children, at least three. I don't know the exact number, and what I don't know for sure I don't say. So, that's how Spinoza came to be my ancestor. So that's why I didn't go to the University of Pennsylvania."

A young girl came in—she couldn't have been more than nineteen. Apparently she had been living in the Pierre apartment with Lawrence since he came to New York for the rehearsals. Lawrence was delighted to see her. He kissed her and caressed her. "God, darling, I wish you wouldn't stay away so long."

"I was gone only three hours, maybe three and a half hours," she said. "I had to see my mother. After all, she wants to know where I am, you know, and I had to tell her all sorts of things, you know. After all, darling . . ."

"I know, I know," Lawrence said, kissing her again and again. "Now you're here and you stay here. Sit down, darling. Charlie got me all upset. He said I don't really know what I think I know, and Phil Goodman was talking again about his ancestor Spinoza."

The girl smiled. "Spinoza," she said. "We're reading him in my philosophy class at Barnard." She turned to Goodman. "You're the Spinoza man, eh?"

"I wish you wouldn't talk lightly about my ancestor," said Goodman.

Suddenly Lawrence kissed the girl full on the lips, patted her rump, and said, "Rush down, dear, and get me an evening paper. I forgot to buy one."

She went to buy the paper, and was back in less than five minutes. She turned to Goodman and said, "You still think women are inferior?"

"God forbid," said Goodman. "Without women where would I be? What fun would there be? And where would *Washington Heights* be?"

"How is it going?" she asked.

"Terrible," said Lawrence. "Terrible, and I'm banking on it to get me out of Hollywood. It mustn't fail. I feel there's something missing. I think it's sex, plain, female sex, breasts and thighs, plain sex. It's in my play, but not on the stage."

"It will do all right," said Goodman. "It'll come through."

"Are you sure of it, Phil?" pleaded Lawrence.

"I'm sure," said Goodman.

"God," said Lawrence. "I don't know. Maybe I never should have left New York. Maybe I should have starved here, like O'Neill. But I said to myself, I'll go to Hollywood, make some money, and come back to New York and work on my plays. But I didn't do it. I stayed on out there. I wrote in my spare time. I was only fooling myself. Just fooling myself. I screwed around, loafed, and I kidded myself I was getting material. That's a riot. Material comes from your guts, not from your experiences. Reporters get material from experiences. Novelists and playwrights get it from their guts, and you can get at your guts only when you're alone. Being alone is a church. It's the only church I give a god-damn about. Jesus himself had to be alone. On the mountain, in the deserts. He wasn't looking for experiences.

Hell, no. He was no reporter. He was an artist. O'Neill is like Jesus. He was alone. Women fooled me, too. I talked myself into thinking that sleeping with a woman was being alone. It isn't. It's more company than any man can afford for very long."

"Thanks, dear," said the girl.

"I don't mean you," said Lawrence. "Being alone, starving, digging into your guts, that's writing, that's what a man needs to write. I don't know, Phil, I might as well tell you, maybe the play is no damn good. I've been away from life too long. I've been too happy, too content, on the outside, that is. You know something, Phil? I'll tell you. I represent the tragedy of a whole generation of cowards and whores, men and women who have some talent but no character, no guts. That's me, that's me all over. You see, I buy things out there. And art can't be bought. It has to be found. My wife out there wants to live like a success. That's how little she knows. She thinks I'm a success. She's all right. But hell, where am I? That's what I want to know. We all stink. We are cowards, with little talents, without the courage to dig and dig. Oh, hell, I'll go to sleep."

He walked out of the room, and the girl followed him, after saying good-night to Goodman and me.

Washington Heights was a total flop, commercially and critically. I believe it ran less than two weeks to virtually empty houses. Mencken, Cain and I discussed it later. Mencken merely said, "Hell, it's a lousy play, but so is all of Broadway. But, still and all, it's no worse than some other turkeys I have seen and that have been praised as immortal." Cain hemmed and hawed and then said, "I don't understand. It listened well. The acting was acceptable, at the very least. I don't understand. It's a mystery to me."

Goodman took it philosophically. I took a long and silent walk with him in Central Park. We barely talked about the play, which had just closed. Then Goodman said, "I guess they didn't like Our Nell."

"No," I said, not knowing what else to say.

Goodman didn't talk about it again for several weeks. I talked to Lawrence on the telephone several times after the opening. He was miserable. "Did I really miss, Charlie, did I really miss?" he kept on asking.

"I don't know," I said. "I honestly don't know. I'm not a theatre man. I mean I go often, but I don't know the insides."

"I know, I know, but you're a cultured man, and you heard it, and Goodman is no fool, and . . ."

"I don't know what to say," I repeated. "I thought the production was fine."

"But the critics didn't like that either. They didn't like a god-damn thing about the play."

"I guess they didn't."

"Charlie, that was my best play, believe me. I banked on it, Charlie, to get me out of that hell-hole out West. To get me out of other troubles, all sorts of troubles. Maybe I haven't got it, maybe that's it."

"I wouldn't say that," I said lamely.

"That's what the critics say. They say I used to be weak in my second acts and my third acts, or something like that, but they nearly always liked my first acts. Now they say it's all no good. All the acts. And this was my best play."

"I don't know what to say, Vince. You just have to try again. These things happen."

"I know. They happen, yes, they happen. But to me they happen all the time. Remember that. All the time. That's what hurts. It hurts deep, deep, all the way down. But maybe it's all my fault."

"What do you mean?"

"Oh, never mind, Charlie. I'm just talking."

A few weeks later I got a brief note from him. He was back in Hollywood. He said, "Maybe this is where I belong. Maybe I did it all to myself."

I never heard from him again.

Mike Gold:
Leader of Proletarian Culture

T HE THIRTIES—CERTAINLY THE FIRST FIVE YEARS—WERE, IN A
sense, the Middle Ages of American literary culture. The literary
landscape seemed to be a desert. There were oases here and there—
Thornton Wilder, Eugene O'Neill, the early William Saroyan,
Robert Frost, Dr. William Carlos Williams—but the dominant force
was that of the so-called proletarian writers. It appeared that they
controlled many of the magazines of opinion and many of the
influential newspapers. They also appeared to control several
important publishing houses. The organs of the Communist party,
especially the *New Masses* and the *Daily Worker,* had relatively
small circulations but were influential. It would probably be only a
mild exaggeration to say that important editors in the publishing
world in the United States followed both periodicals carefully to
know just where the wind of literary favoritism was blowing. A bad
review of a novel or play or book of poems or book of essays in
either was a serious matter—and a favorable review meant good
sales and "good reception" all over—at least in the more vocal
metropolitan circles of culture.

There were several left-wing cultural leaders. There was John L.
Spivak, a reporter, who had something of a reputation as being "a
man who digs up the truth." He misled several editors into thinking

he was something of a genius, and I'm afraid I was one of them. There was Kyle Crichton, who doubled as an editor of *Scribner's Magazine*, a conservative periodical, and a columnist for the *New Masses* and the *Daily Worker*. He made a reputation as a satirist by his spoof of Stark Young's *So Red the Rose*. It now makes embarrassing reading, but at the time it was considered very brilliant. There was Granville Hicks, who wrote a fairly useful book, *The Genteel Tradition*, and who startled some New York intellectuals with strange pronouncements, among them that Gustave Flaubert was little more than a capitalist lickspittle, and *Madame Bovary* a shameless kow-towing to capitalist morality, or something of the sort.

But the real symbol of proletarian culture—and of the genuine proletarian man in general—was Michael Gold, or, as he was affectionately called, Mike Gold. What Mike said may not have been as profound as what Granville Hicks said, for instance, but it had more influence. When he sneered at Thornton Wilder in the *New Republic* for writing things that were "not real," for "living in an ivory tower," the New York intellectuals trembled and gaped in admiration of Mike's bravery at daring to go at the author of *The Cabala* and *The Bridge of San Luis Rey*. Mike was the Ilya Ehrenburg and the Karl Radek of the American Communist world and of the American fellow-traveling world.

Mike came within my ken with a series of sketches that Mencken thought were good and that he published over my violent but vain objections. The sketches later formed part of his book, *Jews Without Money*. I objected to printing any of the sketches on the ground that they did not represent a true picture of life on the East Side, as Mike Gold claimed. Besides, I asked Mencken what he knew about East Side life, how much Yiddish he knew, how much he had read of East Side history. He admitted he knew nothing of Yiddish or of the East Side, but, he added, "I don't have to know any of this stuff to know that Mike is telling the truth. The trouble with you, Angoff, is that you're too academic."

Mike, Mencken, and I went out to lunch together several times. The impression I had of him, at first, was that he was rather simple-minded, not too well-informed—but at the same time a bit slippery. I had a hunch that the slipperiness was not, so to speak, native to him but imposed upon him by the tactics of the Communist party. Our conversations, however, were revealing. Mencken made fun of the whole Communist ideology. "They're just a bunch of Tammany politicians," said Mencken, "those Communist friends of yours, in this country and in Russia. The only difference is that Russian Communists are worse than American Communists, and the only reason they're worse is that there they have the run of the country. Here the Communists are a small minority, thank God, and they're held in check by more decent people."

"Like the Republicans?" said Mike, smiling.

"Yes, like the Republicans," said Mencken. "Mind you, I agree that Hoover and Coolidge are pretty disgraceful. If I had a daughter, which I may have somewhere, and she came home and told me that she was planning to marry either Hoover or Coolidge, I'd feel dreadful. That I admit. But bad as they are, they're better than Stalin. Stalin is a gangster. Hoover and Coolidge are just dummies."

"And Judge Gary of U.S. Steel?" persisted Mike. "Isn't he a gangster, a cruel man?"

"I suppose so," said Mencken. "I hold no brief for Judge Gary. He's a jackass. But you and I and everybody else has a right to lambast him. In Russia nobody has that right."

Mike hesitated. "They do have the right. In the local Soviets."

"Local Soviets?" asked Mencken. "You mean the local clubs."

"I suppose so," said Mike, "I'm not too well up on the Soviet political setup."

"I thought you were an authority," I said.

Mike smiled again innocently. "No, I'm not an authority on anything. I'm just interested in peace and in people. That's all. Even here, in the party, they call me naïve; they want me to read political tracts, you know. I can't read that stuff. It's important, of course, these things, but I barely understand them. I don't even know all the features of the Soviet Constitution. I just know it's good."

"How do you know that?" I asked.

"They tell me. Browder tells me things once in a while. That's how I know what I know."

Mencken and I looked at each other.

"Mike, how can you believe in the materialistic concept of history?" I asked. "In history, everybody knows that there have been other factors at work, factors like religion, like pride of race, like love of country, I mean patriotism."

"No Charlie, you're wrong. All these other factors are unimportant. I mean all that counts, at bottom, is a man's economic security. That's what breaks up homes, that's what brings on all kinds of diseases, that's what even makes mental troubles. Yes, mental troubles, too. Listen, it stands to reason, if a man has no money to pay his bills, his bills for food and clothing and sending the kids to school, and paying the doctor bills, that man goes crazy, and being crazy is mental, isn't it?"

"Yes, that's mental," said Mencken, looking at me.

"I think it's mental, too," I chimed in.

"But, Mike, you look like a decent sort," said Mencken. "You don't beat your mother, you don't rape too many women, at least not older women."

"Only under forty," said Mike, smiling. "Forty is the age limit with women."

"But you look like a good sort," continued Mencken. "You pay your taxes. You . . ."

"I don't pay taxes," said Mike smiling.

"No income taxes?" said Mencken.

"I don't believe in income taxes," said Mike.

"You don't?" said Mencken.

"Never paid income taxes," said Mike. "I don't make enough."

"I'll report you to the Internal Revenue Service," said Mencken. "But how can you believe in all the Communist rubbish?"

"Listen, both of you," said Mike. "Are you for peace?"

"Yes," I said.

"Up to a point," said Mencken. "I'm not fanatical about anything."

"Do you believe in people having all the necessary things in life,

I mean, the bare minimum, you know, food and things like that, do you believe that?"

"Yes," I said.

"Up to a point," said Mencken. "I'm against sticking my neck out on any intellectual issue."

"All right," said Mike. "So you believe in all these things. And the Communist party believes in all these things. So how can you not be a Communist?"

Mencken and I looked at each other. Neither of us knew just how to answer Mike without insulting him. I was totally bewildered.

Mencken came to my rescue. He said, "You know, Mike, now that you put it this way, I'm stymied. You may be right. You really may be right. You put it very potently."

To this day I think Mike thought that Mencken had been won over to Communism, at least a tiny bit. I think I saw a look of victory on his face.

A few weeks later Mike called me up and asked me to lunch with him. I was surprised, chiefly because I had opposed the publication of his article-sketches. I knew he didn't know my attitude, but I felt strange accepting a lunch engagement with a man whose work I held in little respect. I did get to like him personally, but still I was troubled.

He took me to lunch at a celebrated proletarian place, a speakeasy in downtown New York. Let's call it Moshe's, which wasn't its name. I had never been there before. I liked it at once.

Mike ordered for me. He ordered chopped chicken liver, mandel soup, boiled beef with "real horseradish—not horseradish sauce"— cheese cake, and coffee. I reminded Mike that, having been brought up as an Orthodox Jew, I couldn't very well eat cheese cake with boiled beef.

"Do you want to make a *goy* out of me?" I asked in mock consternation.

He smiled. He said, "I know, I know." There was something sweet and appealing about the way he said this. "I know," he repeated. "I was brought up as an Orthodox Jew, too. I know about *kashruth*.

It's all silly, I know. But I always feel funny about eating *milchig* (dairy) right after *flaishig* (meat). Now isn't that strange? I feel like a *goy*."

I was curious about the reason behind his call. When we came to the boiled beef he said, "Charlie, is Mencken anti-Semitic?"

I was startled. "I don't know, Mike," I said, "I've been wondering."

"Well, Charlie, I don't know. It's a terrible thing to say. I've been hearing things. I have no proof. But you know, I was a little disappointed about his taking sketches of mine, I mean about the Jews on the East Side."

"What do you mean?"

"Well," said Mike, "this will surprise you. I wanted to appear in the *Mercury*. After all, you know. . . . But I've been troubled. I've been saying to myself that maybe he took them because the sketches seemed to make fun of the Jews, well, not exactly fun, you know what I mean?"

"Yes."

"I knew you were for them, but he, that was different," said Mike.

"I don't know what to say," I said. "I'm in a funny spot."

Mike looked at me for one concentrated moment and said, "I understand completely."

"Maybe I ought to explain," I began. "You see, Mike . . ."

"You don't have to explain," said Mike. "I don't have to hear your explanations. I don't want to embarrass you. I understand."

I felt a little relieved, but not as much as I wanted to be. "Thanks," I said.

Mike continued with his eating. Then he looked up and said, smiling, "It takes all kinds to make a world."

"Yes."

Then he said, "Charlie, why don't you join us?"

"Mike, I can't. The Communists are against so many things I hold dear. I mean free speech. I mean free press. I mean, oh, hell, you know what I mean."

"Charlie, you're wrong. There's free speech and free press in Soviet Russia."

"Mike, can I get up in Red Square and say that Stalin is a murderer?"

"No, I guess you can't. But why should you want to?"

"Well, because I feel that way. I don't like him. I think he's ignorant and cruel, and I want to say that. Why shouldn't I have that right?"

"Do you want to say a lie?"

"It's not a lie to me. I really feel that way. And I want to be able to say that without being thrown into jail or killed."

Mike smiled. "You don't believe everything you read in the *Times*, do you?"

I looked at him, and decided there was no point in continuing this line of talk. "Oh, Mike, to hell with it all," I said. "Let's talk about literature."

"There isn't much right now. It's all capitalist literature. Willa Cather is a capitalist author. Sinclair Lewis is a capitalist author. Eugene O'Neill is a capitalist author. I mean deep down. We need a new group, a new line of writers, writers who say the truth about workingmen, who don't kowtow to capitalists. I'm only asking for writers to tell the truth. That's all. Anything wrong in that?"

"But Mike, the truth is more complicated than that."

"Is it?" he asked. Then he said, "Well, I like you anyway, Charlie."

Somehow I was deeply stirred by this expression of love. I didn't know what to say. I did say, "Mike, I like you, too. But I guess there are some things about which we don't agree or ever will agree."

"Maybe."

"You know something, Mike?"

"What?"

"I was just thinking that there's one area where you and I could agree."

"What's that?"

"I think we would both have a good time at a *Pesach seder*." (Passover festival meal)

He smiled. "I think so, too," he said.

Jim Tully

HE WAS A LITTLE MAN WITH A HUGE MANE OF RED, WIRY HAIR.
His face looked more like that of a lion than any face I had ever
seen. His eyes were large, yet strangely innocent. He was famous
for only a short while. Maxwell Anderson had dramatized his novel,
Jarnegan, dealing with a prize fighter, and while the play was one
of Anderson's feebler efforts and did not run long on Broadway, it
gave Tully the Broadway reclame that his lonely and ebullient heart
craved. "Now," as he told me a week after *Jarnegan* opened,
"Broadway will always be mine. I mean I won't be afraid of it. It
really doesn't matter whether it's a hit or not. I mean it. I want it to
be a hit, but it doesn't matter, you know what I mean, don't you?"

He was already famous when he wrote a series of interviews for
Vanity Fair, when Frank Crowninshield was editor, and it looked
as if the magazine just couldn't ever die. He wrote largely about
movie actors—about Jack Gilbert and Ina Claire and Mae West and
their professional brothers and sisters. Jim was the master of the
short clipped sentence.

"Are you happy, Miss West?"

"Happy?"

"Yes, happy?"

"Oh, I guess not. How can a lonely person feel happy ever?"

"What is happiness, Miss West?"

"Does anybody know? When I'm alone, I'm lonely, not happy. And I'm alone a good deal."

Tully's interviews were the talk of New York sophisticate society. He liked that. I had the feeling that the acclaim of society meant more to him than the acclaim of the critics. Actually, most critics paid little attention to him. Except one: H. L. Mencken, who called him "the American Maxim Gorki." Nathan befriended Tully, but secretly, as he told me at the time and later, he didn't think much of his "proletarian lyricism," a phrase that Nathan used sneeringly.

My first encounter with Tully was in 1925, via the mails. I had just been hired by Mencken on the *Mercury* and I read all the manuscripts that came in. One morning I got a manuscript from Mencken, to send to the printer. It was called "Bright Eyes." I recalled having read it about two months before. I had rejected it, because I thought it was a sugary, sentimental story of poverty, involving a little boy. Quickly I reconstructed in my mind what had happened. When I had got on the *Mercury* I had not heard of Tully, though he already had been appearing in magazines, and I had not known that Mencken had befriended him. Clearly what had happened was that Tully was astonished by my rejection of "Bright Eyes," since Mencken has specifically said he wanted to see it. Tully sent it to the New York office, without a covering letter. Mencken had said nothing about my rejection when he sent me the manuscript. When he came up I asked him about it. He said, "Yes, I asked Tully to show it to me."

"I rejected it," I said lamely.

"I know," said Mencken without a trace of displeasure.

"Do you like it?" I asked.

Mencken looked at me, hesitated, then said, "Yes."

"I still think it's rather sentimental," I said.

"It is," said Mencken, "but only in part. There's good feeling in it."

Tully never mentioned the incident to me. We got to know each other shortly afterward at a party that Mencken gave for him at the Algonquin Hotel. It was a small party. Only six of us were present:

Mencken, the actress Aileen Pringle (with whom Mencken was friendly for a while), George Jean Nathan, some very young actress (whom Nathan brought along and whose name I have forgotten) Philip Goodman (a very close friend of Mencken), and myself. Mencken had ordered dinner for all of us in his room. Mencken did most of the talking. He talked and laughed and talked and laughed. He told again about Dr. Welch of John Hopkins, who did so much for the young university and especially for its medical school. He was an authority in bacteriology and in public health, yet he personally was a model of uncleanliness. He seldom took haircuts, he washed only casually, he ate fruit he had bought at pushcarts and seldom took the trouble to wash the fruit ("I'm immune to disease," he once explained), and he almost never cleaned his living quarters. Apparently Dr. Welch had lately fallen under the spell of a very young girl, who turned out to be a manicurist, and this manicurist who rather liked the old doctor, as a grand-daughter would like her grandfather, influenced him to have his nails trimmed. Dr. Welch submitted to this indignity and was heart-broken that she would not look upon him as a suitor. According to Mencken, Dr. Welch was at first greatly depressed by this experi-ence, but later had learned one lesson from it. Dr. Welch had learned, according to Mencken, "Women can never be trusted." Mencken told this story over and over again, and whenever he came to the lesson that Dr. Welch had learned he would burst out laugh-ing. Aileen Pringle and George Nathan and Philip Goodman had heard this story many times before, and they smiled politely. I had also heard it before. Nathan's girl saw nothing to laugh at. She merely giggled. Tully laughed out loud with Mencken.

By this time Mencken and Nathan and Goodman and Tully had had quite a bit to drink. Tully tried several times to interrupt Mencken. Finally he succeeded. He said, "But there are women who can be trusted and who are grateful. Young ones, old ones. I remember a Baptist preacher's wife in Indiana, where I used to steal books in the local library, I forget the name of the town. I was walking down the street. I must have been only seventeen, and she was maybe twenty-two but she was married to an old preacher, maybe he was thirty-five, and she saw me from her window, and she asked me in to have coffee with her. She was sorry for me. I looked hungry, I guess. So we ate, and then we went to bed, at her insistence and my acquiescence. So help me, she was a virgin. But I accommodated her for a month, maybe, and her preacher husband never knew the difference. I could trust her, and she was grateful."

Mencken tried to make Tully stop, because Mencken was a Southern gentleman when women were around—he didn't like to tell sex stories in their presence. Tully refused to stop. He told other stories of the same nature. He also told the story of his life, or what he claimed was the story of his life. He had been born in Oklahoma (during the telling he also said he had been born in Kansas and in Nevada). His father was a drunk and his mother was "a woman who had no taste at all in anything, couldn't cook, couldn't take care of a house, and I'm sure was no damn good in bed. Why my drunken father married her I'll never know." Tully had a brother "who died in the electric chair for something or other, and my sister became a whore." His parents died when Tully was twelve. He immediately took to the road where he became a bum, hopping freight cars, stealing food from grocery stores, sleeping in parks and in stables. "I learned to read from another bum. Then I began to steal books in libraries, but I promised myself I would return the books when I got around to it. And I did return them or their equivalent in money, didn't I, Henry?" Mencken agreed that he had.

Tully then began to write a book about his experiences. He had worked occasionally in circuses, as an all-round helper, he had been a prize fighter, he had been a teamster, and "once I was a pimp. I really was a helper to a bigger and older pimp. He made me hunt up men who liked to sleep with hunchback girls. This big pimp had a half dozen hunchback girls, and he would pay them well, because men who want to sleep with hunchback girls are willing to pay big fees, as much as $25 a piece."

When Tully was finished with his book he sent it to Rupert Hughes. The book was just one paragraph—extending to some 300 pages. Hughes helped him and that's how Tully's first book was published. Then came his best-known book, *Circus Parade*, made up of his own experiences in circuses. Then came other books, but not one of them equalled *Circus Parade* in sales or in critical reception. At the time of this party he had just jublished *Circus Parade,* and he was, as the saying goes, riding high. After Tully's recital of his life, the party fizzled out, and we all went our separate ways.

I had suspicions about Tully's veracity, and I said so to Mencken. "Well, he does edit his stories a little bit," said Mencken, "but that's all right. The Apostles did plenty of editing of what Jesus said, assuming He said anything worth remembering. But Jim is all right. You're hard on him."

Philip Goodman had other ideas. He said, "Tully is an out and out liar. I don't even believe his name is Tully. I wouldn't be surprised it's Goldberg or Cohen, and I am sure he was born in the Bronx or in Staten Island, where all liars are born." Goodman told Mencken precisely how he felt about Tully. Mencken merely smiled. Goodman insulted Tully to his face and in company. At another party at the Algonquin, where almost thirty people were present, Tully came up to Goodman and said, "You don't like me, do you?"

"I wouldn't say that," said Goodman. "I hardly know you, and I am perfectly willing to leave things stand as they are."

"I mean you don't like my work," said Tully.

"I wouldn't say that, either," said Goodman. "What you do is not work. It's not writing."

"Then what is it?"

"I'd rather not say," said Goodman and walked off.

Goodman was too harsh with Tully. Tully obviously manufactured a good deal of his autobiography. He wrote with bathos, most of the time. He had hardly any feeling for words. He had hardly any profound experiences to draw upon. Very likely, he worked but a brief time in a circus, and hence knew little about circus life. Much of what he wrote about that life was probably fiction. The same with his prize fighting experiences. The same, perhaps, with his boasted stealing of books and food. The same, even more probably, with his boasted sexual conquests. But the trouble with Tully really was not that he fictionized experiences he did not have. The trouble is that the quality of his fictionizing was so low. Tully's standing as a writer is thus very modest. Yet he did personify, in his very failings, a large group of writers, who sweat and manipulate and twist the facts of their lives, hoping that something lasting will come out of their tortures—and little of real value does.

Toward the end of his days Tully's life seemed to become what he had claimed his early life was. One of his sons, according to him, was in jail on a multiplicity of charges, including rape and dope peddling. And a young daughter, his only one, I believe, had strayed from "the decent and moral path." Tully's affairs with women were becoming pointless. Actually, as he freely admitted, "I am having trouble getting anybody, not a professional or an amateur whore, to go to bed with me. I am having worse trouble getting women just to talk with me." His health was poor—stomach, heart, kidney.

So low had his reputation become that when he came to New York he hardly had anybody to see. George Jean Nathan wouldn't see him, concocting all kinds of reasons for avoiding him. Former girl friends avoided him, too. They were either married by then, or they simply saw no "profit" in meeting with a man who obviously was no more a literary light. Mencken was in Baltimore most of the time now, and Tully confided to me that Mencken's last few notes to him were strangely brief.

Sometime in 1940 he came to New York. He hadn't written to me of his coming, as he had been doing. He called me and said, "Charlie, go easy on me. I've been here for a few days, staying at a cheap hotel, and I have been drunk. So forgive me. I know you will. Jews are as forgiving as Irishmen. They're probably related. I suppose Irishmen are just lowdown Jews. Anyway, let's get together." I said sure. Whereupon he suggested that we meet at the home of the then publisher of *The Living Age*. When I arrived Tully had already been drinking heavily and his eyes shone brightly and I saw at once he was miserable. He greeted me by embracing me and mumbling, "I love you, Charlie, I just love you. God, it's good you came."

The party was rather dull. The women especially were dull. The host was not drinking and this perplexed Tully. "Imagine it, Charlie, a man who calls a party, and he isn't drinking." As the party dragged on Tully became interested in one of the girls, a rather dumpy, not very intelligent woman of perhaps forty. I thought she was not too keen on Tully, but since there was nobody else in sight, she submitted to his attentions. Suddenly Tully said to her, "Honey, are you a virgin?"

She blushed. "I better not answer that," she finally said.

Tully smiled and snarled. "You've answered that already. You need go no further, sugar."

"What do you mean, Mr. Tully?" she asked.

"What do I mean?" mumbled Tully. Then he turned to me. "Charlie, tell her what I mean."

"I don't know what you mean, Jim."

"Always the diplomat, Charlie." He turned to the girl, who apparently was nameless. "What I mean, sugar, is that you haven't been a virgin since coal was $2 a ton. Understand?"

"No," said the anonymous girl.

"You really mean that?" insisted Tully.

"Yes."

"Well, I love you just the same, and I would like to baptise you sexually."

"I don't understand," insisted the woman.

Tully turned to me again. "If I told you this, you wouldn't believe me, would you?"

"Frankly, no."

Tully went home with the woman-girl, and later he said he had no difficulty. He added, "But she didn't love me, even verbally. She was like a dog in the street, not in an alley, but in the street."

We met the following day for lunch. He was staying at a very modest mid-Forties Hotel in Manhattan. I wanted to take him to the Blue Ribbon Restaurant on West Forty-fourth Street. He refused, and would give me no reason. Instead we went to the Automat on Sixth Avenue, directly opposite the Public Library. Tully was morose.

"Last night was the first time I didn't enjoy sinful sex," he said. "That's a bad omen."

"What do you mean?"

"I didn't like it. It was dull. I used to like sex for its own sake. Now I don't. Either I'm growing up, or I'm dying. Which do you think it is?"

"I don't know."

"I don't either, Charlie. I'm worried. She was all right, but . . . oh, well, I couldn't cry for her. Did you know that I always cry after I lay a whore? I mean I always used to. With her I didn't cry. That worries me, it really does. Something is wrong. I've lost out all around. The whole world is a whore, and I don't feel at home any more."

I didn't see him again for some five or six years. When he died in the spring of 1947 I remembered the last line he spoke to me, "The whole world is a whore, and I don't feel at home any more."

Isaac Goldberg

O NE OF THE SADDEST CAREERS I HAVE KNOWN WAS THAT OF Isaac Goldberg. He was not a success, he was not a failure, he was above the average, he was a truly useful citizen—but he is totally forgotten. Ask a hundred people of above average education, picked at random, and it would be a miracle if a single one of them would know who Isaac Goldberg was. Was he important in his day? It's hard to say. He was, and he wasn't. He meant something, and he meant nothing; he had influence, and he had no influence; he left his mark upon his generation, and he didn't. He was always on the verge of doing something truly important, and he never really did.

When I lived in Boston I had heard vaguely about him. He had written this, and he had written that, but nobody who spoke about him really took seriously a single thing that he had written. Nobody knew exactly what he did to earn a living. Nobody knew exactly what he was a doctor of. For a long while I thought he was a Ph.D. in philosophy, and I asked several people who knew him well, but they weren't quite sure. Some said he was a Ph.D. in languages, but they weren't quite sure what languages. "I know it's not French," said one. "I know it's not German," said another. When I finally learned that Dr. Goldberg's languages were Spanish and Portuguese I was disappointed. I don't know why. And when I was told that in Brazil he was considered a great authority on Brazilian literature, that he had written "a classic" about that literature, I didn't believe it. It seemed bizarre. Finally, I did read his book on Brazilian literature, and I was bored. Not because I didn't know the subject, but because Dr. Goldberg's treatment of it was so uninspiring. The man was just dull, I thought to myself.

I moved, as the phrase goes, in the intellectual circles of Boston, but I had not met him. I thought that perhaps the circles I moved in were not sufficiently important for a man of his stature to move in. Then I did meet him, but only through correspondence. I had gone on the editorial staff of the *American Mercury*. Mencken had published some things by Dr. Goldberg. Then I wrote an article on Boston, "Boston Twilight." It was, alas, a poor article, though it caused something of a stir in the Boston of those days—way back in 1925. Shortly after the issue of the *Mercury,* with my article in it, went on the stands, I got a letter from Dr. Goldberg. It was brief. I haven't got it with me any more, but I remember every word of it: "Dear Mr. Angoff: I salute you, as one Bostonian to another. Your article tells the unvarnished truth. We must meet soon. Sincerely yours. Isaac Goldberg. P.S. The next time you are in Boston, do call on me. My name is in the Boston telephone directory."

I couldn't see him the next time I was in Boston, but the result of my not seeing him was a correspondence that lasted till his death in 1938 at the age of fifty-one. He would write me little notes about the state of culture in Boston, for example: "Censorship is still bad here. The police arrested a new-born babe on a charge of nudity. . . . I hear that the Bible will soon be banned. Remember the story about King David and Uriah?" These notes embarrassed me. I had been hearing similar "humorous" remarks from Mencken and Nathan. I had grown tired of them. Hearing them from Goldberg made me still more tired.

Then he came to New York to interview Mencken (and later Nathan) for the biographies he was writing of them. I saw a good deal of Dr. Goldberg then. I told Mencken and Nathan about my meetings with Goldberg, and both were troubled. I asked them why.

"How can you stand him?" asked Mencken.

"Are you a pea-and-carrot eater, too, Angoff?" asked Nathan.

They were referring to Goldberg's strange eating habits. Goldberg, as well as I could make out, was not a vegetarian, but he was very close to it. He was a food faddist of a strange sort. Mostly he ate dairy products, some vegetables, and lots of fruit—but only certain kinds of fruit, precisely what kinds I don't remember after all these years. But I do remember that he was a devotee of yoghurt.

Mencken and Nathan actually had reference, not so much to Goldberg's eating habits, as to his conversation. The man was simply dull. He had a knack of missing the point in whatever book he read. I remember he once spoke about Dreiser's *Sister Carrie,* and he said it was "a work of realistic fantasy, without moral implications, thank God." Of Sherwood Anderson he said, "I call him a throwback to Greek classical morality." I asked him what he meant and he said, "Well, *Winesburg, Ohio* is a kind of mystical realism." I told Mencken what Goldberg had said, and Mencken said, "He talks like a Reform rabbi who has read more than is good for him. Worse, he talks like the Rev. Dr. John Haynes Holmes." Nathan didn't bother to characterize Goldberg's conversation in any detail. He merely said, "Oh, my God!"

When the Mencken biography came out, Mencken said, "May the Lord help me and Goldberg, too. I'm sorry for the poor slob." The book got middling reviews. Mencken wasn't surprised. "The poor man just doesn't understand a thing of what I am trying to do. He might as well write about Ghenghis Khan or Michelangelo or the Pope as about me."

Mencken, however, continued to see Goldberg on occasion. They would have dinner together in New York two or three times a year. Mencken came to New York about once every three weeks, and Goldberg came to New York three or four times a year. Mencken always came back from a meeting with Goldberg, determined he would never see him again. But Mencken did not keep his resolve. He did see and correspond with Goldberg till Goldberg's death.

Nathan was cruel. He saw Goldberg as long as he thought Goldberg needed material for his Nathan biography, but once the book was published—it, too, got only middling reviews—Nathan stopped seeing Goldberg abruptly. Nathan at first stalled Goldberg with pleas that he was busy, that he had to go to Philadelphia to see his mother—and then he merely stopped answering Goldberg's letters completely. Goldberg was hurt. "I feel humiliated. I feel I have been used," he said to me.

Goldberg was a professional writer, that is, when he finished one writing assignment he began another. He wrote a number of books, in addition to his biographies of Mencken and Nathan and his history of Brazilian literature. Perhaps his best known other books are those on Gilbert and Sullivan and George Gershwin. I remember what Mencken said about each, as it came out: "A still-birth. Strange how little life Goldberg can put into a man or a situation. He writes vegetarian books. A Pullman porter could have written livelier books on Gilbert and Sullivan and Gershwin. I read them and didn't hear a single tune." Nathan dismissed both books with one word: "Trash."

But Goldberg's reputation, such as it was, did not suffer from his poor books. At the same time, it did not increase, and it never did reach the more discriminating readers. They knew of him, but thought little of him. But the middle-brows, to borrow a phrase from Dwight McDonald, talked more and more about him—at least, this was the case of the middle-brows in Boston. Whenever I visited Boston I heard his name mentioned in various circles. They who talked about him were graduates of Wentworth Institute and Tufts College and Suffolk Law School of a generation back. They went a great deal to lectures at the Ford Hall Forum. They bought the *Nation* and the *New Republic,* and they read here and there in them—they were samplers of magazines and books. They preferred to talk about articles and books to reading them carefully. But even they did not ever get enthusiastic about Goldberg.

Perhaps the only writings of Goldberg's that they did get a trifle excited about were his writings on sex. Goldberg and Dr. Schnitkind edited some pamphlets and books dealing with "the modern attitude toward sex." They pleaded for more "freedom" and less "obscurantism and Middle Ages barbarism." It is to be doubted that many of the middle-brows who discussed this "freedom" themselves practiced it to any considerable extent, but they looked up to Goldberg and Schnitkind for "daring to state the issue."

I told this to Mencken and he said, "That's a laugh. Goldberg has no more sex in him than a cockroach with a sour stomach, and he preaches sex freedom! What a world!" Nathan thought the whole subject of Goldberg and sex was too vulgar for him to discuss.

So Goldberg continued to be a literary man. He wrote on many subjects. It was generally impossible to disagree with Goldberg, or even to argue with him seriously, because he was hardly ever "wrong." He said the "right" things, but they were clichés or otherwise not very illuminating. To repeat over and over again that Mencken was a "gadfly" is not to make Mencken interesting or important, unless his gadfly character is detailed and placed in proper perspective. To say that Gershwin reflected the "musical consciousness of the time" makes little sense, too, unless the musical consciousness of the time is properly described and evaluated, and this Goldberg didn't do, no matter how hard he tried. Goldberg couldn't even dramatize sex. Bertrand Russell and the Rev. Dr. Percy Stickney Grant, a "liberal" Episcopalian preacher of the time, said little more that was new about sex than Goldberg, but they said it excitingly. They really brought sin into the discussion. Goldberg only leered at it. And when, as he sometimes did, he wrote or spoke about "wholesome sex" one had the feeling that "wholesome" and "dull" were synonymous.

Then Goldberg became an editor and publisher. He founded the magazine *Panorama*. It was a monthly and it specialized in "civilized" writings. It came out against "sex enslavement," it came out against all censorship, it was for "the free life," and so on. It was in somewhat enlarged tabloid form, and so it didn't look "popular," but neither did it look "cultural." As I look back, it probably reflected Goldberg perfectly, who was neither popular nor profoundly cultural. The magazine was not worthless, but neither was there much point in reading it.

Goldberg had apparently always wanted to have his own magazine. There was journalistic blood in him. He had written for the high-tone Boston *Evening Transcript,* and this had helped him to obtain whatever reputation he had. What did he write? He wrote book reviews, he wrote articles about Spanish and Brazilian literature, he wrote "general cultural" articles on love and freedom and democracy and education.

Panorama, I believe, lasted for a little over a year. I wrote an article for it. I have lost the issue containing my article, but I believe it was about Boston, how it had declined over the years. I also recall faintly that it was a poor article, a tired article, which I apparently wrote to please Goldberg, because he asked for it. I didn't get a single letter commenting on the article. At the time I was disappointed. I felt that I might as well have thrown the article in the Hudson river. Now I am glad.

When *Panorama* died, Goldberg returned to being Goldberg. But now he wrote more and more for Haldeman-Julius, who was the publisher of the Little Blue Books, which in ten or twelve or fourteen pages told one all about the History of France or Astronomy or Science or Greed or Religion. Goldberg wrote many such Little Blue Books on his favorite subjects—Love and Freedom and Liberalism. He also wrote for the Haldeman-Julius magazine, *Appeal to Reason.* Then the Little Blue Books and the *Appeal to Reason* began to fade from the market. I don't know why. Probably only because nothing lasts forever. The books and the magazine were purposeful, though not very good; one learned something from them, though not very much; they were on the "right" side, but they made that side seem a little seedy and unappetizing—just like Goldberg.

Now Goldberg came more and more to New York with all kinds of book and magazine projects, except now he had more difficulty in getting editors interested. But his reputation did not suffer, certainly not in Boston. People still knew about Goldberg, though if one asked them what they knew, they would be hard put to it to say. Then Goldberg came less frequently to New York—once every two months, once every three months, once every five months. Then I got a letter from him that he didn't "know exactly when I'll be seeing you again. I'm a bit under the weather."

Then, one morning, I opened my *Times,* and I read that Goldberg was dead, aged 51.

William Saroyan: Some Footnotes

THE OTHER DAY I SAW WILLIAM SAROYAN'S PICTURE IN THE New York *Times.* I was astonished, for a while, at what time had done to his face. He is an old man now, in his late fifties, I guess. And yet he didn't look too much different, internally, so to speak, than he did when I last saw him in the middle Thirties. A slight touch of phoniness seemed to be all around his picture as it seemed to be around him some thirty years before. Perhaps phoniness is too harsh a word, but I can't think of another word.

How did I first meet him? For a long time, when I was editor of the old *American Mercury,* somebody in Fresno, California, had been sending me strange short stories on yellow butcher paper, single-spaced, and with hardly any margin. I read them all the way through, because there was something about them that interested me—but not enough for me to want to buy them. Then a manuscript came in entitled, "Aspirin is a Member of the NRA." I instantly fell in love with the title. We were in the throes of the Depression. Everything had been put under the Blue Eagle of the NRA— National Recovery Act.

I read the story and when I had finished I felt strange: I didn't know what I had read but I had been moved. I turned to my secretary and said that I had just read a good story and I wanted to buy it.

"What's it about?" she asked.

"I don't know," I said.

"You don't know?" she said. "And you want to buy it."

"Yes. You read it."

She read it and she said, "I like it, I like very much."

"What's it about?"

She smiled. "I don't know, but I like it."

When the story was published a large number of letters of comment came in, most of them favorable and all of them asking me what the story was about.

That's how William Saroyan came to my attention. Shortly thereafter I bought two other stories from him: "Ah-hah, Ah-hah" and "Myself Upon the Earth." When Saroyan's first book of short stories, *The Daring Young Man on the Flying Trapeze,* appeared, these three stories, I believe, were included and received almost unanimous approbation.

Not long afterward Saroyan came to New York, and he wrote to me ahead of time. The one time he and I could meet, in New York, was a Tuesday—a day I somehow remember. On that day I had to see another author, let's call her Mrs. Larkin, and I asked her if she would mind meeting Saroyan. He had already said he would be glad to. We met at Mrs. Larkin's apartment in New York City. She had a fine phonograph and excellent records. Mrs. Larkin served coffee and cake, and then she played some Mozart—actually, Mozart's Symphony in G-minor, No. 40.

As the music continued Saroyan kept on shaking his head, and neither Mrs. Larkin nor I could quite make out what he was trying to express. Between the first and second movements Saroyan exclaimed, "Isn't that just wonderful? How can anything be so wonderful? Does Mozart write more things like this?"

We assured him that Mozart had written a good deal, and Saroyan was pleased. The music continued but now Saroyan did not shake his head any more. I got the idea that he had tired of that which he had thought was wonderful. We continued talking about various composers and music in general. It was clear that Saroyan knew little about music. I was disappointed. Later I asked Mrs. Larkin what she had to say about the matter. She looked at me and said, "He's a phony. At least as far as music is concerned. That's a great writer for you!"

Several months later Whit Burnett, Martha Foley and I had dinner at a pleasant French restaurant in the Fifties. Our guest was William Saroyan. The Burnetts had known Saroyan longer than I did. Indeed, I think they printed him a month or so earlier than I did. It was they, too, I believe, who influenced Bennett Cerf to print Saroyan's first collection of short stories, *The Daring Young Man on the Flying Trapeze,* under the imprint of Random House.

It was a bizarre evening. We all felt high, not so much because of liquor but for some vague reason. It was one of the most pleasant and most confused evenings I had ever had. Whit and Martha were, as usual, excited about their magazine *Story.* They mentioned one "great" writer after another whom they had discovered—three months ago, six weeks ago, last week, only this morning. We all smiled. I don't recall what was said verbatim—this happened about thirty years ago, but I do remember the substance and I'm quite sure about the nuances.

"Well, everybody's great, really great," exclaimed Saroyan. "The man serving us now, he's great. The cab driver who brought us over here, he's great. We are living in great times, but all times are great times, because people are great at all times. Everybody's great."

"That includes you," said Whit.

"Sure, especially you," said Martha.

"I make it unanimous," I said. "Only I wish it were not true."

"Why?" said Saroyan.

"I don't know," I said. "The truth frightens me. It means it's running out, no more true, and its opposite is coming."

"Say, Charlie has something there," said Whit.

"The truth is fragile, always was and always will be. It's the nature of truth to be that way," I said.

"I think Charlie is right, and I think Whit is right, and I think

Bill is right, and I'm frightened, too," said Martha. "Being right is a terrible thing."

"I'm frightened, I'm very frightened," said Saroyan.

"Remember," I warned, "that what is true to us may not be true to God or to other creatures, other than we are. Truth is a relative thing. What is true is true to somebody, not just by itself. So we may all be wrong as far as horses and angels are concerned."

"I'm frightened, I'm very frightened," said Saroyan again.

"Are you sure about what you're saying?" asked Whit.

"I'm not," I said. "It's philosophy. It's epistemology."

"Is it good?" asked Saroyan.

"I don't know," I said. "I'll say this, it's not bad, but neither is it good."

"Then what is it?" asked Martha.

"I'm frightened, I'm very frightened," repeated Saroyan.

"Philosophy is not good for anybody," said Whit.

"I don't know of a single philosopher who has ever written a good short story," said Martha.

"I don't like that, either," said Saroyan. "I always thought philosophy was a special kind of short story. Now you tell me this. I'm frightened, I'm very frightened."

"Bill," said Whit, "what is a short story?"

"That's easy," said Saroyan. "A short story is a short poem told the long way."

"I like that," said Whit.

"I do, too," said Martha.

"I think it's marvelous," I said.

"But there's more to it than that," said Saroyan. "Some poems have to be told the long way. Poems that are told the short way are just poems. Both are good. Everything good is poetry. The rest is business."

"I like that," said Whit.

"I do, too," said Martha.

"I think it's marvelous," I said.

"But I'm frightened by the truth," said Saroyan. "Poetry never frightens me. The truth does."

"What we need is another drink," said Martha.

We all had another drink, and somehow we did not come back to the subject of poetry and truth.

Many months later I saw Saroyan with George Jean Nathan. I encountered them at the entrance to the Royalton Hotel, where Nathan lived. I could stop for only a few moments.

"George said there's no hereafter," said Saroyan.

Nathan smiled.

"I said he's the hereafter, and I'm the hereafter, and yesterday is the hereafter. How do you feel about it, Charlie?" said Saroyan.

"The hereafter is always dying," I said, trying to enter into the spirit of Saroyan's talk.

"Nothing ever dies," said Saroyan.

"Nothing?" asked Nathan.

"No, nothing ever dies," said Saroyan. "Things only get older."

"Bill, you're just using words, and hoping they will make people say you're profound," said Nathan.

I winced. I thought Saroyan would take offense. Instead he smiled and said, "I know, I know. Lots of people say that. For effect, eh? Well, I mean it. I never say anything I don't mean, even when I know it's foolish. I like to believe some foolish things, if they're beautiful. Believe them and they come true. I mean they really are true. I mean a beautiful thing is beautiful, and what is beautiful is true. Anyway, the beautiful is truer than the true. Truth is unimportant. Poetry is important. The beautiful is important."

"Bill," said Nathan, "the trouble with you is that you use words as if they were aspirin. They ease the pain, as you use words, but in a while the pain comes back, and people feel swindled by your words. You're a temporary poet, to use your lingo."

"What's wrong with that?" said Saroyan. "There is nothing that is temporary. Everything is immortal. Just being is immortal. That's the miracle of it all."

"The miracle of what?" asked Nathan.

"Everything," said Saroyan.

"More aspirin," said Nathan.

"Maybe," said Saroyan. "But that doesn't matter. Aspirin is aspirin."

"Do you use it ever?" asked Nathan.

"Sure, and it helps," said Saroyan. "Poetry should help, true or not, and if it helps it's true; if it doesn't help, it isn't true. That's everything I know. Everything else isn't worth knowing."

"That's aspirin, too," said Nathan. "You should use more discipline in your thinking as well as in your writing."

"I don't use discipline in anything. I write and talk the way it comes to me. Everything anybody says or writes is good."

"Angoff, remember what you've heard," said Nathan. "You are hearing tragic words. Bill is writing his own death sentence. It's a real shame."

Saroyan laughed. "You talk like an Armenian preacher," he said.

I left them, because I had an appointment.

A few days later I saw Nathan, who had done a great deal to place Saroyan before the New York theatre-going public, especially in connection with *My Heart's in the Highlands* and *The Time of Your Life*. We talked briefly about Saroyan. "He's a fluke, I fear," said Nathan. "Life Can Be Beautiful is no philosophy for any genuine artist. It is with Bill Saroyan. You and I witnessed his death. From now on he'll be no better than an inspirational columnist for country weeklies."

Francis Hackett

Francis Hackett was one of my heroes when I was still in my teens. I used to rush to the Boston Public Library in Copley Square Friday evenings to get the *New Republic,* which then usually came in that very morning, in order to read Hackett and Walter Lippmann, but chiefly Hackett. I had read Lippmann's *A Preface to Politics,* and was entranced with its clarity. Lippmann made politics exciting . . . he brought it right into my parents' kitchen. But, somewhere in my unconscious, I suppose, I wasn't profoundly interested. Some anarchistic streak in me said that politics wasn't really important, what was important was art—in the widest sense of the word . . . writing, painting, sculpture . . . and some devil within me told me that the artist was "above politics." Politics was sober, and art was mad and wild and carefree. It was this sense of wildness and madness that I got from the reviews and literary articles of Francis Hackett.

I used to read and re-read every line he wrote, especially when he wrote about Joyce and Gogarty and AE and the whole Dublin world. I loved him when he wrote about Shaw and Yeats and a certain young writer by the name of Sean O'Casey. Hackett got magic into his lines, and I could almost see the leprechauns dancing all over the page. It was all so many years ago, and I hardly remember what I read, I mean the precise words, but I remember very well what new zest in sheer living his words gave to me . . . what an abiding love for literature and for writers and for the whole magnificent world of art.

It was therefore with considerable expectation that I looked forward to his joining the editorial staff of the *American Mercury* in 1944. He was to come to the office three times a week, and help me out in the reading of manuscripts. The publisher told me that James Reston of the *New York Times* had recommended Hackett.

"That speaks well for Reston," I said. "Hackett is one of the finest literary critics we have ever had in the United States."

"That could be," he said, "but I can barely understand what he's writing about in the *Times.*" At the time Hackett was writing an occasional daily review for the *Times.* I had been about to praise these reviews, but in view of what he said, I desisted. Not that I didn't want to contradict him. I did that frequently. His idea of running the *Mercury* and mine were often different . . . and I had resigned myself to working on the magazine. I looked upon it merely as a job, not as a professional position. I desisted from contradicting him because I didn't want to hurt Hackett's chances of landing the job and staying on it. I knew he was along in years and I sensed that he had money problems. So—may God forgive me— I said in reply, "Well, Hackett is a little difficult at times, but he has excellent judgment."

The first day Hackett went on the job the publisher took him and me to the Grill Room at the Waldorf Astoria. Hackett was all politeness, with the charm of the cultured Irishman who is being shown the town. The publisher asked him if he wanted a drink. Hackett did order a drink, a Scotch highball. I ordered a Manhattan. The publisher ordered an orange juice. Hackett said, "I always feel a little adulterous when I drink a Scotch and soda instead of an Irish and soda."

I laughed. I thought it was a witty remark. The publisher barely moved his lips.

Then Hackett said, "And you, Mr. Angoff, with a name like that, how come you order a Manhattan, a sweet drink? And for lunch, too?"

"I don't know why I ordered a Manhattan," I said. "I really wanted a sherry."

"Really," said Hackett. "You and the Queen."

"The Queen?" I asked puzzled.

"Yes," he said. "Queen Mary always has a sherry for lunch and one for dinner. So you're in good company."

I liked Hackett very much. But I was sure that he wouldn't be long on the job. The publisher was uneasy with him, especially with the twinkle in his eyes. I had the feeling that Hackett had the same feeling that I had.

About a week after he was on the job Hackett came into my office and asked, "How is your astral body?"

"My astral body?" I asked in puzzlement.

"Yes. My wife is a spiritualist, a little bit of one, and when she thinks I drink too much she says my astral body won't like it. Well, so it goes. Do you mind if I sit down?"

"Please do. I want to be interrupted. I have just begun to think how senseless all I'm doing is. Reading manuscripts, reading proof, and just sitting here. Sitting on a chair in an office is foolish."

"Yes, it is. When you get to feel that way, think instead of a pretty girl. That will save you lots of agony. I saw one this morning, on the way in from Connecticut. Her hips were much more interesting than her face. That always bothers me, about women. It's the fault of girdles. They're deceiving." He smiled. "My astral body. That sounds a little odd for me. My astral body."

We got to talking about his review of *Boston Adventure*, by Jean Stafford, in the *Times*. He and Orville Prescott more or less alternated with their reviews. Hackett had been very harsh with Miss Stafford. He pointed out that she was juvenile, coy, and almost totally dense in her observations. I said, cautiously, "She won't forget what you said about her."

He smiled and a strange hesitation leaped over his rimless glasses.

"I really was annoyed with that book," he said. "It was bad as a novel but that wasn't what annoyed me chiefly. What annoyed me was that she tried to be profound, and I can't stand that in a woman. It is enough for a woman to be lovely. That's hard enough in a world that is really run by men, not by women, as women think and as some men imagine. You know, that's why I dislike Mary Colum so much. She tries so hard to be a William Hazlitt. But, then, I suppose, she's really a man psychologically. But Padraic is a sweet person. He's really more profound than Mary is, and in addition he's also a wonderfully kind man."

Now and then the name of Mencken would come up. Apparently he and Mencken had had considerable correspondence when *Henry the Eighth* came out. Then they stopped writing to each other. That was not surprising. Mencken wrote with a meat axe; Hackett wrote with a scalpel. "Frankly," said Hackett, "I never did take to him. He was a longshoreman as a writer. He was a vaudevillian at best. I never respected his scholarship. I never respected his literary criticism. I believe he and I did exchange some notes about James Joyce, whom he called a mountebank. That was inexcusable. Joyce was a great writer."

Joyce was the cause of the only tiff that Hackett and I had. When *Finnegan's Wake* came out I tried several times to read it, but got nowhere. I said so to Hackett. Whereupon the good man began to explain the book to me. He had been explaining for almost an hour, when I said, "I still don't understand." He became angry for a moment. He said, "Then you're hopeless."

Often when he made ready to go back to Connecticut he carried two packages: a bottle of Scotch and a bouquet of flowers for his wife. Once he said, looking at his two packages. "That's what keeps our marriage going smoothly." He did not elaborate. I had learned some time before that his wife was rather active in the spiritualistic movement in the United States. One person told me that she was also a medium. I never had the heart to discuss this with Hackett.

The topic of Zionism once came up. Hackett knew a great deal about it. I imagine he got this information through his friendship with Associate Justice Felix Frankfurter of the United States Supreme Court. He said, "The Jewish people are very fortunate in their top Zionist leader. Dr. Weizmann is a scholar, a learned man, a worldly man, a man who can smile, a man, I imagine, who has known sin. But De Valera is a fanatic ignoramus. It's bad enough he's a devout Catholic and does whatever the Vatican says; he's worse, in that his own native fanaticism and barbarism are worse than the Vatican's. The Vatican now and then—rarely, to be sure— compromises, and compromise is a mark of the civilized man. De Valera never compromises. He is ruled by the same fanaticism now as when he was a young boy."

Hackett had known Shaw and corresponded with him over a considerable period of time. Once Hackett said, "Shaw was the only atheistical Irishman I have ever known who I was sure would stay atheistical. The others secretly, as they get older, began to doubt their atheism. But I suppose that's the penalty of being born a Catholic. Catholics generally go back, as they near the end. Shaw was a Protestant, or his parents were. Protestantism hasn't got the iron hold on its believers that Catholicism has. I suppose he really had only one religion. George Bernard Shaw."

Once Hackett and Lowell Brentano were in my office. Brentano, when he was associated with the book firm bearing his name, had published Shaw's books and had met him many times. "I did love that man," said Lowell. "He was a gentleman all the way through, a shrewd business man, of course, but he cared less for money than some people think. He had a childish desire to best business men at their own game. He had little respect for business men and he wanted to show them that making money required so little brains that even a writer, on his off days, that is, could beat them at it.

"He and his wife had a strange relationship. I think Mrs. Shaw loved her husband, but I'm not sure about him loving her. Anyway, whenever I would visit Shaw, he and I would eat at one table, you know, vegetables, peas, cabbage, and oranges, and sometimes some light tea. It was really quite tasteless. But that's what I had to eat. A few feet away from us would sit Mrs. Shaw, eating a steak or some chicken with potatoes, you know, and I would be jealous. And once Mrs. Shaw called over to us—she would eat alone—she called over, 'What a foolish way for a man to live!' He, I mean Shaw, only smiled. I was embarrassed, but I don't think either one of them was embarrassed. I have the feeling they always ate separately that way at different tables."

"Did you know, Mr. Brentano, that Mrs. Shaw was a Christian Scientist?"

"Oh, yes. She told me so, and he told me so. But, you know, I think he was a little bit that way, too. Not out and out, you know, but he saw a lot in it. They were a strange pair, a very strange pair."

Hackett said, "He was full of contradictions. He liked high living, he liked to live in a neat and roomy flat, but I do believe he was a genuine Socialist. I asked him several times about his Socialism, and I got the impression he really believed. In any case, I think he was the only Socialist in England who had truly read the whole of *Das Kapital*. I have a theory about him. I don't think he was at all Irish."

"What do you mean?" asked Brentano.

"All Irish people, I mean full-blooded Irish people, believe in fairies and gnomes and leprechauns. I believe in them. If anything is part of the Irish character, that's it. You see, that's one of the reasons why De Valera is really not Irish. He doesn't altogether believe in gnomes and fairies. He believes in them a little, though. Some Irish blood did creep into his system. I don't know exactly how, but it did. But Shaw, without meaning disrespect to his parents, I sometimes don't think there is any Irish blood in him at all—if any, just a few drops that hardly count. He really doesn't believe in fairies at all, he just doesn't. He's a rationalist, and no real Irishman is wholly a rationalist, or even to a great extent. That's their failing and their glory. They let the superstitious Catholic church run them, which means they have no reason. But they really don't believe all that the church tells them. The Church is against fairies and gnomes and leprechauns, that's paganism, you know, it really is. But the in many ways, a miserable and ugly era, but it also had its more favorable aspects.

There was a speakeasy on West Fifty-Sixth Street, between Fifth and Sixth Avenues. It was called the Napoleon. It occupied a whole building, which formerly had been the residence of an ancient and moneyed Manhattan family. The ground floor was a huge reading room, with books and magazines in sufficient numbers to have rivalled a small town library. The middle floor was the main floor. It was divided into two large rooms, a restaurant and grill, and the bar. The top floor was empty. I was there once and found only chairs and tables in disarray.

George Jean Nathan used to take me there occasionally. We usually went to the middle floor and stood at the bar, for a while, then took our drinks to a nearby table. The bar was built in the form of half the number eight, cut down the middle. Behind the bar were mirrors and always there were phrases written on them in soap, remarks by celebrated writers or artists. One that sticks in my mind across the years was Oscar Wilde's: "There are two great tragedies in life, one is not reaching your goal, the other is reaching it." Another was that attributed to King Gustavus Adolphus of Sweden: "Remember, my son, gold sinks in the sea, but elephant refuse floats. It is God's will." A third was the one whose authorship is problematical: "Heavenly father, give us serenity to accept what cannot be changed, courage to change what should be changed, and wisdom to know one from the other."

One evening Nathan and I were sitting alone at a table. He had just introduced me to a drink I had not had before: poussé-café, a mountainous glass with one color on top of another. The taste was somewhat sweeter than I liked, and I said so to Nathan. He smiled and said, "Wait, my boy, wait, the sweetness will soon become tart, and then bitter. Like women."

He was right. The sweetness soon became bitter.

"Angoff," he said, "that's the tragedy of women, they nearly always become bitter, sooner or later, and if they don't become bitter, they become dull. That's how women differ from men. Men improve with age, women degenerate, and they degenerate early in

Catholic priests know they can't root out this paganism. If they tried they'd find themselves with empty churches. So they humor the Irish with their fairies, just like the early Christians humored the pagan Romans and the pagan vandals and the others in the so-called barbarian world who were the first converts. They were the first rice Christians, the first Mexican Christians, you know what I mean. Now Shaw is no such Christian at all. He's no Christian at all, and he means his atheism and agnosticism. But neither has he any truck with fairies."

Brentano was impressed. "I never thought of that," he said.

"But I don't mean to be wholly friendly to Shaw, I mean favorable," smiled Hackett. "His failure to believe in fairies keeps him from being a great poet as well as a good playwright. You see, he knows that Shakespeare is his superior in spite of what he says. He knows that Shakespeare was a poet over and above his being a playwright. Being a playwright is inferior to being a poet. Now Yeats believes in fairies and other little people. He believes in more of them than is proper for any Irishman, you know what I mean. But that has helped him to be the great poet that he is. That Shaw lacks."

Hackett was enormously fond of Justice Frankfurter. He could quote phrase upon phrase from his opinions and from his table talk. Once he told me that Justice Frankfurter was the finest thing that ever happened to the Harvard Law School. I once asked Hackett if he thought equally highly of Professor Morris Cohen, who was a friend of Justice Frankfurter, and whom Hackett had seen several times. Hackett hesitated and then said, "I don't know, I don't know what to say. Professor Cohen is, of course, a great philosopher. I know Bertrand Russell has called him one of the greatest the United States has produced. But I can't get close to him. Maybe he has no humor, or too little. I don't know. In all frankness Justice Frankfurter is not given to jokes such as even Yeats and AE told each other, and yet I detect hidden humor in him. So that's how I feel about Professor Cohen. But he really does have a razor-edge mind."

For some reason I don't recall, Hackett once came into my office and sat down and at once began to talk enthusiastically about an elderly nun he had just heard from. Apparently he had been corresponding with her for many years—she lived in a convent not far from Dublin. I was waiting for him to tell me something special that was in her last letter. Apparently there wasn't. He merely felt warm all over because of the letter. "A strange woman," he said thoughtfully. "She must be nearly eighty, about my height, quite thin, and lovely, kindly eyes. When I last saw her, about ten years ago, maybe more, she hardly had any wrinkles. Not even on her forehead, where women get wrinkles before men do. I once said to my wife that women's heads shrink faster, and she didn't like that. But this nun, Mother Anthony, is so gentle, and so worldly, really. She reads a great deal, and is not at all afraid of the atheism that is in intellectual Ireland. She seems to think that God's love will conquer even Irishmen's atheism. She knows I haven't been to mass for fifty years. She knows what I think of the Irish cardinals and archbishops and of the terrible Catholic Church censorship, but she never discusses it in her letters. Just gossipy letters, about an old nun who's died, and about a young nun who seems to be having doubts, and she sends me clippings from newspapers and magazines, some of them Catholic but many non-Catholic, or lay. I miss her letters when I don't get them, and I welcome them when I do get them. I hope she'll be alive when I next get to Ireland. But that probably will not be for a long, long time. I am more eager to get back to Denmark. That's one of the most remarkable countries in human history." His wife came from there. He did go back there. He died there. He never saw Mother Anthony again.

Prohibition Days

MANY PEOPLE THINK ALL SPEAKEASIES WERE LOW, LURID, AND immoral places, among the many evils of the twenties and thirties. Dens of iniquity. Cesspools of sin. Many, perhaps most, of them were just that. The food and the drink in them were truly dreadful. So was the clientele.

But there were other speakeasies that were charming places where men and women of breeding met. They were less drinking places than salons in the grand European sense. In fact, it may well be that these better speakeasies were the only grand salons, on a large scale, that the United States has ever had. There were salons, in the great days, in Boston and in Philadelphia and in Baltimore, and perhaps in Chicago, but these were confined to literary and artistic folk and the attendance at them was relatively small. The salons of the speakeasy days were numerous and they were democratic. Unlettered people and people of modest means, but who had good taste and wanted to be in superior intellectual surroundings, could go to the speakeasies and be engulfed in refined atmosphere and occasionally overhear soaring conversation, indulged in by men and women in the arts or in the various professions. These speakeasy salons thus gardens of general popular good taste. The Prohibition era

life. No woman can ever forgive God for giving her gray hair. Every woman is an atheist the first time she notices a gray hair in her head."

"I thought women take to the church more readily than men," I said hesitantly.

"I know, I know," said Nathan, "but that does not disprove what I have said. Women go to church but still are atheists. Women can do a thing like that. By the way, do you know who are the most atheistical women in creation?"

"Who?"

"Dancers."

"Dancers?"

"Yes, dancers," said Nathan.

He was about to continue with his philosophising when a man from an adjacent table said, "That's true. Dancers believe in nothing, not even in themselves."

The man got up and walked over to our table. He introduced himself, and the name at once registered something in my mind. I knew his name vaguely as that of an eminent choreographer. He asked us over to his table, where sat another man and two young and beautiful women. The tall man, who had come over to our table, said, "We couldn't help overhearing what you were saying about atheism and dancers, and we recognized you, Mr. Nathan. And all I want to say is that what you say is right, as far as I know dancers. The only change I would make in your statement, Mr. Nathan, is that male dancers are just as atheistical as women dancers. I have known women writers and women sculptors and women musicians, you know, and women teachers, and all of them believed in God, I don't mean they necessarily went to church, but they were believers, silent believers, non-joiners, you know; but believers. But I have never known a dancer who believed a single word in the Bible, I mean the believing parts, about the Virgin Birth, the Resurrection, and so on."

"That is the truth," said the other man, "I have seen icons in the rooms of Russian ballet dancers, and you know what they say about Russians, how they always pray and bless themselves and carry huge crucifixes, but Russian ballet dancers just look upon their icons as ornaments, like rabbits' feet or charms, ordinary charms, like dragons' teeth. They believe nothing."

The two young women merely smiled.

"What do you think?" asked Nathan of the woman with the red hair.

"I really don't know, Mr. Nathan," she said, smiling. "It never occurred to me to think about such things. I mean I don't know."

Nathan asked the other woman, the one with the black hair.

"It's hard to say," she said. "I believe in something, but what it is I can't say. Maybe it is God. Maybe it's something else."

"I have a theory," said the tall man. "Listen. Dancers, male and female, are so deeply involved with or in, whatever it is, so deeply involved in their bodies, motion, you know, are so often in the nude, almost nude, so dependent upon motion, expression through motion, that's dancing, that they simply cannot think of anything incorporeal, spiritual, God. See? People who sit believe in God, people who move around don't believe in him, or anything of that sort. I suppose, on that theory, athletes and locomotive engineers and policemen should all be atheists. But, of course, they're not. That hurts my theory, but I still think there's something in it, don't you, Mr. Nathan?"

"I like your theory," said Nathan. "I like theories that don't hold up, because theories that do hold up are surely wrong."

The conversation went on far into the night, and it mounted in interest and excitement. Nathan wanted to know if dancers ever worry that their "immortality is brief." He said, "You are here today, gone tomorrow. Nijinsky can be seen no more. He can only be read about. Anna Pavlova the same. And so on."

"No," said the tall man, who appeared to be the spokesman-philosopher for the group. "We don't worry about that except when a man like you brings it up. I guess we just don't think about it. We do what we do because we like it. That's all, I guess. But what you say is probably true. We dancers are not remembered as dancers, I mean people do not see us dance after we are gone the way people read Shakespeare and Dickens and the other writers long after they're gone. But maybe that will be changed with the movies or television, if it develops to the extent that some people think it will.

I don't know. In a way I hope so. In a way, I'm really not too worried. After all, what you say applies equally to actors, don't you think?"

"Oh, yes, actors, too," said Nathan, "and that's a pity."

Suddenly Nathan said, "I have a theory, too, ladies and gentlemen, and that is that all art, all the arts, are immoral. I mean that they feel hemmed in by the ordinary codes. Art essentially is anarchistic, and all artists are anarchists. No real artist believes in monogamy or in honesty or in politeness or in voting or in paying debts."

"I think that's true," said the girl with the red hair.

"I do, too," said the girl with the black hair.

"Well," said the tall man, "I don't know. Some artists are anarchists, others are not. I should say dancers are, I should say sculptors and painters are, but what about writers? I really don't know too much about them. But I seem to remember from my school days that John Bunyan was a very religious man, and I think Milton was too, wasn't he?"

"There you have me," said Nathan. "You're spoiling my theory. Perhaps my eminent colleague, Mr. Angoff, can enlighten us."

I hesitated to say anything, because I preferred to listen. But I did say something to this effect: "It's true, I'm afraid, that Milton and Bunyan were believers, in their own way, of course. Milton had his own brand of Christianity, but he believed. And I think Bunyan was a believer and Coleridge, of course. He was a minister for a while. At first he was a Unitarian, then he became a Trinitarian, or maybe it was the other way around. At least he believed, I mean, anyway he believed. But there is a great deal to Mr. Nathan's theory. Even Milton and Bunyan and Coleridge were essentially anarchistic. And I suppose it can be said that an artist, more or less instinctively, follows his own mood, wherever it may lead him, rather than the customs and beliefs of his time."

And so the discussion went on, helped along by fresh drinks. As Nathan and I walked back to his hotel, the Royalton, he said, "Maybe Prohibition is a good thing, maybe it should continue, for the

artistic good of the country. Besides, I like the idea of people disobeying a foolish law."

One morning an old contributor showed up at the *Mercury*
office. He was in a state of panic. He literally shook all over. He
pleaded with me to tell him of the nearest speakeasy. He had
bummed his way all the way from a Western city, "and all I could
get," he told me, trembling, "was a little bathtub gin and some
burning alcohol."

I told him about a speakeasy not far from the *Mercury* office.
Actually it was right behind the Ziegfeld Theatre, and it was
frequented by judges and policemen off duty, as well as newspaper
and magazine people. The prices were reasonable and the food and
drinks were good, too. The walls were a bit shabby, and the chairs
and tables were far from sturdy, but otherwise it was an ideal place
for men and women in modest financial circumstances or eminent
personages who didn't care to be seen by "superior" people, as they
were disobeying the law. It was also the sort of place where men of
means took their temporary lady loves.

I told Sandy, which was not his name, to tell whatever person
asked him, that "Boston Butch" had sent him and that he, Sandy,
was "all right." "Boston Butch" was a name I sometimes used as
my identification at speakeasies. From his later report I gathered
that Sandy was made supremely happy at this speakeasy, the name
of which, incidentally, was The Beautiful Sahara. In gratitude
Sandy took me to this speakeasy two weeks later, and plied me with
food and drinks. I gathered immediately that Sandy had been a daily
visitor at The Beautiful Sahara, and that he had made many friends.

Sandy was a fine writer on the plane between the popular and the
medium quality. He had written some first-rate articles about subjects
he knew; loggers' camps, saloons, brothels, and orphan asylums. He
had been an orphan since the age of ten and had wandered from
one orphanage to another. He had had no schooling beyond the
fourth grade grammar school, but he had read a great deal in public
libraries. In fact, he was so fond of libraries that he frequently
"borrowed" books from various municipal libraries and had "forgotten" to return them. "You see," he told me, "I liked to re-read

some of these books and I just didn't want to go through the trouble of returning them and then taking them out again. There was always the danger that somebody else would take them out while I was waiting to take them out again myself. Besides, why put those overworked library clerks to all that unnecessary work? It makes no sense, does it?"

Sandy had an audience when he and I came in. There were older people present and there were young people present. Altogether, there were about twenty. The whiskey and the beer, as the saying goes, flowed freely. Sandy had had several drinks before he met me, and he began to replenish his supply. It was the middle of the afternoon . . . not many customers were expected till after dinner time. All the people gathered around a table, and Sandy held forth. It was one of the finest hymns to America I had ever heard. Sandy talked about the folklore of the Far West, about the loggers and about the salmon fishermen and about the skidrow characters and about the vanishing cowboys and about the vanishing camp followers of the loggers, and he talked about the saloons and about the various grades of brothels in the Far West and how they differed from the brothels in the East, and he talked about the medicine shows and the minstrel shows and the circuses and the shanty towns and the itinerant preachers and the lady loves of some of them, and he talked about the good work of the Salvation Army and the Volunteers of America, and he talked about the various churches, what good deeds they did and what lengths they went to to save "lost souls." On and on he went to a rapt audience. His precise words, of course, elude me, but the essence of what he said, especially toward the end, still lingers with me.

"This, my friends, is truly God's country, God's footstool, God's big acre and His little acre. You can keep Europe, you can keep Asia, you can keep Africa, you can keep all the oceans and all the seas and all the mountains and all the valleys beyond the confines and beyond the borders of this land. I say to you, from a full heart and an empty purse, from an overflowing soul and innermost being, I say to you, If God chose the Jews of old as His chosen people, He chose this country as His chosen land. The signs are all about us of

His favors to us. All about us, my friends. There is bounty a-plenty all around. Bounty-a-plenty.

"Here, in the United States, a man is a man, and a woman is a woman. And they can embrace under the finest and most glorious canopy in creation, the canopy of the forty-eight stars of the Federal union, and those stars, these forty-eight stars, are my galaxy, my milky way, my Paradise, my home and your home, and the home of every free soul in creation. And those stripes are the broad lands of freedom and opportunity and the finest song of expansion and exhiliration known to man from the days of Adam and Eve down to now.

"My friends, America is a song, a silent song and a mighty song and a symphonic song and a great chorus and a great Hosanah to the past and the present and the future till time unending. What do you hear on the Mississippi? A song of glory to all that is best in man. What do you hear on the Missouri River? A song of splendor and sheer delight to every heaving breast on every shy and desirable woman. What do you hear in the Grand Canyon, that dwelling place of the American Moses and the American Apostles? You hear, especially in the twilight, my friends I know, the Grand Canyon wail, you hear the echoes, the lifting, mounting echoes of all time past.

"Yes, sir, yes ma'am, I'm a drunkard, but so was Noah and so was Edgar Allen Poe and so was Shakespeare and so were the Apostles and so were all the great people of the world. The good are drinkers, the bad are non-drinkers and dull. Women know. Women love drinkers. Women hate Prohibitionists. Women hate politicians. Women like anarchists. Women love artists. And, I tell you, my friends, women love this country. They know. Their judgment is sound and true and good. And I listen to women when they love something and somebody.

"And that's what I hear all over the land, women singing their love for America. My friends, have you ever seen a young married woman with a child at her breast and another in her womb looking across the great prairie or the great Mississippi, at twilight or at high noon or any sunrise, watching her man going on to get the bacon,

have you seen her? I have. There is no lovelier sight in creation. It
is a singing face she has, and her baby at her breast is singing, and
her baby in her womb is singing, and his song comes from the womb
through her and through her face. Yes, and her husband is singing
as he goes farther off and farther off, and the whole prairie is singing.
What are they singing about? They are singing about themselves,
their love is for one another, and they are singing for another love,
the love for this land of ours, the love for the nation, the love for
every one of the forty-eight stars, and those forty-eight stars, my
friends, shine more brightly than any stars in the heavens above.
And now let us have another drink, each of us, and all on me . . ."

There was a speakeasy in the East Fifties. Its name escapes me,
but I think it was something like The Seven Deadly Sins. It was on
the ground floor. Always there was a gaudy door-opener in front;
he looked like a grand admiral. The door leading into The Seven
Deadly Sins was painted light blue, with two lamps on both sides.
A bit in front of the door was an iron gate, decorated with iron
lattice work. The grand admiral stood directly behind the gate, and
opened it when a customer arrived. One of his functions was to make
sure that no "strangers" or Prohibition agents tried to get in.
Another was to keep sight-seers from stopping too long in front of
The Seven Deadly Sins. Too much publicity was not desired by the
management. It invited attention from the police and the Prohibition
agents. The local police were "taken care of," and it was to be
presumed that some of the Federal agents were also "taken care of."
But one couldn't always be sure that these police and agents would
stay "taken care of." A new precinct captain or Federal supervisor
might be appointed and he would set about doing his duty, and there
could be trouble.

The Seven Deadly Sins could seat only about fifty people at most.
The food was superb. It was prepared in the Viennese style. The
waiters were uniformed. Young girls, dressed in Viennese fashion,
were the bus-girls, and they also sold cigarettes and candy. The
Seven Deadly Sins was open for lunch, but it did little in the afternoon. It did most of its business at night. The chief attraction, next

to the good food and the good drinks, was the musical concert and
the dancing. There was a four-piece orchestra, which played waltzes
and other nostalgic European music. And always there was a singer,
male or female, who joined the orchestra several times a night. There
was another attraction in The Seven Deadly Sins: the huge table of
snacks against the wall. There was herring and there was potato
salad and there was *tort* of all sorts and there was wonderful cole
slaw and there was a constantly hot pot of specially brewed coffee.
One could have a full meal from this snack table alone. Indeed, some
people did. There was a flat charge of $1.50 for a meal obtained this
way and one could come back to the table as often as one wanted.

I was introduced to The Seven Deadly Sins by the late Stewart
Holbrook, who came from the Pacific Coast. I hadn't known about
it, but he had heard about it from several people in Oregon.
Holbrook was a heavy drinker, well into his middle life, when he
began to "take account" of himself. But he never drank when we
went to The Seven Deadly Sins. I asked him why, and he answered
me somewhat in this manner: "The first time I came I liked it so
much here that I decided to be like these people, drink like a decent
human being. But I knew I just couldn't drink moderately. One
drink led to another and you know the rest. So I made a compromise.
I said to myself I wouldn't drink at all here, and enjoy myself, and
do my drinking outside. And not drinking here does me good, honest.
I think it helps me to drink a little less outside. This is too wonderful
a place for me to spoil with my drinking. You know what I like
especially here?"

"What?"

"I like it because it shows me how ordinary people can live. This
is the way a whole nation should be—polite, quiet, gently gay, nice
music, nice dancing, good singing, good food. You know what I
think?"

"What?"

"This country could be another Greece, another Rome, no,
Greece is what I mean, and another Paris and Berlin and another
London in the great days of these cities, spread all over the country,
setting an example to everybody. The horrible thing about Holly-

wood is that it sets an example of living and dreaming to the United States, and that example is bad, very bad. This is a much better example for Main Street. You know, Prohibition has been a good thing in many ways, a really good thing. I don't mean the bootleg gin, the terrible joints all over the country. New York City is full of them. I mean places like this. And I'm worried."

"Worried about what?"

"That Prohibition will be repealed. Of course, Charlie, it will be. This can't go on. And I'm for repeal. But I'll be a little sorry when it happens. Places like this will vanish. The saloon will come back. Well, I'm old enough to remember the saloon. There were good ones. Good places for lonely men to come to. I mean some of them, maybe many of them. But they didn't have the class that a place like this has. You see, saloons had no orchestra music and no nice singing like here, and there were no nice, white table-cloths on the tables. A saloon is a place where you rush in and rush out, where you stand up and figure how you're gonna meet the wife and her yipping, how you're gonna meet the kids and all their yelling. It's not a home where you can spend two, three hours, being a civilized human being, where you can regain your self-respect. This place is just that. I love it."

The Proletarian Bohemia

THE 1929 DEPRESSION USHERED INTO AMERICAN LITERARY LIFE—
as into the broad cultural life—something new: the so-called
proletarian point of view. For about ten years thereafter a considerable number of "proletarian" novels and short stories were published, there was a vociferous group of "proletarian" critics, and
there was a "proletarian" theatre. The general attitude in all these
endeavors was pretty much the same: that the workers are better
people than the employers; that what is good for the workers, by
and large, is good for the country and for the world as a whole; that
the basic morality of the bourgeoisie needs revising to bring it more
in line with the "true values" of civilized man, who is best represented by the worker; that all the arts had better give up their
"ivory tower seclusion" and try to achieve "a closer relationship"
with the life of the workers—that art must hereafter have some
"relevance" to "the common man"; and that what was being done
in Russia, at the time, despite its obvious (and largely excusable)
"excesses" had many valuable lessons for the United States and for
the rest of the Western capitalist world. All this is a simplification
of the proletarian attitude, but substantially it is probably more
correct than incorrect.

This attitude is now pretty much no more. It is doubtful that the proletarian movement had any lasting influence on the stream of American culture, especially literary culture. But for a while it did have a vogue, and "proletarian" critics could do much to "make or kill" a book or a play that did not follow the "proletarian line." Many of them occupied positions of authority in publishing houses, on magazines, and on newspapers. It must quickly be added that the more intelligent ones among them eventually saw the light and severed all connection with their past foolishness, and some are now doing useful work on the very same capitalist publications that they had hitherto denounced as "tools of capitalist imperialism." It is for this reason that I desist from mentioning any of them by name. I believe that the tone of their movement, insofar as it was a movement, was perhaps best reflected in their actions and talk away from what they used to call "the firing line," where the "proletarian stalwarts" met the "capitalist enemy" as represented by those writers and composers and playwrights who had grave doubts about every one of the assumptions of the proletarian movement.

Perhaps a word is necessary to explain why I was admitted to their parties and gab-fests. I was antipathetic to their ideas, I was largely ignorant of politics as a whole and of their special and peculiar politics, I openly talked about Russia as I would about any police state, I said publicly that I saw little difference between the Russian police state and the Fascist police state, and I also openly and in writing said some sharp things about the proletarian novels and short stories and plays, claiming that most of them were poor as art and incorrect as reporting. I did something else that must have galled them very much: In a long essay review in the old *American Mercury,* shortly after I took over as editor, I denounced Russian historians for belittling and falsifying the role of Trotsky in the Russian revolution. I did not claim to be an authority on the Russian Revolution, but it was obvious to me that the ruling Bolsheviks were making a mockery of the writing of history, and I wanted to voice my protest.

Then why did the "proletarians" allow me to go to their parties and listen in to their discussions in the various bistros? They didn't tell me the reason, but I knew it: They wanted to indoctrinate me

with their ideas so that they could use the *American Mercury* as a
vehicle for their movement. They wanted to "educate" me. They
wanted me to see that they were my "friends," that they wanted to
"show me around" the labyrinth of capitalist tricks to enslave the
workers. "You're a fine editor and a good writer," they said to me,
"but about what's going on in the world of politics and economics
you know nothing," and they implied that they alone had the truth
and they were ready to teach me the truth for my own sake, for
the sake of the United States, and for the sake of the working class
the world over. They probably did hoodwink me on several occasions, and for all I know I did print things now and then that had
within them "hidden propaganda." But on the basic ideas I remained adamant. I saw some sense in theoretical collectivism, but
I saw no sense in Russian Communism. My volunteer mentors
smiled at me, and continued to try to "educate" me, but in the end
they gave me up as more or less of a "congenital capitalist lackey."

There was a basement restaurant-speakeasy in the Village called
Danny's, which was not its name. The writers and cartoonists of the
New Masses and the *Daily Worker* and their wives and sweethearts
and mistresses used to meet there. Danny himself was a man in his
middle forties. He claimed he had been an anarchist "when I had no
better sense. Now I'm a complete and absolute Stalinist. God, was
I a fool once! I actually thought that Emma Goldman and Sasha
Berkman were on the right track. Now I wouldn't want to be caught
dead with a book by Emma Goldman." But apparently Danny did
not abandon all of Emma Goldman's ideas—certainly not those
relating to sexual relations. He boasted that he lived with three
women: one was his legal wife ("I married her when I was very
young and subject to bourgeois morality; besides, her people
insisted we get married by a rabbi, you know."), another was an
"active worker" in the Communist cause, and a third was a colored
girl who was doing recruiting for the Communist party in Harlem.
Danny's legal residence, of course, was with his first wife ("I still
like her, I admit, and she's reading more good books, by Marx and
Foster and Browder, you know, and she's getting more intelligent,

and she's a good mother to our two kids, that I admit"), but he had two rooms above his restaurant, and that's where he kept his other two "wives." These two other "wives" knew about each other, and at least outwardly they said nothing. In any case, all who went to Danny's knew about his women, for he made it a point to boast about them to all newcomers and to remind old friends about his state of emancipation. Whether or not his legal wife knew about the other two women I don't know for sure. But old habitues were sure that she did. As one of them said, "Bessie knows. She's a smart Jewish girl. She hardly ever comes here, and when she does, which isn't often, Danny says nothing about the other women. But Bessie knows, of that I'm sure. As a matter of fact, she may be glad there are two other women. If there were only one, she'd have reason to worry. You know what I mean. Women are smart that way. Anyway, she has the kids, she is the Mrs., and she gets the money. I hear he gives her every nickel he makes, only takes expense money for himself. And on Sunday, like clockwork, he goes home to his wife and the kids, and many times he goes during the week, too, and during the summer he takes the whole family for a month's vacation."

Danny told me about his amours the second time I saw him. I expressed surprise. He looked at me and said, "Hell, Charlie, you're joking, tell me you're joking."

I told him I wasn't joking.

He said, "Well, I'll be damned. The editor of The *American Mercury*, a nice bourgeois Jewish boy, who believes in monogamy and all that rot. Grow up, man, grow up. This isn't the Middle Ages!"

A former Unitarian clergyman, who had become something of an atheist, for a while taught at several women's colleges, had married three times and at the moment was relaxing between marriages, finally joined the Communist party, and became one of the most prominent literary and art critics in the Communist world. He and I had met several times before he had joined the Communist Party, and we had established a not-too-distant and somewhat pleasant relationship. He puzzled me always. He seemed to be the last person in the world who would find any pleasure in the Communist-Bohemian life. He seemed so shy, so eager for seclusion, so much the scholar. We met a few times after he joined the party, but we were no more as we had been before. I felt ill at ease with a man who appeared to accept all the barbarity of the Stalin regime. I told him as much. He smiled at me and said, "Eh, Charlie, you're naïve. You don't understand the logic of history. Sometimes, as Lenin said, history makes a sharp 45 degree angle turn, and strong people have to hold on not to fall off." I told him I couldn't follow his reasoning: "Dictatorship is dictatorship. I'm against any government that doesn't permit me to say it's no good out in public and with impunity." He smiled and kept quiet.

Months passed by. Then we met at Danny's. He was with a Korean girl. The Korean girl at once tried to sell me on the virtues of a man called Rhee, who, she said, was as great as Gandhi. I had never before heard of Rhee, and she smiled at me, in pity. The Korean girl had her hand on my friend's thigh, and I was offended. Now and then she used dirty Anglo-Saxon words, and I was even more offended. My friend was all smiles. Then he suddenly asked me, "Charlie, what do you think of Hardy's *Jude the Obscure?*" I answered at once, "I think it is one of the finest realistic novels of English life ever written, and done so well, it's really about all life everywhere."

"So you like it?"

"Sure."

"You ought to be ashamed of yourself, Charlie," he said. "Hardy was no genuine artist. He was a lackey of the capitalist class. He is no more interested in poor decent people than the late Czar. He is a fool of capitalism."

"You can't be serious," I said. "You know better than that."

We did not meet again for many years.

When we finally did meet again he had left the party, had remarried his first wife, now occasionally preached at a local Unitarian church, and he was a regular reviewer for that "arch example of corrupt capitalist journalism, the *New York Times Book Review*."

Neither of us brought up the past. Somehow we were not able to resume our pristine relationship.

His second wife, with whom he had two children, and who had been an ardent Communist organizer in New Jersey, married a copywriter for a prosperous advertising agency, and shortly afterward I saw her name mentioned as a member of the committee of a church group whose aim was "to extirpate immorality among innocent young girls who seek false glamor in the life of the remnants of Greenwich Village." Wife number three calls me occasionally to ask me to read the short stories of her high school daughter. Her new husband owns three dry cleaning establishments in Manhattan. What happened to the Korean girl I don't know.

Esther Strachey, the former wife of John Strachey, used to run a sort of literary salon in the Upper Fifties, but many of the people who went to it were Greenwich Villagers. She was a tall woman, and very imperious in her manner and in her talk. It was clear that she had a sharp mind but I wasn't too sure how much she actually knew of politics or literature. It was from her that I first heard the phrase "within the framework," and at the time I thought that was a profound way of viewing things: "within the framework." To this day I'm not sure I know what it means, though I use it now and then to impress academic colleagues who, I think, look upon me, now and then, as a bit of an interloper, since I have not gone through the academic wringer of degree-earning that they have.

Esther Strachey's parties were at times very noisy, and at other times they were quite interesting and informative. Apparently she was still on friendly terms with her former husband, whose book, *The Coming Struggle for Power,* was at the time the proverbial Bible of the more intellectually pretentious Communists, and he asked some of his English friends to visit her. I was present when some of them held forth, and they were uniformaly worth hearing. Actually very few of them were card-carrying Communists, but all of them were enormously well-informed, far more so than the general run of American Communist leaders. One of them, something of a maverick, one night spoke for almost an hour straight on

Trotsky's *Literature and Revolution,* one of Trotsky's less-well-known but extremely brilliant works. The Orthodox American Communists couldn't agree with this maverick, but they were obviously impressed. I hardly remember the occasion for his oration, for that was what it was, but I think he was annoyed by the remarks of one of the Americans about literary criticism, namely, that it was and should be a tool of the class struggle. The Englishman stopped him short, and then proceeded to enlighten him, more or less this wise: "Art is never a tool of anything. Art is an expression of an individual living at a certain time, and its maturity and stature are determined more by his own individuality than by his times. The times are always no more than a background. I dare say that as soon as art becomes a tool of the class struggle or of the church or of a form of government, then it withers away. That is why, I firmly believe, no truly devout Catholic can ever be a good novelist. He may be a good Catholic novelist, which is, to me, a contradiction in terms, but he's a poor novelist. He views everything through the spectacles of Holy Mother Church, and those spectacles are tinted Vatican-color. Similarly no devout Lutheran can be a good poet. Gerard Manley Hopkins? Yes, he was a Catholic priest. But was he really a good poet? I'm not so sure. But whatever little quality there was in him was written in those moments when he was a, well, non-Catholic, or a Catholic in abeyance. The same with a devout Communist. That's where Trotsky is wrong, dead wrong. But his analysis of capitalist novelists, that is, novelists who are first, consciously or unconsciously capitalists, and second novelists, is brilliant.

"I have a theory that all art is atheistical, at least from the point of view of the Church. Artists believe in God, but to them Art and God are synonymous. Artists look upon priests and ministers and rabbis as fools and knaves, either or both. Michelangelo's *Pieta* is not Catholic. Goodness, no. He didn't believe in the Virgin Birth or the Immaculate Conception. No artist does. Goodness, no. They've slept with too many women. They know how eager women are to be seduced. Really. Michelangelo's *Pieta* is about a woman who has lost her son. He used the Catholic fable for his figures. He used the Catholic myth to get for his work the attention it deserved. That is all. He was no more a Catholic than was, say, Correli, or Vivaldi, or Palestrina. They pretended to be believers, they pretended to be priests, but they really were not. They had to be pretenders in order to get attention, as musicians, as sculptors, as painters. Some day I hope some real scholar will do a masterwork on the meaning of atheism in the history of art. And by atheism I do not merely mean atheism as regards religion. I also mean atheism as regards politics and economics."

One of the women present at this party was a Southern divorcee whom I had seen at Mrs. Strachey's house many times before. She told her troubles freely to anybody who would listen. She was nearly always on the verge of becoming intoxicated. She was probably in her late thirties, but she looked as if she were ten years older. She had a drinking woman's face: round and rosy and a little bulgy at the neck and feverish of eye. The first night she told me about her divorce: "My husband never trusted me after the birth of our first son. We had three children altogether. You know why he didn't trust me?"

"Why?"

"He once saw me in the arms of his best friend. I don't mean sleeping with him. Heavens, no. We had gone over to this friend's house. We knew his wife, we knew him. For years. Yes, years. So we had some drinks, and I did sort of like him and I said to him, 'Kiss me, you lug.' Anything wrong in that?"

"Well . . ."

"Of course, not. Well, he smiled, but he came over to where I was sitting, and I pulled him over and kissed him. And that was all. That's all there was. So help me. My husband said I had touched him all over. Oh, you know. But it wasn't so. It wasn't. It just wasn't. I do get a little friendly with people. I'm that kind. Maybe I did touch him, this friend. I don't know. And my husband caught me kissing this friend of his again, one time when they were over at our house. Anything wrong with that?"

"Oh . . ."

"Of course, there's nothing wrong. But he divorced me, my

husband did. Well, that's just as well. He has no social conscience, no feeling for social values, he wouldn't be at home here. He's a golf player, you know. He'd puke if he went down into the slums of New York or anywhere else. The only place he can eat is at Sherry's or the Waldorf."

Later that night she asked me to take her home. Her home at the moment was at a very expensive hotel not far away. She asked me if I wanted a nightcap. She had a three-room apartment all to herself. On the table were copies of the *Wall Street Journal, Business Week,* the *Daily Worker,* and the *New Masses.* She was getting more intoxicated by the minute. She asked me to go to bed with her. I pleaded I was tired and had to be in the office early the following morning.

"Are you sure you're not suffering from middle-class morality?" she asked haltingly.

I had to control myself to keep from smiling.

She looked at me with an ill-hidden sneer. "You know what people have been saying about you?"

"No. What have they been saying?"

"They've been calling you a social-fascist."

"Who has said this?"

"Never mind who," she said. "I've heard it. And I believe it."

"You do, eh?"

"Yes, I do."

"Well, I'm really tired," I said. "I have to go."

"Angry with me?"

"Oh, no. I'm tired. Honest."

"Don't you love me a little bit?"

"Of course, I do, but . . ."

"You lie. You know you lie."

"Not at all. But I really must go."

"Goodnight," she said, and I left.

I didn't see her for many months. In that time I heard that she had "played the field." Then I heard that she had married a house-painter. That marriage apparently lasted only a few months. Not long afterward word reached me that she had married another time, but it wasn't clear exactly what her new husband was doing.

Some months later I accidentally met her on Fifth Avenue. She had become quite stout. Her face had the plumpness of the heavy drinker. She told me about her several marriages since I last saw her. She added that she had just divorced her last husband. "His name was Fox, is Fox," she said, smiling. "I suppose you can call me, Mrs. Fox."

"What's funny about that?" I asked.

"When I first married him I said he was Jewish, and he jumped at me."

"Was he Jewish?"

"Oh my God, no. That he wasn't. He was everything else, a liar, and a drunkard, and a thief, but he wasn't Jewish."

One of the heroes of the Proletarian Bohemia was Heywood Broun. He died in 1939, at the age of fifty-one. He is now barely remembered, except by newspaper men, who are grateful for the part he played in the establishment of the Newspaper Guild. But when he was thirty he was already a potent force in the journalistic world of New York, largely through his celebrated column in the *New York World,* called "It Seems to Me." He achieved perhaps his greatest renown at the time of the Sacco-Vanzetti trial, when he differed sharply with his editors. He asked for a more vigorous stand against Judge Webster Thayer, the trial judge, and Abbott Lawrence Lowell, President of Harvard, chairman of the committee of three appointed by Governor Alvan T. Fuller of Massachusetts to review the case, and which found against the defendants. Broun's stay on the *World* became precarious, and he had to leave, going first to the New York *Telegram* and then to the *Post.* While he was now in more congenial editorial company, his influence waned gradually, even after he joined the editorial board of the *Nation.* I think it would be accurate to say that as he was going down in influence, he became more and more interested in "radical" causes.

I got to know him fairly well when I was on the *Nation,* but I had met him several times while I was still on the *American Mercury.* He was a tall, clumsy man, whose shirt had probably not been washed or even removed for several days, and the tie knot was often on a level with the lapels of his jacket. Somebody said he looked like an unmade bed. He smoked cigarettes incessantly, he often had liquor on his breath, and the general aroma that came from him was more often than not rather unpleasant. But I don't know anyone who met him who was not attracted and sometimes very much impressed. He was obviously a troubled man. After his death it was revealed that he had sought psychiatric aid. His marital life was ruffled. He had had an attachment with another woman that had stretched over a long time. He finally divorced his wife and re-married. About the same time, more or less in secret, he had become more and more uneasy in the agnostic-atheistic world he had built up for himself, and sought for comfort elsewhere. He took instruc-tions from Bishop Sheen, and eventually was received into the Catholic Church. How much comfort he did find in Catholicism is problematical. The friends of his agnostic-atheist days were reluctant to discuss the matter with him in any depth, and others respected his privacy. In any case, he died not long after embracing Catholicism.

Broun was not a well-read man. He appeared to be allergic to books. He read mostly newspapers and magazines. In the main his opinions about matters of national and international importance were based upon his intuitions. He said that there was only one choice before every intelligent man or woman: Communism or Fascism. He said this at editorial meetings of the *Nation*. I objected. I said there were other choices, one especially, liberalism. He smiled at me. "Liberalism hasn't got us anywhere, has it?" he asked.

"I think it has," I said. "It has brought us such democracy as we have."

"Yes, maybe so, but also poverty and injustice."

"That is true. But all that means is that liberals have to work harder. Liberalism is a slow process, but it is, in the main and all in all, the only one with any prospect of enduring success. Communism and Fascism bring food and a sort of peace quickly, but they don't last. Besides, Communism and Fascism also bring with them a total denial of civil liberties, free speech, free press, free assembly, free-dom of religion."

"That is true, but only partly true," said Broun. "The only suppression in Russia is against the *kulaks*. The common people have considerable liberty."

"What would happen to any one of the common people if he got up in Red Square and said Stalin was a killer?"

"I suppose he would be arrested and shot. But he wouldn't say it."

Some time later I became editor of *The American Spectator*. I wrote an article in it on the intellectuals in Left Wing Bohemia and I called Broun "an amateur radical," and I politely suggested that he do a little more reading. Shortly afterward he wrote an article in the *Nation* in which he made light of my charge. A few weeks later I met him at a *kaffee-klatch* in the Village. It was at somebody's home. Broun was the "lion" of the party. He moved about lumberingly—puffing away at his ever-present cigarette and munching cookies and little sandwiches. That's when I saw him listen attentively to a man propound the doctrine that "Twentieth Century Americanism is Communism." Broun was impressed. "That may be an overly dramatic way of putting it," he said. "But it's true, very true."

He spied me, and came over. We shook hands, and exchanged pleasantries. Then he said, "You shouldn't have called me 'an amateur radical.'"

I was uneasy, and began to apologize. He stopped me. "That's all right," he said. "I'm doing a little more reading now." He said he had a hard time reading Marx's *Das Kapital*. I told him I had tried to read it myself once and gave it up after fifty pages. I suggested he read Veblen's *The Theory of the Leisure Class* and some of Norman Thomas's books.

He smiled. "I'll read that Veblen book," he said. "But Thomas, never. He's a naïve preacher. He doesn't understand the world he's living in."

"I wouldn't say that," I ventured.

"People like Thomas are, wittingly or unwittingly, the tools of the capitalists," he said.

There is a belief among some extremist rabble-rousers that Jews, as a people, are especially prone to radical ideas. Strangely enough, the same rabble rousers also preach that the money of the world is largely in the hands of Jews: "international bankers." Actually, the whole Jewish tradition is against the infringement of personal liberties, against all tyrannies, and against atheistical systems. It is impossible for a Jew who is true to his tradition to be an honest Communist. Are there, then, no Jews in the radical world? Of course, there are. But they are not representative Jews. They are, so to speak, aberrant Jews.

Such radical Jewish Bohemias as there were in New York in the thirties were few in number and very small. Perhaps most of them met in the offices of the Daily *Freiheit*, the only Yiddish Communist newspaper of any importance in America (and nearly always in dire financial circumstances), or in the homes of the *Freiheit* editors or of some of its small coterie of readers.

Many Yiddish Communists, when they wanted to participate in political discussions, went to the Cafe Royal on Lower Second Avenue. The Cafe Royal was for years a center for Jewish artists and writers and political philosophers. The legend is that Leon Trotsky was a frequenter and used to draw on the tablecloth his plans for the prospective Red Army's onslaughts upon the Czarist soldiers. I used to go to the Cafe Royal once every two months or so, because I liked the food and I liked the general talk and noise even more. Further, I enjoyed the Yiddish spoken there—it was a lively American-style Yiddish. I have gone there with other "social-fascists," I have gone there with radicals who looked upon me as a "sell-out to the capitalist bosses," and I have gone there with girls who knew nothing about politics but simply wanted to see the place I used to talk to them about.

Few of the *Freiheit* Jews tried to do any converting at the Cafe Royal. They were outnumbered by those who looked upon the *Freiheit* as a foolish, worthless, and anti-Semitic paper—chiefly because of Stalin's known anti-Semitism and his murder of Jewish doctors on the absurd charge that they had poisoned or planned to poison Communist leaders. But now and then a hardy *Freiheit* editor or reader did try to defend his paper for supporting Stalin's anti-Semitism. I once heard such a defense. The defender said, "Stalin is not an anti-Semite. He's only against those Jews who are enemies of Russia."

"And who told you these doctors that Stalin killed are enemies of Russia?"

"Who told me? The Russian courts. They were tried in court and they admitted they killed men high up in the government. What more proof do you want?"

The opponent laughed, and as he did so others of his view joined him. "All trials in Russia are false, criminal. Where else in the world do people confess to such terrible things? Where else?"

"Because they're guilty, that's why they confess."

"Yes, they're guilty. Then I'm guilty, if they're guilty. And let me ask you about the Jews, the other Jews, Radek and Alter and the others? Where are they? I'll tell you where they are. In Siberia, or they're killed. Why? I'll tell you why. Because they're Jews and because they're Socialists, and Stalin the murderer doesn't like Jews and he doesn't like Socialists."

"Why should he like Socialists? They're the enemies of the people," said the defendant.

"You should be ashamed of yourself, a Jew, a man with a Jewish head believing such lies. I'm a Socialist, my friends here are Socialists, most of the people here are Socialists. Do I look like an enemy of the people? Does anybody here look like an enemy of the people? What kind of *meshugaas* are you saying? And tell me about Trotzky, go ahead and tell me."

"Trotzky, he's the worst. He was collaborating with the capitalists."

"You believe that, heh, you believe that?"

"It's a fact."

"All the enemies of the Jews should live so long, that Trotzky was an enemy of the people, collaborating with Capitalists. Stalin exiled him because he was opposed to Stalin's murders, because he, Trotzky, was a Jew. Stalin can't stand anybody who's against his ideas. That's why he hates Jews and Socialists, because they're against him, most of them except the foolish Jews who read the filthy *Freiheit*."

"You don't have to insult me. This is a free country and I can read anything I want."

"Of course, you can read anything you want. And that's good. Read the *Freiheit*, read anything you want. But have you ever asked yourself if any Jew can read the *Forward* in Russia? Tell me that."

"The *Forward* tells lies about Russia."

"I tell you the *Forward* tells the truth. But that's not the question. If Russia is a democracy, the way Stalin and the other murderers say it is, then a person should have the right to read anything he wants, not just one side, Stalin's side. Isn't that right?"

"Not if it tells lies, what he reads."

The opponent looked at the defendant in disgust, and said, "I'm a fool for wasting my breath on you," spat on the floor and walked off. His friends followed him, and the *Freiheit* Communist Jew remained alone.

One of the most interesting frequenters of the proletarian Bohemias was a former "left-winger" who had become a sharp critic of the Communists and Communist sympathisers. He seemed to seek out the haunts of his former friends to have battle with them—even though he often told his new anti-Communist friends that anybody who spent time with Communists or their tools was "a damn fool."

Benjamin Stolberg, who died at the age of sixty, was a mysterious character. Nobody knew exactly how he earned his living. Nobody knew how he paid his bills, how he managed to be so well-dressed. Some said that "rich women and widows," who were drawn to him sexually, took care of his financial problems. But that seems unlikely—at least, it seems unlikely that they paid all his bills all the time. For there were long stretches of time when his only female friends were women of modest means, who had troubles of their own. It is true that Stolberg "borrowed" money from friends and did not repay them, but the sums he thus "borrowed," as I can personally testify, were quite small—$5 or $10 generally. In all the years I knew him he "borrowed" from me a total of, I should say, not more than $100, and throughout that time he was living at the

Chelsea Hotel—not a wealthy hotel, but certainly not a slum hotel. And Stolberg always looked well-fed.

He had a reputation of being "brilliant," and his admirers sometimes quoted remarks of his. These brilliant remarks were of this order: "F.D.R. is the result of a marriage between Andrew Jackson and Woodrow Wilson . . . President Green of the A.F.L. is a talking Golem . . . Emma Goldman is a spiritual hemophiliac . . . Karl Marx, by a different turn of the wheel of fate, would have made a fanatical Orthodox rabbi . . . I don't trust anybody who converts from the religion of his birth to another religion: he takes religion too seriously . . . A woman who's no good in bed is generally no good in the kitchen, too; but it doesn't work the other way around." Such remarks appeared in his few published articles.

I first got to know him in my *American Mercury* days. I forget who first introduced us, but we became quite friendly. He, in turn, introduced me to some of the more intellectual, anti-Communist radicals and also to various labor lawyers and labor organizers. He also introduced me to Negro professors and writers, and they, in turn, made me comfortable at the homes of professors at Howard University in Washington. It was at a gathering of such Negro intellectuals that I first met Dr. Ralph Bunche. When I met Dr. Bunche many years later at the U.N. we spoke about Stolberg and he agreed that Stolberg was a fascinating man, though at the moment he didn't specify what it was that made him fascinating. I also spent some time alone with Stolberg: we'd meet at his apartment or at mine (at the time we were both bachelors), we'd have dinner, and take in a movie or a Broadway show. Stolberg didn't like movies or plays, but he would give in to me on both—and I would give in to him when he asked me to go with him to some Communist meeting or festival: "Let's see how the Stalin dupes carry on," he'd say.

Stolberg was always in the process of writing an article for some magazine or a book for some publisher. Nearly all the time he got advances, not only for the books but also for the articles. Magazine editors seldom give advances for articles: whatever money they do pay out in advance is generally only for expenses. But Stolberg got outright advances. How did he do it? It's hard to say. His reputation for "brilliance" was so widespread over so long a period of time—more than ten years—that editors vied with one another to tie him down to do an article. Each editor thought that Stolberg was doing this or that article for him alone. Alas, more than once Stolberg would promise the same article to more than one editor—and get advances from each—and not deliver the article to any one of them. The editors would badger him for months and months and then they'd give up. They'd ask Stolberg to return the advance, but I don't know of a single instance when he returned it. I had such experiences with him three times, and finally had no more business dealings with him. He was not at all offended when I refused to give him other advances on other articles that I was sure he wouldn't do—and that I was sure he knew he wouldn't do. He continued to call me on the telephone, asking me to meet him socially. And I did, as other editors, who had had similar troubles with him.

Why? There are many reasons. First of all, he was a charming rogue, utterly anarchistic, utterly amoral. And secretly, I presume, all of us have a streak of the amoral in us, and we are fearful of acting amorally, and we mollify our sense of cowardice by applauding those who do act amorally. Stolberg was also a cynic. He trusted nobody, he pooh-poohed the pretensions of the Liberal Left almost as much as those of the Communist Left. I once heard him say, "Eh, give a Liberal enough power, and he becomes power-drunk, and soon he's talking and acting like Stalin." He refused to be taken in by anybody. Not even by F.D.R. "Wait," he would admonish us. "Don't worship. I don't like his smile. It's the smile of a demagogue. Yes, he's better than Hoover, but who wouldn't be? But F.D.R. holds hands with Hague of Jersey City, and that I don't like. A decent man wouldn't want to be in the same city with Hague." I liked to hear this kind of talk. All of us liked to hear it. Because we believed at least some of it. Stolberg liked to argue with the Communists and Communist sympathisers, I suspect, because he liked their abiding distrust of Capitalist philosophers and apologists. He liked all people who distrust "leaders" and "professional way-showers." What hurt him most about the Communists, I suspect,

even more than their political superstitions, was that they didn't
extend their distrust to include Stalin and the whole Soviet Tammany
Hall. To Stolberg distrust of the sheer human was an integral part
of the civilized man, and whatever man did not have this distrust
irked him.

His attitude toward women was special. I believe he had been
married when a young man—I once met a woman, with a young
boy, who claimed to be his wife, but the circumstances of our meeting were such that I wasn't sure she was telling the truth. From
information obtained from others I gathered that it was possible
this woman was his wife. But they had not lived together as man
and wife for many years. On one occasion I asked Stolberg directly
if he was married, and he answered, "Yes, sure, I married a woman
who claimed she was part Indian, and I thought it would be nice
for a Jew to marry an Indian, so I tried it. Well, it didn't work out.
I guess that psychologically I'm a bachelor. But she's a very fine
woman. I suppose if she would consent to our living apart and
meeting only occasionally I would agree to continuing the marriage,
as a real marriage, but she won't, and of course, she's right." Still,
as far as I could make out, they were still legally man and wife. He
always spoke well of her, and she always spoke well of him.

Stolberg was a loner intellectually. He probably would have been
most at home in the days of Benvenuto Cellini, when the elegant
rogue was held in high respect, when men and women united
sexually more or less at will and society did not frown too much
upon such liaisons, and when cynicism was a central part of every
man's intellectual armament. He was originally attracted to radicalism and Communism—though I don't think he ever carried a
Communist card—because the world of radicalism, at the beginning,
more or less coincided with the world of spiritual anarchism . . .
and that is why he returned now and then to their Bohemian lairs.
He loved to twit them and to sneer at them—and sometimes his
sneering was sharp and cruel—but he liked them even while he
castigated them. As he once said to me, "These damn Communist
revolutionaries aren't really Communist or Revolutionaries. They're
just annoyed. They're not even angry. Now Dean Swift was angry.

Trotzky, when he was honest, was angry. But Mike Gold isn't angry. Even Jay Lovestone, who's worth a carload of Earl Browders, he isn't angry either. Real anger is non-partisan. It is world-wide, it is cosmic."

Stolberg was a Jew, though he didn't practice any of its rituals. He knew little of Jewish literature or Jewish history or Jewish philosophy. I took him a few times to temple services, and I tried to make him read some Jewish novels. He disliked the novels, including Cahan's *Rise of David Levinsky*. I tried to find out why, but I made little headway. He apparently didn't like fiction in general. As for the temple services his reaction was mixed: "I don't like public prayer. Private prayer, private dreaming and hoping, that's all right, but public prayer, with a baritone-voiced rabbi leading, that I don't like. Besides, the rabbi doesn't mean it, anyway. I get the feeling the rabbis you took me to hear are really floor-walkers. There must be better rabbis. There just must be. But I kept on looking at where the Torah is. That interested me. You see, the Christians have a crucifix and some bread and wine up there. That I don't like. The crucifix is an instrument of torture, and it should not have a place of honor. The bread and wine, that's all superstition. Bless them and you have Christ. Christ would laugh at that, assuming he ever laughed. But the Jews have a book up there, the Torah. The book is in the place of honor. That I like. The book has kept the Jews going for two thousand years. I like that. That's the Jewish part of Judaism that I like. That's what makes me proud of being a Jew."

He and I once went to a Communist basement on West Fourth Street. He took a great deal of insulting from the Communist faithful, and he himself insulted them in return. There was even less genuine argumentation than usual at such meetings. Suddenly Stolberg stood up and asked me to go with him. We walked over to the Cafe Royal. After his second tea and cheese sandwich, he felt better. Then he said, "You know, those people we left, say what you will about them, they were angry about intellectual things. They didn't know what they were talking about, but they pretended to know about good things. That's good in itself. You know what the real trouble was?"

"What?"

"Did you notice that there was only one Jew there?"

"I didn't notice there was even one."

"I think one of them was at least half Jewish. Not entirely Jewish. If he were 100 per cent Jewish he wouldn't be there. That's the trouble. There aren't enough Jews to go around, and the few good Jews don't want to waste their time with such fools. And another thing. *Goyim* don't know how to laugh. Only Jews know how to laugh. Look around you. Notice how happily these Jews laugh. A wonderful people, the Jews, just wonderful."